COLLECTED POEMS

COLLECTED POEMS

EDITED BY TAYLOR STOEHR

WITH A MEMOIR BY GEORGE DENNISON

PAUL GOODMAN

RANDOM HOUSE   NEW YORK

Copyright 1940, 1941, 1942, 1947, 1949, 1950, 1951,
1952, 1954, © 1956, 1957, 1958, 1959, 1960, 1961,
1962, 1963, 1964, 1965, 1966, 1967, 1969, 1970
by Paul Goodman

Copyright © 1972, 1973 by The Estate of
Paul Goodman

All rights reserved under International and
Pan-American Copyright Conventions. Published
in the United States by Random House, Inc.,
New York, and simultaneously in Canada by
Random House of Canada Limited, Toronto.

Library of Congress Cataloging in Publication Data
Goodman, Paul, 1911–1972.
   Collected poems.
   I. Title.
PS3513.O527A17   1973   811'.5'2   73–3979
ISBN 0-394-48358-8

Manufactured in the United States of America
98765432
First Edition

Poems No. 37–60 originally appeared in *Hawkweed*,
published by Random House, Inc.
Poems No. 61–72 from *Little Prayers & Finite
Experience*, Copyright © 1968 by Paul Goodman,
originally appeared in *North Percy*, published
by Black Sparrow Press.
Poems No. 73–85 originally appeared in *Homespun
of Oatmeal Gray*, published by Random House, Inc.
Poems No. 87–110 from *Little Prayers and
Finite Experience* by Paul Goodman, from *Religious
Perspective Series* edited by Ruth Nanda Anshen.
Copyright © 1972 by The Estate of Paul Goodman.
Reprinted by permission of Harper & Row,
Publishers Inc.

EDITOR'S PREFACE

※

PAUL'S PLAN FOR THIS BOOK INCLUDED ALMOST EVERYTHING FROM the four major volumes that came before—*The Lordly Hudson, Hawkweed, Homespun of Oatmeal Gray,* and *Little Prayers and Finite Experience,* along with quite a few new poems. In June 1972 when he packed up the working copies to take to New Hampshire, he left a great many other poems, published and un-published, behind in New York City. He expected to finish the book during the summer, and it was his habit to take everything he needed with him when he went to the "north country." No doubt he would have written a few more poems by the time he had completed the editing, but it is unlikely that he would have dug any deeper in his trunk.

Before he died on August 2, he had finished well over half the book—the first eighteen sections, from "Growing Old" to "Making Love I"—and he left notes for three others—"Making Love II and III" and "My Family of Architects." He said in June that he was experimenting with new thematic subdivisions, and at that time he had already put together the sections called "La Gaya Scienza" and "June and July," the recent poems that pleased him most. Probably several other sections were also finished—"Growing Old" and perhaps "Poems of a Heart Attack," and several cate-gories were given by genre or by groupings in previous volumes. By the end of July he had worked his way through to the first part of "Making Love II" (four of these poems were typed), and every-thing up to that point was revised, arranged, and ready for the press. The order was that followed here, except that "In the Manner of Anacreon" and "Making Love I" had not yet been put in sequence with the other sections. All of this part of the book is probably just as Paul wanted it.

The lists for "Making Love II and III" contained all the remaining love poems he had brought with him, and their order has been retained, although Paul would certainly have tinkered with it (the four poems of "Making Love II" that he typed do not quite match his list). Two poems—"Lilacs" and "Sentences" ("I won't give thee my come")—are also on his list for "My Family of Architects," so that a choice had to be made; they are apt enough for either section. "White Dogwood" does not appear on any list, but is marked for "Pt. III" in a working copy of *The Lordly Hudson,* and obviously goes with the other flower poems— a reason for including "Lilacs" there too.

Paul left no title for the section now called "My Family of Architects," and the list he made seems incomplete, including a little less than half of those I have picked out as belonging there. The sequence is roughly that of earlier publication in *The Lordly Hudson, Hawkweed,* and *Oatmeal Gray,* with some adjustments at the junctures between volumes.

Aside from these, only one other category seemed clear-cut enough to warrant separate status—"Exile," a section already developed in *Hawkweed.* I have included all the poems from that section (except for a few that Paul had already used, e.g., in the new "North Percy"), and have added some poems from the other books and some new poems that go with them.

For the rest, a large body of verse that might be subdivided in any number of ways, I have been unable to find a satisfying principle of sorting, and so print them pretty much in the order of previous publication, with a catch-all title I think Paul would have liked, "To My Only World," the subject of many and the name of one of these poems.

Wordsworth—one of Paul's favorite poets—told Emerson that "he never was in haste to publish; partly because he corrected a good deal, and every alteration is ungraciously received after printing." Paul was always hot to publish, yet he too corrected a good deal, afterwards. Since his poetry never had a wide audience, he risked little except among his friends, who would find copies he had given them annotated with pencil revisions not always to their taste. Some readers will not like to encounter their favorites tampered with again—"The Lordly Hudson," for example, seems to irk people in its new version. This is not my edition however, but Paul's, and the truth is, I prefer the revised poems, even "The Lordly Hudson." So the reader who has his Goodman by heart will notice a great many differences, usually tiny but always altering the effect, in the direction of simplicity and ease. Many more of the poems would have been improved had he lived another month. No doubt they would have undergone still further revision if he had been granted Wordsworth's longevity, as he did share his passion for plain speech and his trust in the Creator Spirit.

❦

I WANT TO THANK GEORGE DENNISON AND SALLY GOODMAN FOR their help in finishing Paul's book. In particular, I am grateful to George for suggesting the title "My Family of Architects," and to Sally for the addition of "Sentences of Nietzsche," a poem that Paul liked very much but happened not to bring with him to New Hampshire.

T.S.

CONTENTS

A MEMOIR AND APPRECIATION
BY GEORGE DENNISON

꽃

PAUL DESCRIBED HIMSELF ONCE AS "AN ORPHAN WHO HAD HAD A home." His father abandoned the family while Paul was still an infant. His older brother set out early on his own, and his mother, "a bourgeois gypsy," was often away. He was cared for—through even his years in college—by his sister Alice, almost ten years his senior. The first book of *The Empire City* is dedicated to her.

Many writers speak of a lonely youth, a flight into books and the world of the imagination. Paul seems instead to have contrived a family of poets and philosophers. His great masters, his fathers, were Aristotle and Kant. If Paul's own work and the many principled examples of his life were not well known, it would be difficult to make believable, in these cynical and very sophisticated times, the simple earnestness with which he pursued his ideals. I met him in 1948. He was then thirty-seven. I was studying with William Troy at the New School, and like several of my classmates was already a Goodman fan (*The Facts of Life, Kafka's Prayer, The Grand Piano, Parents' Day, Art and Social Nature;* two Noh plays at the 91st Street Y; a production of *Faustina* by some poets and artists in a loft on 8th Street). Paul in person was dazzling, bold and iconoclastic, and much given to rearranging or removing entirely the accepted pillars of culture. Yet for all his high spirits and the spontaneity of his thought and wit, there was something about him that seemed willed, willed in exactly the style of an idealistic youth correcting himself continually toward some lofty goal. Ten years later the same thing was visible—and ten years after that. If this was noticeable, a related trait was even more so. Among his age-mates (as one would say: in the egotism of one's own generation) he was combative and arrogant, and could rarely abide to be opposed; but when he felt secure, as before us admiring younger ones who accepted him as a teacher, his egotism vanished, one heard the voice of a selfless, prodigious boy, an angel of mind whose feats of memory and analysis seemed like familiar descriptions of a much-loved home. (This kind of love—comradely, familial and touched by yearning—appears also in a writer who otherwise doesn't resemble him: Maxim Gorky.)

By his own count Paul wrote forty books. His apparent diversity is actually the unfolding of one large underlying theme. In its broadest terms, it was the search for harmony of the life made by man and the life not made but given. More intimately—as is evident in many poems ("long have I labored to make me Goodman") and in the autobiographical *Five Years*—it was the creation also of a self, but a self in the Aristotelian sense that would rather describe *self* as *world*. It might be contrasted with the familiar *persona* of art (as a poet imagines a bardic figure and tries to live it, or protects himself by means of it). It was the transparent or minimal self harmonious with Aristotle's highest good: the unimpeded functioning of the powers that are distinctly human. One need hardly say that our characters—like our laws, politics, mores, architecture, etc.—impede our human powers. Paul was willing to dissolve such aspects of selfhood (which might be called the fleshly forms of received opinion) in order to stand closer to the powers prior to the ego. The task was spiritual, and was technical in the psychotherapeutic sense, and—above all—was philosophic.

But it hardly matters how one puts it. One can say that he lived "the examined life," and that his tools were art, psychotherapy and philosophy. Or one can say simply that thought was real to him, and that the truth as he saw it was never a mere intellectual proposition but a commandment (for he did try to live the Kantian imperative). Or one can say—as Paul does in many poems—that he "staggered from need to need," was an exile among men, had "from another planet," and was deeply obliged to create a self and a task. The fact remains that most of his thought is devoted to the nature that is prior to the ego, its progress through the self, and the requisites of the human home (political, social, ethical, etc.) necessary to fulfillment. (At times, his name for the whole is *Adam*.) These are the subjects not only of his social criticism but also of *Gestalt Therapy*, and in more imaginative forms, of his short fiction and his major work *The Empire City*. Nothing so reveals his central importance to our time as the fact that the task he took up so many years ago is now, under a variety of names, on everyone's lips. Even in its closest terms, that is, in the making of self (the attaching of world, and of work) it has turned out to be—not by force of fashion but simply by the continuing collapse of social values—the very task that faces Everyman.

All of which is to say nothing of the powers that actualized his work, or of his remarkable poetry, which never was a projection of his main task but seems to have been read off straight, or gathered in (I think of Picasso's remark: "I don't search, I find") from the passing days, the "thousand suns falling westward." In its uninhibited, highly detailed telling of a life, his poetic oeuvre is unique. I doubt that he set out to tell the story of his life; rather, it was the kind of poetry that he wrote, and he wrote it all the time. Whatever memories pass through my mind—Paul arriving for a game of poker, or joining friends at a bar, or conducting a session of group therapy, or presiding at dinner—there comes a moment when he hands around five or six sheets of new poems.

Paul's days were extraordinarily varied. Anecdotes, especially in small quantity (as I discovered in earlier versions of this brief memoir), tend to be distorting. Moreover, he was complex—complex beyond description. There are people who knew him, and with cause, as a monster of reason. And others who knew him as a knight of reason. I remember talking with a young woman after seeing the Living Theater production of *The Young Disciple*; she said there was a romantic in him somewhere, and she was right, for though the whole of his work, in surface and in theme, is powerfully rationalistic, it expresses also a deep, deep yearning and unrequited love. He was wholly committed as a therapist, was on call at desperate hours, and often displayed a sweet, paternal kindliness. His dignity was becoming; it was the face of his service, his desire to be used. Yet he could be ruthless and destructive, quite blind to his own motives. On the other hand, he knew his motives: there was never an accusation hurled at him that he hadn't already anatomized in his poems. At times he seemed tossed by obsessions, at other times calmly attentive to the dreamwork of his life. His stability was like the eye of the storm. Then he would stumble with the awkwardness of a man who has mistaken the entire environment.

Many thought Paul pedantic, and were astonished by the lyric turns of his conversation or his art. I remember how, more than twenty years ago, at my place, a scholarly friend, who on the basis of one calamitous argument with Paul detested him and thought he knew all about him, picked up some carbon copies of poems from my table and began showering me with astonished praise; a moment later—"What! *Goodman* wrote this?" If ever a man deserved that marvelous line of Whitman's: "Do I contradict myself? Very well, I contradict myself" it was Paul. He taught the drifting of the Tao and was never at rest, but was strenuous, possessed of enormous will, and of what he often described as puritanical persistence. Yet into his middle forties his gaiety was striking; it amounted to a power.

Into his forties, too, he sailed around on his bike, or, rather, "pedalled like a ferocious fireman," went everywhere, and grew sedate at last by switching to a Lambretta. For years—as he put it—he "looked for love where it can't be found," which, however costly in emotion, added considerably to his sense of the city. But he was a lover of the city itself, knew its history in close detail, and labored much for its possibilities. He foresaw its present condition, which many older residents would simply call its fate. Early in his career he described himself as a "regional poet," and the region, of course, was the city. Those he sought out, either as opponents or colleagues, lovers or companions, spanned an extraordinary range: the universities and City Hall, several of the professions, the literary cliques, the community of the arts and groups of political dissidents, and the wandering youths and semidelinquents of several neighborhoods. It was really his life as a poet—that is, his classical learning and his lively pursuit of so many, including fleshly, interests—that gave such point to his later works of social criticism.

He lacked physical grace, and one was continually surprised by his agility and competence at sports. He was an excellent handball player and was good at the games for which there was room at the place in the country: badminton, croquet, horseshoes. He played with verve, stretching the rules in favor of himself and arguing loudly with the extended, highfalutin legalisms of young boys. He was far more domestic than his poems (especially) would lead one to believe. To see him at home was to understand his deep dependence on his wife, Sally. She abetted and endured his genius, and tended the desperate child in him. The ambience of their home—its hospitality and domestic festivals, its music and love of learning—was very much her character as well as his. In his later years he enjoyed gardening, and traveled to the country ahead of the family to plant the seeds. His poem "Proverbs of a Small Farm" is wise; he includes the A & P in his ecology, the neighbors' preferences in foods, and his own preference for writing books. He enjoyed swimming, small boats, campfires and kites. He never had much feel for making things. I remember how at Wellfleet, at Dyer's Pond, he wanted to make a raft of some timbers and scraps. What seemed to be needed—so the rest of us argued—was a good quantity of small cord. But he wouldn't listen. He went away and came back with a piece of one-inch rope eight feet long. The contraption floated, though not all in the same direction. Nevertheless, he enjoyed it, and even went so far as to say, "I told you so." And he was right. His study in New Hampshire was a cool corner of the barn loft. Where other men of letters would put up shelves and paintings, bring in chairs, sofas, desks and whatnot, he braced a plank against the wall to write on, threw a mattress on the floor, and commenced with letters. Parts of ten or twelve books were produced there.

꧁

PAUL'S LATE CAREER AS A PHILOSOPHER OF SOCIAL CHANGE WAS, IN one sense, a subtraction of picnics, ball games, parties and therapy sessions from what he had always done and their replacement with lecture platforms and large audiences in chairs.

Paul at ease, Paul enjoying himself, was Paul philosophizing. He was rarely silent and never idle.

During the early fifties a crowd of us met annually at Ward's Island for softball and a picnic. Of all the settings I saw him in, these outdoor events and the festivals of the artists and friends at Stony Point, near Bear Mountain—gatherings of a good size, with people of all ages, children, infants, dogs, games and gaiety, erotic possibility, and high talk—seemed most to his liking. Their ambience was that of his lovely early story "A Ceremonial." Stretched on the grass between turns at bat, puffing at his pipe, he would chuckle and anatomize the postures and characters of our opponents in the field, and make humorous predictions of their likely errors; or would notice a youthful black face against the blue of the sky and remark how it retained its aesthetic value, whereas our white faces against that same blue seemed drained. And he would talk at length of the book underway, for his work was with him continually.

At such times his wit could let go into glee, and there was an attractive ease to his gravity. In more contentious settings he behaved quite otherwise. No one listens in New York. But where others say, "Yes, but . . ." and interrupt, Paul would say, "You couldn't be more mistaken" and interrupt. Or would interrupt with a formulation in itself a little gem of contradiction: "By strong you mean weak—no?" He would enter a crowded room shuffling like an old-clothes merchant, smiling to himself, avoiding others' eyes—and abruptly would seize everything. Soon the room would be strewn with bodies, eyes fixed on his. The power of his talk was not its insistence (for anyone could leave), but its clarity, its pertinence, its learning and breadth, its elegant swiftness, its structure—in short, its beauty.

He handled ideas in their potential for use, for structural change in politics, morals, education. And the magnetic attraction of Paul-at-thought was that he did live, both awkwardly and bravely, everything he believed. If this won him admirers, it won him enemies as well. He was harsh in his own defense, and harsh in his loyalties. Many who now praise him once feared his scorn.

Yet even among his detractors he aroused an unusual fascination. It was a response, in good part, to his many-sided combat. The New Critics, the adjustment psychologists, the behaviorists, the architects and planners of centralization, the military-industrial, the schools—to list his opponents is very nearly to write the history of the last thirty years.

But for many the fascination was more personal than that. Paul was living, *was* in himself, an existential drama, the small events of which—the troublesome lusts, the stubborn insistence upon values—were joined both verbally and by demonstration to much larger issues. He rejected Freud's theory of sublimation; he accepted Reich's insight into the continuity of politics and sexuality, and all such beliefs sooner or later showed up in his behavior. He meant to be exemplary, and in exactly the Kantian spirit. He could not live with himself otherwise. The stands he took came to mean a great deal to the country as a whole, and they were costly to him in social ease. His very gestures occasionally seemed didactic. His exemplary demonstrations—life being what it is— sometimes expressed also contempt and spite.

I remember Paul at a party during his forty-sixth year. It was a stressful period. He had written twenty books, among them his best, and had seen no reward. He had much need, certainly, of love and pleasure. The party was lively. There were a great many young women, and they were conventional, were scrubbed and scented and prettily dressed. There were no intellectuals. The young actor he had been waiting for arrived with a woman. And it seemed that all the young men had come with women. He talked with this one and talked with that one. Soon he was looking into the distance, his jaw clenched and his eyes vacant in exasperation. But a handsome mongrel dog, part shepherd, was ambling about, pausing at this one and at that one. Paul by now was sitting on the floor, leaning against the wall, dismayed and contemptuous. The dog went to him and wagged its tail. Paul took its head caressingly in both hands and spoke to it. There was self-pity in his voice, but also admiration and outright gratitude. "Yes, my darling," he said, "you're the prettiest one here." The dog licked him, and Paul licked him back, and for a full twenty minutes they exchanged kisses. The voices in the room fell silent, started up, fell silent. The two red tongues touched again and again, and Paul opened his mouth to the dog's tongue.

He meant to offend the human company. It was an effective display of contempt. But much more than this could be seen. The longing expressed by his open mouth was real, and was disquieting, as of something beyond placation. His affection for the dog was real, too; his fingers liked its fur, and he welcomed the closeness. Yet in the entire event there was a quality of will. I don't mean that he willed to kiss the dog in order to express his contempt, but that he willed—now, and had in the past—to overcome the squeamishness, that is, the way of life, and the entire tradition of that way, that appeared in those other faces. For in fact their fascination—persistently staring eyes, and nauseated mouths—was neurotic disgust: unlived life.

Before taking up Gestalt therapy, Paul had undergone Reichian analysis. He had also performed self-analysis. During his years as a therapist he devoted a great deal of time to the Gestalt exercises, and more time still to an investigation of breathing (about which he had considered writing). Certainly in all this he was concerned with his competence as a therapist; but more deeply it was simply another aspect of the examined life, and, as such, was nothing new, was all of a piece with the task he had long made his own.

The didactic burden of his display with the dog was obvious: if you would affirm and not suppress your animal nature, etc., if you would be as direct as this dog instead of wasting life in idiotic avoidances, the world would be more practicable, and I not so alone. The message, in the event, was both true and false. To some extent his dismay was a private matter. Generalized, the message is true and familiar; it comes from many quarters, not least from Paul.

This little incident with the dog showed still another aspect of Paul's character. I can indicate it best with an anecdote.

When my younger brother was three or four, he and the family bulldog were much enamored of each other. One night my father could bear it no longer, and said, "Stop kissing the dog on the mouth." But the kissing went on. My father grew angry and sent my brother up to bed. Ten minutes went by. They heard his footsteps coming down the stairs, and then he stalked into the room, both fists clenched, and made for the dog shouting ,"I don't care! I love Skippy and I'm gonna kiss 'im on the mouth!"

There really was a child like that alive in Paul, both problematically and as a reservoir of power.

And of course it's a truism—that is to say, difficult to credit—that the child-presence in the artist is a strong resource of his art. It was for Paul. In both his fiction and his poetry, his descriptions of physical events—of crowds in motion, a workman at work, the ocean, a cyclist—have often the freshness of discovery, the surprising physicality that is prior to category and type. In *what* he noticed, too, one sees the instinctive, that is, the *attracted* noticing of a child. It is this that takes him so often through the Every-Day Sublime (for which he much loved Wordsworth), and puts him so acutely in touch with the desperation of ordinary life. He writes learnedly, and with an ease and acuity of analysis that find many readers unprepared. Yet (and this too can be disorienting) one comes frequently upon the sufficient simplicity of the naïve glance—as when the far-off ocean in the sun is not described as water shining in the sun, and in fact is not described at all (for the water is invisible in the distance, and the sun is in the sky) but is *identified,* and by one word, as a child would look and say, "the shining." Phenomenologically such touches are beautifully accurate.

". . . the noiseless points of little rain were drizzling endlessly on roofs and hats." "The sherry had stored in it the weather of an old year and a distant country; and it had burning in it many a better thought, not second thoughts but thoughts that were not even the first thought." "They lay by the fire, the branches crackled and the rising stars continually died upward into the night." These are sentences from *The Empire City.* And of course it is absurd to isolate sentences this way; nevertheless, they display the characteristic effects which are the literary equivalent of some of those childlike paintings of Picasso's, paintings in which we sense everywhere the same radically unconfined source of imagery we see briefly in the paintings of many children, exploited by the artist with enormous knowledge and sophistication. In Paul's poetry and fiction there is much of this very thing: learning and enormous skill at the disposal of a spirit which in some part is still childlike and naïve.

❦

PAUL'S POETRY IS DISTINGUISHED BY ITS IMMEDIACY OF FEELING AND meaning, its daylight actuality, over a wide range of experience. His learning appears unabashedly as the way he looks at things (not as a map of culture), and he suffers no convention of "the poetic," but every significant turn of thought, emotion and event seems to have shaped a poem. The classic themes of love and death recur often, and recur in their classic form, that is, not as themes but as persons and emotions. There are somber prayers, and poems of a lofty nature, and poems of humor, sometimes of a hilarity to make one laugh aloud. At all periods there are simple lyrics beautifully realized: the early "A Cyclist" and "The flashing pigeons as they wheel"; and the late hokku, of which he wrote many:

> In crashing waters
> of the same falls, falling leaves
> of the same forest

> the leaping voyage
> home at last the red salmon
> spawn and faint and fade

He wrote ballades and ballads, sonnets, narrative poems such as the stern and strong "The Well of Bethlehem"; and analytic odes like "The Character of Washington" and the early "Death of Leon Trotsky."

Like D. H. Lawrence, Paul is a poet "without a mask." The voice of the poetry is persuasively the man himself—and he is in the real city of New York. In our present extravagantly metaphoric conventions, with their elaborate *personae,* and multiple (finally rather dim) refractions of experience, I find the brilliant actuality of these poems infinitely refreshing.

Paul's is "occasional poetry" (and he was fond of quoting Goethe: "the highest kind"). Technically, he is often brilliant. The prevailing effect, however, is of spare accuracy capturing experience already deeply felt and thought. Poem by poem his aim is modest. The poems accumulate to an *oeuvre* of striking presence and magnitude; the more so in that the life embodied here was itself a rare venture in our time.

꽃

UNTIL WELL INTO MIDDLE AGE, PAUL'S WORK WAS PRODUCED IN poverty and against a blank of appalling neglect—and it poured out of him: poems, stories, plays, novels, literary criticism, works of psychology, community planning, social criticism, educational theory. He even composed some music. In his forty-ninth year *Growing Up Absurd* made him famous.

One might say of Paul truly, that he was revealed by events. Certainly, he was not thrust forward by publishers. His first small books of poetry (after almost twenty years in little magazines) were published by himself, as was *The Dead of Spring*. For several years *The Empire City* was rejected everywhere. I remember seeing letters from four of the large publishers. Two said it was possibly a great book, the others said it was extremely impressive. All four had reasons for not printing it. These letters, needless to say, were more dismaying than the flat rejections of other publishers. *Growing Up Absurd* was rejected by the publisher who commissioned it, and then was rejected by a dozen more.

As a social critic Paul is a figure of international fame. But as soon as one writes of his fiction one is dealing again with an avant-garde artist whose works are largely unknown. His collected stories, *Adam and His Works*, appeared in 1968, and was not reviewed. *The Empire City,* which was finally published in 1959, was widely praised—and nothing has been said since, partly, I believe, because the avant-garde from which it emerged had by then given way to the hucksters' avant-garde of pop art, and partly because our literary quarterlies in the sixties became on the one hand extravagantly factional, and on the other increasingly academic, while the livelier magazines turned more and more to politics.

The Empire City was composed over a period of more than fifteen years. It makes no effort to "express the age," and is not a work of realism, but takes for granted that we have all shared more or less the same catastrophes and are more or less aware of it. It *responds* to its age, responds overtly, saying, in effect, "I and thou" as it goes. It is certainly a novel: it is an educational romance, and a *picaresque*. Its one grand subject is the conflict that Schiller called "the only significant drama,": the conflict between what man is and what he ought to be. Where in his later works Paul deals with this conflict as it appears on its public stage, he deals with it here on a stage, or against a background, of personal vision. In our own time one must look to Genet for a comparable power of formal invention. What every artist yearns to do—to find a method and a form capable of utilizing the full range of his knowledge and gifts—is accomplished here triumphantly. Paul's essential training was philosophic. (His doctoral thesis, *The Structure of Literature,* was a bold Aristotelian essay in completing the *Poetics* of Aristotle.) His thought was analytic and structural, he had strong lyric gifts, imaginative delight and humor. His genius of invention in this book is to transform analytic insight into narration and lyricism and to transform meanings inherited in tradition (quotations, often) into dramatic metaphor. He wrote of *The Empire City:* "I undertook the task of not giving up *any* claim of culture and humanity . . ." Just this is the triumph of his method, is the range and flexibility of the voice (the vision) against which the characters and their actions appear. And it is even a description of the characters, for they are all paradigms and archetypes of human powers, and their various fates are those precisely of refusing to give up.

The characters began in *The Grand Piano* (Book One) as "sociological humors . . . after Ben Jonson," and soon deepened to grand archetypes. They are vivid and distinct, but are not intended to be "believable," are not "like people," do not demonstrate a personal psychology. But of course they *are* like people, even more so. Long years after one has read this book, they loom in one's memory with unusual power, rather like that of the "inhuman" distortions of Picasso in "Guernica" and in such myth-making works as the Minotaur series. (I have mentioned Picasso twice now. He was important to Paul. The closest formal parallel to *The Empire City* is actually the Cubism of Picasso. I mean that Picasso's attitude toward tradition, his use of it [exactly as a *second* Nature], his overt lyric play with properties abstracted from the history of art, are quite like Paul's in *The Empire City.* There is not the space here to develop this comparison. Paul's characters levitate—after Nietzsche and Cocteau. They encounter "the friend downstairs"—after Freud. Plots are drawn from Buber and Malinowski, props from Kafka. Yet the effect is never one of fantasy, but of true event, clear meaning—and a radical extension of the genre which yet observes structural fidelity to it.)

The truly grand (and perhaps the proper word is great) first effect of Paul's task here of claiming *all* his humanity, *all* his culture, and of inventing characters who themselves do the same, and who persist through hundreds of events in a range from hilarity to tragic grief, is that the total emanation of this book is a spirit of the most beautiful pride, delight and freedom—absolutely unmatched in our recent American decades.

Another, more technical effect, yet one of importance in modern fiction (for since Proust, Dostoyevsky, Freud, and others, novelists are hard put to be interesting in the demonstration of individual psychology), is that psychology is shifted from the characters to the background, that is, to the personal vision against which the characters appear, and is treated there with the finesse and scope of its actual development in history.

This might be said another way. We hear that the social observation of the nineteenth-century novel has vanished, but of course it has not vanished—it has moved into sociology, with no gain at all in interest but considerable gain in detail. And so for analysis of character: it persists—in extremely impressive detail—in the psychoanalytic case history. Perhaps (and maybe not) only a poet-philosopher at home in both fields can win these things back for art.

Paul's fiction is just strange enough, it seems, to require the services of such cohorts as have accompanied the major figures of modernism. His prose in *The Empire City* is one of the truly superb styles of our period, yet it seems to be inaccessible to many readers, not because it is obscure (in an age of obscurity it is crystal clear), but because it moves along very often on the *affect* of meaning—what Nietzsche called "raptures of understanding"—and edification has long been absent from our notions of what the novel may be.

It is worth repeating that the themes Paul took up in *The Grand Piano* in 1941, and deepened through the subsequent books of *The Empire City,* have proven to be the central issues of our time. He dealt with them in unrivaled breadth and detail, and in a voice of great security and finesse. I am tempted here to make an invidious comparison, that is, of Paul's strengths with the weaknesses of some others. Often the incidental flaws of precisely major literary figures show the characteristic stresses of an age: Pound's disfiguring self-conceit, and his consequent lapses into moral parochialism; Lawrence's recurrent crises of self in which he grows hysterical confronting the mores of his tradition; Eliot's remote and willful speculativeness in the dilemmas of faith. This is to say nothing of these artists' enormous genius. My point is that Paul's performance under just these stresses—of the artist embattled among countrymen who cannot know him (Pound would say philistines), of creaturely and passional needs in a repressive tradition, of the self in solitude requiring a present that may promise a future—is not only impressive artistically, but is generous and courageous. His great strength—given his genius—was his broad and modest accountability within the tradition he espoused. His philosophy was no collage of culture, but digested experience. He confronted his fears where they must be confronted—in life, not in art; and he accepted the now massive body of modern psychological thought as being entirely continuous with our tradition as a whole. He was closely engaged in life, and on many fronts of knowledge, well beyond—and often beyond—the confines of his art. His poetic gifts, in short, were in the service of a trained and truly chastened philosophic mind.

What is characteristic of our age in the lapses I have mentioned, of Eliot, Pound and Lawrence, is the encapsulation of modern art. Science, philosophy, history, etc., have been raided for images, parallels and themes, but there is little structural effect on the product, which remains entirely literary, that is, severely isolated from comparable work in other fields. A friendlier description, of course, would be *pure*. In comparison with the great figures of the past, however, the historically inescapable word is "encapsulated." The striking exceptions are precisely our period's greatest figures, Joyce and Proust.

Paul described himself as "a man of letters in the old sense." His writings deal with many subjects and are often practical. But even his art was open to and continuous with the work of masters in other fields. Marx, Freud, Kropotkin, Buber—all make a structural difference, are dealt with in their *presentness* in thought rather than mere place in history. One might say that Paul's accountability within his own tradition was not only a spiritual undertaking, but appeared also in his method, and became audible as voice. It is a voice of moral finesse and amplitude, of rare equanimity, and of rare pleasure in the gifts of mind.

Paul's virtues are not merely striking or praiseworthy. As virtues, they are the virtues of greatness. They were the endowment and the triumphs of a man who, like Coleridge, was also beset by ills and injured by his own age. Both powers and failings are broadly visible in his art. Some of Paul's stories and poems, and the late novel *Making Do,* are very seriously flawed. The best of his short work, however, deserves comparison with that of Melville and Hawthorne. And in the span from Chaucer until now, *The Empire City* must be counted one of our grand eccentric books.

The death of a writer sets his work adrift in time, or rather, as Rank puts it, his work enters the "public space" in which we construct our ongoing human immortality. We judge rather differently now, are comparative on a different scale, and affirm the very inertia we formerly disowned: only a considerable force can move us. Inasmuch as no serious study has yet been made of Paul's fiction, the foregoing remarks amount to little more than assertions and are terribly bare. Yet they may have the point of personal testimony. Our estimation of all works in the public space of history begins with just this. It is the first identification of the force capable of moving us.

※

WHEN I MET HIM, PAUL WAS WRITING *The Dead of Spring,* BOOK Three of *The Empire City*. During the same period he became acquainted with Frederick and Lore Perls, the founders of Gestalt therapy. He agreed to help Fritz with a manuscript, became deeply interested and entered didactic therapy himself. "Novelty, Excitement and Growth"—part two of *Gestalt Therapy* (Perls, Hefferline, Goodman)—is entirely his own. Whatever its flaws of tone (at times it is messianic), one finds again the brilliant structural analysis of *Kafka's Prayer, Art and Social Nature, Communitas* (with Percival Goodman), and *The Structure of Literature*. One finds, too, the acute awareness of the loci of change, the sensitive boundaries of self-and-world, that figures so importantly in the method of *The Empire City. Gestalt Therapy* was published more than twenty years ago, and it offered full-blown the holistic vision of man-in-his-environment (political/historical/social/etc.) which is the tendency at present of the humanistic psychologists. An epigrammatic formula of the overriding dilemma is spoken by one of the characters of *The Empire City:* "If we conformed to the mad society, we became mad; but if we did not conform to the only society that there is, we became mad." ("The solution was to stand in love . . .").

It was while writing *Gestalt Therapy* that Paul commenced his own practice. When he told me of this decision, I asked him what his rates would be. Certainly he was conscious that whatever his theoretical brilliance, he was in the position of an intern. Yet his reply revealed much more than this. It was one of those little moments of principle in which one could almost observe him consulting the examples of his masters—perhaps, especially here, Kropotkin, whom he admired above Tolstoy. It was clear that he meant to reject the monopoly privileges of the profession and apply a standard of more or less honest work. What he said was, "What do electricians get?"

I became his patient, soon his apprentice, and attended his and others' workshops at the New York Institute for Gestalt Therapy. That period of my own life, of being much in Paul's orbit and seeing him frequently, ended around 1960, when I stopped my own work with severely disturbed children. We remained friends, however, until his death.

※

PAUL'S LAST YEARS WERE SOMBER. THE ROTTING AWAY OF NEW YORK affected him deeply. The war was a profound sorrow, a nausea of soul. The death of his twenty-year-old son was a more grievous blow than might be described. His sense of solitude, of exile among men, which (as he revealed in *Five Years*) had assailed him even in times of great public activity, became a more settled state. Where he had once written, in a poem of mixed bitterness and love

Only you

Adam, my red lover made of earth,
I am in love with in this world

he now came to write

> I've come to hate, it is appalling,
> Adam I used to love.
> In the war between mankind
> and the beauty of the world
> I am a traitor, my loyalty
> does not lie with mankind.

He wrote *Speaking and Language: Defence of Poetry* and *Little Prayers and Finite Experience,* mixed poetry and prose. He had finished with social criticism, and spoke of wanting to write an epic narrative poem. He had wanted also to write an ethics.

He continued to write short poems, especially of the New Hampshire countryside, "this pretty land of my exile," poems in which an almost wistful love of the world is mixed with the pain of solitude and the foreboding of death.

> Heart aching for the North Country
> ill as I am is my will to live
> until at least again the spring.
>
> The view is heavy wherever I look
> with those who were and will not be
> on the meadows along the river
>
> five lovers who have drifted
> to other country and my own
> flesh and blood that is dead.
>
> Today I buried as I promised
> Alice's ashes next to her nephew
> in the village graveyard up the hill.
>
> She liked it here. My son had plans
> how *he* would farm it when it was his.
> Here is a red leaf on the lawn.
>
> I am obsessed by the plain facts:
> writing them literally down
> is all the poetry I can.

The solitude he speaks of is the residual, unassimilable solitude of a man who has already confronted the identifiable problems of life and has labored by many means to solve them. It is the source of Paul's many Prayers, and of the strangely vital poems of desperation which appear often as outer limits of both his art and his religious yearning.

> Every gain has its loss, not every loss
>   its gain but sinks into the waste
> the primal pain unplastic the chaos
>   without a future the astounding past
>
> O monument of agony! if I could
>   carve you a few hacking strokes
> unfinished, you'd be worthy to be stood
>   in Florence among the other rocks.

Paul died August 2, 1972, shortly before his sixty-first birthday, and was buried in New Hampshire beside his son and the ashes of his sister.

George Dennison
March 1973

COLLECTED POEMS

GROWING OLD

❧

My anarchy as I grow old
is, Let me alone with my habits
I learned when I was poor
—nor did they ever work.

I like to have a flag,
I too, and hold it up.
I really don't expect
anybody to salute.

❧

BOY SCOUTS

When I was a scout I was our scribe
and that was bully till I lost the books
and quit, I never did become
patrol leader. But now they're plotting
to make me into the scoutmaster.

The patrol leader! he decides
the path to hike in the ferny woods,
he picks the games and chooses up the teams,

and when at night we camp who sleeps with whom
and keeps him company in his pup-tent.

But the scoutmaster, I know his job!
thinks up the trip and buys the tickets
and keeps them out of trouble with the farmer,
frowns at horsing when he has a hard-on himself,
and he sleeps with the boy who has the fits.

⚹

When an irresistible force
meets an immovable object
stick to it, something has got to give.
Maybe you'll get tired.

A farmer had a horse who wouldn't pull
when he loaded up the wagon,
he let her stand there for four days,
and she pulled it.

Except another farmer had a horse
he let stand and she got weak
trying to pull and she fell down
she fell down dead between the shafts.

Such are the pleasing thoughts that fill my mind
on the Pennsylvania railway
in February 1960
going from coast to coast.

⚹

"An average heart
in a life of seventy years
has done the work to lift

4

the largest battleship
fourteen feet out of the water."

Alas, my average heart
has already had it,
why do you tax me further
unresponding wife
sullen play-reviewers?

William Hunter after a heart attack
said, "Now my life is in the hands
of every fool who chooses to annoy me."

O metal battleship
fourteen feet out of the water,
blaze once with all your guns
before with a terrific
splash you flop back dead
and capsize and sink.

※

A POLICY MEETING

All of a sudden I understand
I am too old to love
adolescent boys
and make a fool of myself.

Come three knocks at the door:
Welcome, Age Ambition
and Service to my country!
here is bread and salt.

We four: Age Ambition
Service to my country
and I sit and plot.
But I, since I remember

a merry hour with Billy
quietly and firmly
veto the resentful
measures against the young.

※

EASTER 1968

When young proclaim Make Love Not War
I back them up, I back them up,
and some are brave as they can be.
But they don't make love to me.

He brought petunias to the Be-In
and fed a lump of sugar to the policeman's horse,
but he, he said, he didn't like my vibrations
—for this I didn't need to trudge to Central Park.

Sure I am heartened by my crazy allies
and their long hair looks very nice on some,
but frankly, more of them were interesting persons
before they all began to do their thing.

※

I waited the seven hours till he would come (he said),
tricking myself with phony chores to blank out the time.
Headlights glared up the hill, the car doors slammed,
but those who noisily got out were never he,
and then he didn't come at all.
How could he be so perfidious?
He spoke not only words but with his hard-on.
When I was young we were responsible
to our temptations, not as if we had

a hundred thousand years to go to school,
just as we also had to work for a living.
Suddenly it was still and out of my confused day
I noticed again the black and bright night sky.

※

We have a verb "stood up" it means
I kept the date the other didn't,
and damn if twice a week
somebody doesn't stand me up.
My verses come back in the mail.
The President has lied to us again.
I am at odds and ends
and walk the streets a maze.

Willie the crazy boy
came to see me yesterday
clowning gaily at
his hilarious ineptitude
to get the slightest satisfaction.
Grandly he proclaimed
"I could renounce the world!"
laughing fit to be tied.

※

I didn't think when I gave up
my claim to be, my immortal gripe,
and I began to doubt
that I was worthy but neglected,
that I should feel like this
hit-or-miss and happy-go-
unlucky like an Irish pennant
on Somebody's old satchel.

7

The worst about a big hotel
is the inevitable clientele
of aging folk who have made money
like me. It isn't funny.
Naturally the girl who made the reservation
allotted me as befits my station
and now I am too tired to haul my bag and look
for a more entertaining nook.

When I was trapped, tired, bored
I sent my shadowself abroad,
    went down the street and boldly had
    the simple joys I was afraid

to take that even readily
the world would have given me.
    And he returned and was glad
    and stood beside where I sat sad.

"Why do you come back?" I said,
"and not abandon me for dead
    with this body that I cannot use?"
    But so it was and so it is.

Flames of love licking the rafters
with lurid hopes I waited for our meeting
that came to nothing, as it used.
"What a pity the universe

isn't practical!" I drily said
—I have lost my edge of bitterness
and when I frankly wailed you gazed at me
admiring for an honest ancient knight.
So now another evening, aftermath
of nothing, with my nerves still raw, I spend
without remorse, even without despair,
guessing at the interval between
this hour and death.
                              Yet automatically
—unwilled—from time to time I lift my hands
slowly and swiftly let them drop again.
It has no words.

෴

I bore my baby in my arms through the night
like the cantor the Torah dressed in silk
I used as a boy to look at critically.
But his choir sang large chords
as his figure swung along.
Go to sleep now, daughter. I am old
and very tired carrying you late.
Your father too needs to be comforted.
"I give you good advice," he used to sing,
"do not forsake my law.
She is the tree of life
for those who cleave to her,
her ways are pleasant ways
and all their windings peace."

෴

In that company I was malcontent,
I gave them what I could and pretty freely

but they couldn't give me what they had to give
and therefore feared and hurt me, as they could.
To stay my anger, that was issueless,
I didn't go there any more. So passed a month.

Last night they sent me an ambassador:
what were my grievances? *He* was aggrieved
because I cut them cold, yet it was petty,
he said, to lose for spite without a try
my friendship rich with profit for them all
etcetera—he spoke out frank and fair,
passim milking me for bibliography.

And *still* he did not give me anything,
not even to respect my malcontent.
Now I am burdened also with his plea.
He does the best he can, *I* am to blame.
Good! I have profited these bitter verses.

🌽

Go tell Aunt Rhody, go tell Aunt Rhody,
go tell Aunt Rhody the old gray goose is dead.
I drove my wheel too far when I was a boy
and I jerked off a couple of times too many
I once had an awful scare
and I have been to San Diego.
Oh the number of the speeches I have made
is like the witch-grass in the garden
and the press-conferences for peace
have been almost as many as the wars.
But now my stare is fixed, my blood congeals:
he asks me for another essay on the schools,
his letter flutters from my nerveless fingers.
She died in the mill pond, she died in the mill pond,
she died in the mill pond standing on her head.

LONG LINES ON THE LEFT BANK

These nights get on my nerves, these sleepless nights.
In the day I can sleep, but what to do with the nights?
Alone I'm not lonely, only I don't fall asleep
—when I was lonely and bitter I could fall asleep.
Out is six flights down, it is another world,
so I sit in bed and write, but hotels in Paris
are cold at 3 A.M. What am I doing here?
"Why, you're writing in your lonely bed just like the others."
But I'm not *doing* it, that's just the point.
"Most of the others aren't doing it either."
Ah, then I'm doing it, just like the others.
I wish the pretty Arab who lives in Room 15
would knock and keep me company; I'd knock myself
except he has a friend and they are bound to rob me.
When I think of the long years I have spent of painful nights
and the years of painful days that have been like sleepless nights,
I come to no conclusion. Meaning is another world.

HANDBALL PLAYERS

The ball we bought in December
was tired in the shop
and didn't want to bounce at all
on the below-freezing court.

Arrogant in their hot
youth the Puerto Ricans
challenged us and smashed the wall.
But Dave and I were cold,

steady and intelligent,
and coldly took their nickels

dimes and silver quarters
with small shots in the corners.

※

My missing teeth ache the most,
they are the majority.
My dead friends
do me the worst distress.

Hope, that future vacuum,
I abhor, oh more than thirty feet!
—nor has the real, but,
been a bed of roses.

Where, God, are these thoughts tending
I think aloud for whom?
You who have been absent,
it wasn't I that turned my face away.

Here am I! though I say it
grudgingly and late.
"Yes," agrees my Lord,
"grudgingly and late."

※

Good riddance to bad rubbish O at last
my teeth, for forty years you couldn't crack nuts
nor greedily suck out the sweet juice of corn,
but pain I had from you hundreds of horrible nights
when being poor I couldn't get help
and being puritanical I wouldn't take aspirin.
From the beginning you were misshapen

and a damned baseball broke the best of you
leaving ugly my wasted youth among the Americans
who set great store on regular and flashing teeth.
Now I am rich and an exquisite craftsman
will fashion me a bright smile not my own.
If I had bitten the world angrily,
as it did me, I too might have had vigorous teeth.
But my way is to be patient, and I have survived
even to this year not worse than the last.

✻

OSCAR WILLIAMS

                                    Daily
I read my friends' doing in the *Times*:
Yesterday my brother showed a plan
to the Secretary of the Interior
and Bayard doused a box of dynamite
and kept a boy from blowing up the block.
I see Saul has a play. We are the news
—it's not the world we wanted to be news in—
and here is Oscar's funny face,
his wry sarcastic and fun-loving face,
peering out from the obituaries.
He wrote a letter to me last week
about a piece of mine on Robert Burns.
I understand it less and less
(although it's actuarial),
my rage is all the more outspoken.
I wish I had had courage
when I was young and needed it.
But then I hadn't yet encountered
the high and mighty of this earth,
to learn they are like me or Oscar Williams,
or not even.

P.W.

Tonight a man passed away
in my house, in my own bed.
He rather happily was playing
with my merry daughter
yet he was dead within the hour.
His heart broke. Now my own
body is like an enemy
waiting for me in ambush.

I am smoking the tobacco that he left
and picking up the shoes that he left.
Two men are carrying out
the body that he left.
My merry daughter is asleep
in the other room.
I must be deep in shock
for it is like a dream.

Courage to go into it.
Patience to go bit by bit.

PERSEUS

To my dismay as I become
a spokesman in the nation
I have turned into an evil
old man. I do not care about

the young that I make love to
but pay distractedly attention
and talk my own ideas.
I'm too intelligent, I guess,
and well brought up to do much harm
but less and less in love myself
I lash out at our ugly cities.
Creator Spirit, come.
I think of John who loyally
loved me still while he went mad,
while he went mad and I went sane.
To no one now, never, never,
shall I speak again how it is,
as I used to speak to John,
except to these damned pages
that cannot kiss and come across.
I used to hope because he needed that.
O crazy Hope, where are you lurking lost?
You must be somewhere hiding
for it cannot be I work so hard
just by duty or routine.
No, I have learned to outwit
grisly Disappointment
by working as I look the other way
toward nothing. And loud praise
leaves me also cold.
My name is Perseus. My sword is Simple.
My polished shield is Absence from this world.

I THOUGHT OF THE PHRASE
OF MUSIC

I thought of the phrase of music
   for me to die by
   if it were a play

and it was mine to choose it.
  What friend shall I entrust it to
  to make my ending be just so?

But for this grandiose episode
  maybe I have wept
  enough to accept
to die by the wayside
    as I did when I still had
    a penis that grew hard.

That was before I became
  an important man.
  Now my pen has grown
so savage I'm ashamed
    and sorry by daylight,
    but raven again at night.

Lord God who are history
    including the history of me,
    be all this as it may
or any other way
      that chooses me or I choose it
      as I thought of the phrase of music.

⚹

Yes, when I was twenty
I should have converted to High Church
and gone to the pretty seminary
rich with scholarships on Ninth Avenue
to study Greek and organ
and history of the Councils
in a long black cape lined with red.

Amiable Episcopalians
would have put up with my deviations
to make use of a Jewish boy

with a flair for dogmatics
who could write like an angel,
and damn if by this birthday
I wouldn't be the Bishop of New York
in Wow! the mighty house
of St. John the Divine
on One Hundred Thirteenth Street.

Instead, the road I wended
has led me to my semicircle
of tall maples already scarlet
in the North Country in the early fall
here in the airy barn loft
that I have sparsely furnished.

Six of one and half a dozen of the other!
Creator of the only world!

꿏

SYCAMORES

My way of showing
    my longing for the Americans
was not to give a damn
    for their morals and opinions.

They have read me perfectly
    and have made of me a model
for me to live up to
    like a statue in the park.

But now I am growing old
    and I am ashamed
of my shabby dress and missing teeth
    and my near-sighted eyes.

17

And they will have their statue yet
  made of bronze
standing in the sycamores
  whose yellow bark is peeling.

※

I opened with my key, to my astonished joy
there in the room stood one I love, for whom I have
longed in my lonely exile, but I said perplexed,
"How did *you* get in?" in an interminable moment
I did not clasp him in my arms, and realized
that he was dead and that this was a ghost.
He said, "When you're dead too we'll be together
as we have failed. I love you, Paul," and was not
and I looked at the key that I was holding in my hand.

※

IN THE JURY ROOM, IN PAIN

Waiting to whimper or for Messiah
it doesn't matter much
if I wait in the jury room
of the Criminal Courts Building
until the prosecutor
challenges me again
because I don't believe
in *their* penal system

or if like yesterday I hover
eight miles high until
the iron roc descends
it doesn't matter where.
In between is better
than whence I came or where I go

to be with my headache
alone in purgatory.

Here watchfully I wend
and wander through the wonderful
landscape of Pains
where unexpectedly
the ache-trees in the grove
blossom into flowers
and small birds murmuring
hop from twinge to twinge.

Oh the days have vanished quickly by
during which I made a library
of useful thoughts for the Americans
and became a famous man;
but the one empty night of torment
in which I do not fall asleep
is when I write the poem
that says how my life was.

LONG LINES: YOUTH AND AGE

Like a hot stone your cock weighs on mine, young man,
and your face has become brutish and congested.
I'd draw back and gaze at it but drunk with carbon dioxide
we cannot stop snuffling each other's breath.

I am surprised you lust for a grayhead like me
and what a waste for me to grapple so much pleasure
with sliding palms holding your thin body
firmly while you squirm, till it is time to come.

Come, lad . . . I have come with him for company
to his pounding heart. We are wet. Wistfully

I play with his black hair while he falls asleep
minute by minute, slowly, unlike my restless life.

It is quiet on his little boat. "He's a noisy lover,"
I notice idly—the April air is keen—
"but he has no human speech." It's I who say
the words like "I love you" or "Thank you."

✳

Often a pathetic makeshift,
sometimes nobly I made do,
but I never made arrangements,
I never was that much ahead.

During the idle times
when other men make plans
I grew into a panic
—what did you want to say, O Pan?

"Curly-headed boy!
why do you hold your breath
when I meet you in the woods?
And yet you rove the woods."

Then I fled in confusion
and have lived to tell the tale,
the Americans have profited
by my honest speech.

In pain and panic
I didn't provide for myself
but I hammered out of it
a simple politics:

for God's sake,
in the mathematical

improbability of happiness
don't add new obstacles.

✺

HILLBILLY TUNE

Don' never go with a young man
    your evening will be ruin
for a young man's got ideas
    an' he worries how he's doin'.

But an old man likes warm nookie
    because his toes are cold
an' he'll take care o' you, honey,
    he may be bald but he's bold.

I use to go with a young man
    an' he never did come across
but my oh my with my old man
    it's pitch an' toss, pitch an' toss.

Because the near he gets to the grave
    he wants to have it. Period.
There's lots o' fuck in a well-used cock
    before he's dead but good.

LONGER POEMS

SAINT CECILIA'S DAY, 1941

"Admit that it means something!"
—Beethoven, to Goethe

They all looked dead with tingling ears,
close-eyed and open-mouthed, or open-eyed
with mouths closed, their limbs involuntary.
The voices of the instruments harmonized
the ages and sexes of humanity
squeals of little children and the clear
warbling of women and sonorous males.
You would not think the world was at war.
Lastly silence, which is quiet
only after music or when the passions
are finished.   The flood of life returned
into our brains and we were separate,
into our legs we rose and came outside.
But it was the holiday of Saint Harmony
and after saying nothing for awhile
drinking our drinks we said in praise of music:

I.

Lothario said, "Heaven and hell, I was
so sensitive sometimes a major triad
of wooden oboes drilled me like a toothache,

they added fourths and my head split. The chaos
of mixed timbres, say the whine of strings
with a piano, oh it separated
my organism into protozoa,
a horn croaked and they curled their feet and died.
Naturally, when I was in school
they called me tone-deaf and told me not to sing.
What the teacher used to call a unison
was a chasm you could drop a desk and chair in.

"If in this agony I inwardly
would close my ears as I can,
as others close their nostrils against a stink,
then could I hear the music of the spheres.
For know that the creator of the heavens
standing on Canto Fermo forth first breathed
the solemn vibration of the sun
alla breve and filled it out with planets
and passing notes of comets with long tails.
These tones are sustained. Millennia
elapse to the measure, and there is no
cadence yet—the cadence is to come.
The ear hears nothing of it, but the body
flows in tides.
        "I can't," he bitterly
whispered, "hear that music any more.
But I am wiser than I was. To noises!
noises of fire, void, and violence
and interminable continuity
God listens patiently. A stretto trill
in all the voices. Surely the frame
is strong or would by now have cracked, and man
man have fragmented into fractional
intervals and evaporated—"
                He paused;
for everywhere the Man was waging war
but had not yet dropped the first atom bomb.

"At other times, as mildly tonight,
I hear such tones: *'who listens to these tones*

will never know sorrow more.' "
                              "Why do you say it
with death in your eyes if it is so?"
"No. It is so. It is really so."

II.

The architect began more merrily.
"You know Amphion built Thebes with a song,
by harmony on the Boeotian plain.
Now I have had the happy thought of him
standing in a rowboat on the Hudson
while all the fishes look with open mouths
untuning with a supersonic lyre
a thing or two or three or four or five.

"His nail is screeching on the wire strings
and the tip-top of the Empire State Building
conceived as a mooring-mast for Zeppelins
falls like they. The gilt Prometheus
sinks in the pond. Columbia's South Hall
—now there's a building where you could not change
a line without improving the proportions—
he ruins with a flourish, all the fishes
joyfully leap out of the water to see.

"Now Central Park, it once was wild and gay
with bushes for the privacy of love
before another Moses gave it laws
and subsidized the hotels—therefore praise,
you fairies and sailorboys and little whores,
Amphion's name forevermore! he doused
the officious lights, but left the silent moon.
He rubbed the prude off Fiorello's face,
Thomas Dewey he left half a mustache.
My friends! let me have another drink.

"With a large arm Amphion sweeps the strings!
The modulus, the modulus take not

from iron girders or a two-by-four,
take it from the grandeur of a man
standard of doorways. Let the outside in
and inside out, so the space can move;
measure it, so the space can dance.
What is proportion? Lay out twos and threes
on the horizontal for the walking, skipping,
instantaneously leaping eyes,
and where we see perspectively draw in
irrational diagonals. All masses
want finally to rest, do not thwart them;
but passion and pleasure, they are curves that wander,
let them soar—
                    "Where was I?" he asked
and then like Palinurus drowsed and drowned.

III.

I said, "I pass. After that, I pass.
However, let me ask Herman a question:
that music that you played tonight,
what does that music mean?"

"Say, have you ever watched him, bow in hand,
for the florid Concert in the Key of D?
—suddenly the symphony's alive
without the solo, all its veiny tendrils
ramifying into foliage
and rosebuds without Herman! he must wait.
'There goes my tune,' he mutters in his mustache,
'if I'd a known it I'd a stood in bed.'
His bow hangs down forgotten. Finally
he drops the fiddle from his chin and listens.
'This is so strong and sweet that I could listen
to only this.' No, no, now Herman play!
it's time.
                    "We know his phrases, how they pause
in the air, like flowers, in still air, in June."
I turned to him.

25

IV.

But in his changing eyes
were many thoughts and he said in a voice of pain
—so it sounded, but he is hard to read—
"The first years that I played the Quartet
in C-Sharp Minor that we played tonight
—and who knows these tones will know no sorrow more—
I thought, This is just absent-mindedness,
heat lightning, a jig for a carousel;
along with the great heart the mind got tired,
and that is what's written in the score.

"I bent my head. His faults also were songs.
Jokes are the poetry of desperation.
Lapses are the poetry of fatigue.
Heat lightning is a memory of power.
Son, whatever is lost is the meaning of music
and agony is written in the score.
When I play it, if I sometimes weep
my tears are not for only Beethoven."

"Who knows these tones," Lothario assured him,
"will never know sorrow more."
                                    "After a while
I myself played it better, and I thought:
Here's an ingenious machine for Joy,
to force the joy to be where no joy is.
Every part of it is put together
with the cunning of a man who knew himself
and therefore knew how to distract himself.
Explaining it, Beethoven quickly said,
'It's made of what I picked up here and there.'
Yes, he had lots of notebooks to ransack
in winter like a squirrel. He kept busy.
I too kept busy, twenty seven times
around the world, a virtuoso fiddler!

"It happened one day that I ceased to think
and listened—as he listened who was deaf—

where beyond these tones opens the silent world,
and suddenly, like a sick memory
that strikes a patient and the veil is raised,
I saw again the horrifying scene
when Goethe burst in tears and Beethoven
leapt from the piano where he was improvising
and shook him and cried out, 'Admit! admit!
admit! admit! admit that it means something!'

Something is there. Something *must* be there.

and what if it's nothing?

          "I'll play these tones no more!
I felt the weakness creep into my hand
and with an awful sound the G-string broke."

"No, Herman, but you didn't play at all."

"I didn't hold a bow for seven years."

"Ah! ah, I thought that it was longer."

"I didn't try each impasse to the end
but only till I got the idea."

"What! have you tried them all?" I cried in envy.

"Yes."
      Yes!? what was this simple Yes?
the appetite of man is infinite.
But I held my peace.
        He said, "Who knows these tones
will know no sorrow more. If you would know,
if you would know these tones!—
a pleasing truth is written in the score,
all that is best is easiest.
Your ordinary mind, *that* is the Way!
when you feel sleepy sleep, etcetera,

if you are dying whimper.
Who *knows* these tones will never know sorrow more."

⚘

THE WELL OF BETHLEHEM

1 *Chronicles xi, 15–19*

Under the hot sun the reeking battle
in the barley-field the soaking blood
was sickening, and by dusk
the warriors were no longer fascinated.
Their souls were empty and dubious.
The Philistine fled from Pasdammim
leaving many silent bodies
and some whimpering that had been shrieking.
And David the young king the new
went hurrying to the cave his hold
as if he the victor were pursued.

His body-captains have preceded him:
"The King comes! for God's sake, water!
give us clothes without blood on them.
Thee God we praise, but—" they have lapsed
into a blank, being alive
but not much otherwise than those who lie
on the barley-field.

The women and the boys move busily
bringing water and blowing up the fires
and now here spoke King David
in the gateway, in a choking voice:
"I thirst. I am thirsty."

Instantaneously (like a picture)
two women are standing before him
with toward his lips a pitcher of water

and a pitcher of wine. Upon these pitchers,
not taking them, and past them at the women
looking for a long moment with glazed eyes,
David said, "From whence is this water?"
She said it was the water from the well.
His eyebrows met. He said an awful oath
dangerous from the mouth of the anointed,
and with a large arm struck
the pitchers from their hands.

The women's faces are white and open-mouthed.
It is still. The earthen pitchers
lie shattered on the stone floor
and the women have withdrawn into the shadows.
Nevertheless, here is another damsel
standing before him with a pitcher raised,
"My lord, this is water from Adullam."
He did not strike her but he spoke a groan,
he did not whimper but some tears
were rolling down his cheeks in his young beard.
"Will no one give me water
out of the Well of Bethlehem?"

Step back his soldiers from him, for that well
that well is in the camp of the Philistine
by the gate. A mother of grown sons
looks at him with wide eyes across her shoulder
seeing that he too is mad, like Saul.

Here he is standing silently self-pitying
because he had fought hard. There is an hour
in battle when the impetus is lost,
we have really been defeated and are as good as dead,
there is nothing to do but strike another blow
and strike another blow and still another
wearier blow, but we do not have another.
Thee God we praise!—the shout is ours
but not from our throats, and it penetrates
hardly to our hearing, but far off.

Now I am thirsty but what is the good of water
not the water of my home where I was born?
I am already dead and what is the good
holding water toward my lips that is not the water of life?

Then the three captains of the King's body,
Eleazar, Jeshobeam, and Joab
—whom Joab was the first to scale Mt. Zion—
looked at their charge the body of the King
and very wearily but not reluctantly
they girded on their swords and took up pitchers.
They brushed by King David in the gateway
not rudely but not considerately,
it was just how it was.
                    It is no matter
for the King is not there where he seemed to be.
Was looking but he is not seeing anything.
It is too late to help him any more,
the King has already died of thirst,
now he is inventing songs and verses.
"As the hart," he sings, "panteth after water-brooks
—the voice of the Lord maketh the hinds to calve."
He is quenching his thirst
with language! See, his orange lip
is curling with satisfaction.
"I laid me down and slept; I awaked!"
(He sang it when he fled from Absalom.)

Little spoke the three Mighties on their way
to fetch the water from the well of Bethlehem.
Jeshobeam—at whom the people look
askance because he slew three hundred men—
he said, "I go each time involuntarily
but as I go get deeper into it."
And Eleazar said, "He would do well
to quench his thirst with the available!
he is sullen and peevish not toward enemies
but just toward us who are his present help."
But Joab said, "It is the Lord's anointed,

hush. Hush!"—for even as he said it
they came on the first sentries.

The King has sat down, and the frightened women
still stunned get out their brooms
to sweep the shards of the broken pitchers.
These shards of a brown glaze are still so soon
after the crash that they possess, each shard,
around it a bright outline; and hovering
close above them all a Violence.

As with their brooms the women sweep them up
the earthen shards turn simply into earth,
but the Violence on the newly cleaned floor
burns, if anything, colder in the broom-tracks
and in the room there is the echo of a shout.
But when the women wept, the Violence left.

It was hard for the handmaidens of David
to please him, though they also did their best.

The three Mighties came back with one pitcher,
water from the well of Bethlehem.
They were bleeding darkly from old wounds
and bleeding brighter from new wounds.
The King sat half-reclined on his couch
looking out and seeing everything clear,
whom Joab came and offered him the water.
"Water from the well of Bethlehem."
Then David roused himself and bowed his head
deep in shame. And he stood up at once
and took the pitcher from him, lest his Captain
might stand in front of him humiliated
by offering and not being accepted.
He accepted the gift with an obeisance
but he would not drink. In a deep voice he said:
"My God forbid it I should do this thing.
Shall I drink the blood of these men
that have put their lives in jeopardy?

for with their lives they brought it.
Therefore I will not drink it."

What shall I do with this water?
embarrassed that I have it in my hands
and I am hot with shame.
Lack and loss may be consoled, but success
—only God can console.
                    So King David
poured out the water on the ground to God.
And the women again brought him a pitcher of water,
"Here my lord, this is the common water."
But the King said, "Thank you; later.
I no longer thirst."

I no longer thirst! spiteful that I am!
Even so, let me be magnanimous
and drink and try and slake my burning thirst.

※

THE DEATH OF LEON TROTSKY, 1940

I.

What burnt? a meteor close?
or a premonitory comet
that will in fifty years return and burn?
or an old light-bulb in the house?

A peculiar song for a hero
with an ambiguous mind I start.
Trotsky to the end he hated
went fiercely struggling still;
I am suspicious, tentatively
excited weigh the evidence,
quite stirred on one hypothesis.

II.

In France, Norway, and Mexico
in sovereign states by wit and private arms
he warded off the murder day by day.

In every article and speech
we heard the rhythm and cry
of a man at bay, a man at bay.

The initiative is the assassin's
the initiative is always the assassin's
every night and day the initiative is the assassin's.

III.

So now is the time to grieve or rejoice
or be complacent, finally give up,
or shrug. To take advantage
for loyalty or pragmatically
of his name, of his corpse (who can condemn it?)
to reserve judgment (who can condemn it?)
for a week or for a year or history
to institute another inquiry.
To choose the style of ambiguity.
Now is the time to shrug.

If the case is as Lev Davidovich said
now, comrades, is the time to mourn
for the inventor of insurrection is dead.
Unmoving lies the chief of our excitement
and the infernal time-bomb
everywhere doesn't know when to explode.
If the documents should be authenticated
and if the facts confirm the theory
—what month and year is it? August 1940!
if France could have been freed in 1936!
and Russia saved in 1926!
But mourning isn't fatal: in his books

is an analysis and the next step
and on his dying lips there was an urgent call.

But if all of this was lies and spite,
or self-deception, the most likely.
A man who used to have the power
embarks on desperate adventures
the final hero-crimes. His mania
in the end was obvious, when to go forward
was easier than back or hold,
until the last minority of fractions
is estranged.—Yet what heroic perfidy
to even a prepared statement for his deathbed
with copies for the press
—and now whispered mechanically, for whom?

But if neither truth nor lies but only error
men in this unprophetic man believed,
if all are in danger for another reason
and some already dying in a different war,
nor is the end desirable he hoped
nor would, thank God, the method lead to it,
now is the time to be still at a loss
for an explanation of a senseless world.

IV.

Nevertheless!
Trotsky is glorious
    because the present hour
    was not in his power;

at worst, at most
—a poet may securely boast—
    he didn't govern that society
    nor ratify the treaty;

it was not he who set the time
to guarantee the maximum

of disaster, and his alleged plot
before its moment was cut short.

v.

The soul, the art of dissidence,
is by a hatchet blow destroyed.
Unmoving lies the chief of excitement
and his voluble speech is mute.

Of those who struggle to live an hour longer
and choose to live the hour close to death,
how recklessly and fiercely he cringed
from the ending he methodically sought.

Thee God we praise! there is an insurrection
of the body and the brain that worked too hard
and the exhausted refuse thrown away,
as Emma said, as if by capitalists,

a general strike! no longer rallying!
no longer rallying to policy
—this is freedom, and the tyranny
can never be established again.

Shall not we, brothers, for a moment still
our living fears in praise of freedom death,
revolution death? Oh let's declare
—at last when he cannot dissent again—

the war is over and that we have won.
I praise no uncertain victory,
no conditions, not an armistice,
but unconditional and absolute,

given to us, just as grace is given,
not made by us—though many lend a hand.
This victory is small,
nobody would deny it to anybody,

but it is not hypothetical.

VI.

But Trotsky's body too was an object of contention. Three days after the assassination in Coyoacan, Albert Goldman and other American Trotskyist leaders made a bid to bring the body to New York for a public funeral. There was dissension also among the leaders—nearly half the American members had just seceded from the Fourth International.

The State Department of the United States, however, that had previously denied asylum to Trotsky himself, would not permit the importation of his corpse to be a center of street fighting between Trotskyists and Stalinists in New York City. Goldman thought of appealing the decision to the courts, but in the end the body was burned and the ashes given to Trotsky's widow.

VII.

The Jews have a pioneering song
    I'll sing for him and us all,
its lilt is light, its beat is strong,
    and it has a dying fall:

        Up into our land we go
        up into our land

        we have already plowed it
        and we have seeded it

        but we haven't yet harvested
        have not yet harvested.

꙳

GENERAL WASHINGTON

Hot-headed patriots, many of them bigoted
and avaricious narrow tradesmen
—it was a contradiction, petty bourgeois

impetuously taking the big risks
of war with stingy measures. Much they did
who can praise? and yet they did one deed
wise beyond praise as if inspired
by an uncanny forethought Congress chose
Washington. Not a New Englander
but from a class and country that bred soldiers,
a character in history unique
to be among stubborn freemen
Commander-in-Chief for seven awful years,
and then go home.

He was prudent to a fault in the short run.
But falling back across New York and Jersey
he guarded there would be a longer run
and did not wait too long, but fell on Trenton.

Diffident he was, like one who thinks
of everything where much must be in doubt,
and so he listened too much to his staff
when his own judgment was superior;
yet—sharing blunders he made officers
for the war that had to drag in any case
till the King gave up at his slow-witted speed.

And isn't it beautiful and noteworthy
how youngsters, the adventurous and brilliant,
the Hamiltons and Lafayettes, adored him
(I choose the word with care) not servilely?
He must have been like a father to them
so that they also grew into the future.

So we can guess his heartsick shock
come to West Point and Arnold wasn't there.
"My mind misgave me," said the General,
"I had no idea of the real cause,"
although methodically he had observed
all the small signs, but he was not suspicious.
Then Washington's dismay it was, I think,

bursting into the tears he never shed,
that scalded André, whom he wouldn't yield
even a military death but hanged him
from a gallows. (Gentlemen of those times
set store upon the style, though dead is dead.)
He was merciless, not like himself.
When Lee fell back for no good reason at Monmouth,
he "swore until the leaves shook on the trees"
and held the line and rallied, for the men
were awestruck. Mostly, but, he was unmoved
by a mischance and did the best he could,
except it was different before Yorktown!
"I am distressed beyond expression!"
he fretted like a child as he flew south,
and laid his careful plans, the time he scented,
but would not own it yet, the victory.
By this time he was flexible like lightning
that leaps the high potential.
                              Washington's
integrity in all the other things,
money, rank, or the nice points of honor
—among the graspers in and out of Congress
and in the army (and the King of England
still thought to make George Washington a duke!
but not hereditary! said the King)
—was so Olympian that he was spared
intrigues, they dissipated when he looked.

Nor did he threaten once—this is remarkable!—
to quit, as a weapon, though he was
sometimes in despair
and truly might, though not a praying man,
have knelt in the snow, as in the picture.

So might a poet, avid to praise,
avid to praise loud but hard to please,
praise Washington and call the Congress wise.
And still he looms there in the dubious past
real. He does not need interpretation.

Transparent in his virtues and his limits,
not greatly superior in any crisis,
superior enough in every crisis,
a Commander-in-Chief! it is a man whose peers
or abler men in this and that respect,
do not need to make allowances for him
but confidently speak and will be heard.
For war is senseless, its suffering is senseless,
but it is demonic, it is mankind gone mad,
and lucky is the people if its leaders
warrant ordinary admiration
as noble honest men who are not fools.

Such, he seemed like a god to wise old tired
Europe, where we meet, with pleased surprise,
our Washington on little village squares.
It's reasonable that his statue is there.

NORTH COUNTRY

꿏

    Sowing, ignorant
of the method—maybe it
    will grow anyway.

꿏

I slowed the car.
A doe bounded
across the road
and ducking under
the badminton net
went in the woods.
I speeded up.

꿏

THE FIREFLY

Mostly I let be, when a snake
is horribly swallowing a frog,
when flocking sparrows peck in anger
out the eyes of a murderous kitten,

I take no sides. The nature of things is deadly.
I shudder, but it does not fascinate me
and I go away, not to put a stop.

Yet I have rescued from the octagonal web
of the pinching spider this sick firefly,
I hope in time. I have taken sides.
For late last night this one or one like him
amazed my lonely room with a blue bolt
of lightning, when I was half asleep.

𛀁

The porch in prudence I repaired last summer
serves me this as the solid state of things
that have been always so.
Evenly gray is the sheen of all the boards
old and new weathered by the winter,
and the post that I made no longer mentions
how the roof was falling down in ruins.
The backyard is quiet. I have mowed it.
The giant leaves of the red rhubarb spread
their palms out to the sun, and the enormous muzzle
of Henry's cow is munching the bamboo
succulent to her, across my fence.

𛀁

Our house in the hollow is hemmed in
    also by immense maple trees
but walk a short ways to the meadows
    or up the hill and skies

shatter the world, it cannot hold
    against the gales of openness

whose clouds appear from nowhere
and drift away southwest.

But by the road a small daisy
stands up among the horizons,
a still wheel of eighteen spokes
and a yellow hub that spins.

※

It is peaceful coming home across the meadow,
the flowers are continuous as I come.
My bounding beagle somewhere in the hay
is invisible, except her flapping ears
and the white curl of her happy tail
moving through the swaying sea.
The yellow flowers are closing in the evening.
I am not lonely for my only world
is softly singing to me as I come.
They who know me as a bitter critic
who is impractical to serve his country
know me poorly; I am freeborn and pleased
with this world that I have inherited.
And ever my little dog is looking back
with her gleaming eye, and waits if I am coming.

※

In July the tawny hawkweed
hieracium Canadense
rioting before the hayer
lays it low, it is on fire
far into the field
where it is peaceful like a world
where there are no human beings.

❦

Sweet as the meadow smells and lovely
as its variety of flowers
was the hour we trudged across the sweet
and various meadow often pausing,
and oh this truthful sentence is
past tense the while I trudge across,
often pausing, the sweet-smelling meadow
lovely with a variety of flowers.

❦

It was good when you were here,
  I am lonely now.
Nighttime is the worst
  when the light drops out of the sky

and the colored fields that were
  company vanish.
I dislike to go out
  into the dark open

but in my empty house
  is the presence of your not-being,
the speech we do not sound,
  the touch I cannot reach.

Surely long ago
  I wrongly set out toward
this familiar encounter
  with no one at all.

During my prime years
  my country passed me by.
I made do. (America
  alas has not made do.)

43

God bless you who from time to time
    have brought me peace for a day
and saved me from writing only prose
    while my hair turns gray

and may to me God give
    the grace of the poor:
to praise without a grudge
    the facts just as they are.

❧

To this mosquito my vast flesh
is a rich acre like where we pick squash
and my slap is an earthquake—missed.
Another way of looking at it
is that her resolute intelligence
and mine are matched in a serious duel
that she or I will surely win tonight,
she feints and vanishes into the shadows
—got her.
Like us they go to slaughter and are legion.

❧

"Your ordinary mind, that is the Way.
When you feel sleepy, sleep, et cetera."
It comes to being sleepy, though I still
stagger to the stove to get my dinner.
Three years I made a thousand pages
and a hundred flights across America
and kept an ill-starred love affair alive.
Being alone at last, I droop and drowse.

※

Sit still. Soon a hummingbird
hovers on the phlox.
A chipmunk scampers
away with a butternut.
The first line of a poem visits.
Peace not yet.

※

Clutched in the hot hand
of the child, the flowers wilt
before we get home.

※

On the Coös meadows along the Connecticut
a week after haying the stubble is soft again.
The misty evening is falling down
from the big sky in big sections.
My dog Daisy daintily puts her paws
far afield into the crashing stillness
where the mowers left an edge of stars
—like the daffodils beside the lake he saw.

※

BRUNSWICK SPRINGS

It isn't Delphi, though it has
sulphurous springs from seven spouts
and ruins of an hotel
burned down by the Hoodoo,

yet it is pretty with its pines
and tranquil pond of white lilies
   like the that blind Monet
   painted by telepathy.

It was religious to cleanse
the spa of vandal beer-cans
   as Sally did today
   housewifely for the county.

❧

Though I have gone to Glendalough
and Trunk Bay of the Virgin Islands
and come around the head at Makapuu
where the Pacific Ocean
springs open like a door,

yet the Connecticut at Stratford
is just as fair and will be famous
when tourists come to see the very spot
like the relic in the crypt
where he wrote *North Percy*.

Oh this will serve me nothing then,
but today it is a consolation
for a writer in a generation
that can't read English
—God, are they boring.

❧

PROVERBS OF A SMALL FARM

If the raccoon gnaws ten percent of the corn,
don't set a trap, plant another row.

If spinach goes to seed too soon,
try it twice, then plant chard.

Don't fight the cabbage worms
if store-bought is good and cheap.

Do very little "on principle",
life is hard enough as it is.

Honor the weeds that love your land
and call them flowers, they seed themselves.

When phoebes nest in the barn, you have no choice
but to leave the big door open also to thieves.

Many things will grow in the North Country
that they don't grow,
but then it's hard to give away your surplus
that they won't eat.

Nature is profligate, usury is natural,
but *you* must not pocket the increase.

One spring when the snow melts, my asparagus
will finally be big enough for someone else to eat.

༾

TWO SENTENCES

But I'm a summer gardener:
though I ruthlessly swat
the flies in my house,
in my field I will not shoot
the chucks but let them eat.
To Alvin, acres that he farms
are home—he has the joy of hunting
with a flushed face and a loud gun.

My hunting is to notice
my loud gun is to say,
and so I immortalize
details of this world.
Some I have made
into fur hats,
others are stuffed
and stare from the walls.

☀

This tree descends, I guess,
from Johnny Appleseed's seeds
along the valley road
that must have come through here.
The fruit is small, the tree unpruned,
the fruit is sweet, delicious baked,
the tree is like, dotted with red
dots, a piece of jewelry.

☀

SEPTEMBER 9, 1964

My birthday was a beautiful day this year
cloudy and blue and the river cool and soft
there were few insects after the cold nights
the corn was ripe and the tomatoes red

the weather held after dark
Jupiter rose among the Pleiades
at midnight, and the sandy road shone
under the dark trees in the starshine.

I love this country whose low hills enclose
my roomy house and serviceable car,

it is here that I choose to be buried
in the far corner of my fertile field.

Here I have assiduously cultivated
being depressed and the bawling inside me
I do not yet know what it is about
though I have been doing it for fifty years.

※

Connary, Blodgett, Day, Hapgood
and Dennis are the names in the graveyard
of the abandoned church. The local French
are buried Catholic with their own.
A Jew newcomer, I have also chosen
to lie in this pretty land of my exile.
"Goodman" will look as quiet
as the rest under the maple trees.

※

SAWYER

These people came up here
only two hundred years ago.
A half a dozen names
of fathers in the graveyard
have brought us to the farmer
who used to be my neighbor.

But now his sons have quit
the beautiful North Country
for Boston where they will not find
a living or even safety.
The boy has joined the Navy

49

to bomb other farmers
where our Navy ought not to be.

"I set my mind on Richie.
I bought all the machinery for him
and the blue-ribbon cattle.
Now it has no point."
So they have sold and gone
to San Diego
to see the boy on leave.

There will not be another
generation in America,
not as we have known it,
of persons and community
and continuity.
This poetry I write
is like the busy baler
that Sawyer bought for Richie,
what is the use of it?

But I am unwilling to be Virgil
resigned and praise what is no good.
Nor has the President invited me.

    ❧

    Monarch and sulphur
sip the withering clover
    and flops of cow dung,

    The fixed hills around
impassively attentive
    as God is to me.

※

I walked across the yellow lea
    heavy for my loss
but the stubborn peace persuaded me
    as I walked across

that my mother Nature isn't really
    stingy and mean to me,
she obviously loves me dearly
    but the cupboard is often empty.

And God my watchful teacher
    has been earnest to attend
to the slow growth of His creature
    He doesn't much understand.

Hundreds of months of empty beauty
    and a few flashes of life
are a truer biography
    than my usual gripe.

Another year let me live on
    and slowly come to move again
in the stars' circular motion
    that is also mine.

※

Garnered in twenty books
that I count in the barn,
these are the daisies cut
and withered that were beautiful
before the mower passed;
and of the field afire
with hawkweed I extinguished
is neither scent nor glow.

The clover the hawkweed
have burst into bloom
after the hayer
as if summer
could come again,
but the river is cold
and I have eaten
the last raspberry.

HOKKU

※

In crashing waters
of the same falls, falling leaves
of the same forest

the leaping voyage
home at last the red salmon
spawn and faint and fade

※

Irises in hand
Alice used to visit us
on Easter morning

a speechless color
is the absence on the shelf
of the blue flowers

※

From a high mountain
are visible near and far
many high mountains

avoid scholarship
in the valley, rather farm
and swim in the stream

❧

Drifting out of sight
these daffodils sit too light
in a dark green vase

April more real
when it is slightly wilted
the morning after

Wordsworth came on them
by surprise and kept them in
a glass memory

❧

Blue through the tinted
windshield—the wheels wildly
skidded in the storm

❧

The foundering ship
falls behind and the ship that
sank cannot catch up

※

Bang the bell at dusk
and drown out the shrill crickets
and shrieking werewolves

※

Who in the starshine
where only the gross bulk looms
is it? Ah, it's you

※

A lighthouse keeper
his portly friends like dreadnoughts
pass by in the night

※

Sprayed with strong poison
my roses are crisp this year
in the crystal vase

※

Your fists are ablaze
with letters and colored stamps
beautiful mailman

✻

The black shepherd-dog
shakes the water off his fur
in a round rainbow

✻

One a day westward
a thousand suns are falling
blindly we advance

✻

If they were to say
that this hokku was the last
poem that he wrote

✻

HOKKU FOR DAISY

my Now the rainbow
in the falls is growing dim
the sun clouds over

the tons of water
my Future vanishes past
loud and indistinct

nodding on the edge
a white and yellow daisy
unwet by the mist

my little daughter
beside herself is throwing
sticks in the torrent

※

HOKKU FOR MATHEW

ending of August
still wandering in freedom
the fens and meadows

summer in his pail
raspberries and blueberries
and first blackberries

three stripes of passage
in our pails as we flounder
through thorny patches

sick at heart am I
for my son in the autumn
of the unjust war

※

HOKKU FOR ME

In the bright twilight
the branches in silhouette
of my maple trees

my murky old mind
is growing blank for the facts
are impractical

nothing happening
to know in this world I doze
   like a wooden post

the colorless moon
illumines the fieldflowers
   with colorless truth.

RICHARD SAVAGE HOKKU

When I fell awake
the two soaring gulls became
   my new white sneakers

from far off my feet
walked slowly back into them
   I lurching stood up

I spoke my rage out
—a small girl conducted me
   like an orchestra

the song of the spheres
was jangling in common day
   in parallel fifths.

Lying on a dock
I was dreaming that I was
   lying on a dock

the gulls were screaming
and they are screaming and I
   seem to be screaming.

HOKKU OF FALLING ASLEEP

I'm ever ready
to play handball or make love
or talk with scholars

lucky is the man
whose good things alternate
without a conflict

orderly we are
our ritual game and lust
and western culture.

On such crazy hours
temperately drunken I
have curled up asleep

I dream my country
has quit her desperate course
and is now at peace

my people now take
a lively satisfaction
in one another

my people greet me
when I walk out the doorway
well pleased with myself

imagine, only
useful machines are now seen
that I can repair

I wake with rapture
into a rational world
to be put to use.

Alas, the dreams of
good digestion sadden me
    when I fall awake

    in New York City
    in Nineteen Sixty.

❦

HOKKU OF FALLING AWAKE

    Deep sleep is honey
the buzzing flies of troubled
    dreams awakened me

    I scowl at the day
I am at a loss with this
    bright stripe in the dark

    better blind and deaf
if friends cannot come across
    if that's how it is

    God guard me from hope
and be absent from me O
    creator spirit

    I know no poem
nor plan except for people
    I can't live with birds

    birds fly in the air
and enjoy a lovely view
    of things as a map

    when I come downtown
I am blind with confusion
    and stupid with rage.

✻

The sweet sonata
was Mozart's and of Mozart's
naturally F

✻

It is smoke and dust
objectively, and you are
the starry heavens

✻

Swiftly the sand-crab
scurrying across the beach
stopped in the ripple

✻

History is brief
your grandfather might have known
Thomas Jefferson

our busy busy
species fills up big books
with the same story

✻

When Harvey published
his clients left him, hearing
that he was crack-brained

King Charles appointed
Harvey as court physician
and lost his own head

※

"It could have been worse"
we congratulated him
on his great bad luck

※

Wallabies are cute
but kangaroos are too big
for that kind of thing

※

ON A SENTENCE OF PYRRHO

Don't you understand?
Scylla was no more real
than the Chimera.

POEMS OF A HEART ATTACK

※

An hour of panic while I fight
for breath and then all night
   in detail, rib by rib,
   exquisitely my muscles pick

themselves apart until at dawn
I sink exhausted down.
   No doubt, Lord, though I do not see,
   that this is useful to me.

※

In the little mirror
an inch-square window
shows bright the dancing
leaves of a birch
and two electric wires:
a cheerful picture
till it fades in the twilight
and nothing cheerful in the mirror.

※

My barn roof is a mighty ribbed shield
and sheds the drumming rain

from the roomy loft where I lie flat
on a blanket from Oaxaca—the rough floor
sustains against the gravity of the earth
softly my aching body.
                    Pale day
from the oblong window leaks into
the corners. I was one to dart my eyes
and seek out moving things of interest,
but now the dynamic
stability floods mercifully my mind
and my pulse is fluttering regularly.

⁂

Up that hillside stand many birches but
the nearmost out the window rises dead
slim, white, precise in the twilight
no foliage hides the wiry beauty
of her branches and I love her,
bawling, more than all the others.
Death is looking at me.
I meant in May to start a longer poem
here in the North Country with my friend
but no such ambition occupies me tonight
any more than I dare to make love.
Oh I don't know if the sadness that is storming
my breast will kill me, anyway I can't
cut it short.
                    No, it is nothing new
it has been there a long time.

⁂

As soon as we are born
out of the salty ocean

we are like landed fish
gasping till we perish.
It is unphilosophical
to take my heart trouble
as unusual
just because it could be fatal.

※

Our spacemen roving on the moon
(on the TV screen) are like old pictures
of spacemen roving on the moon,
and this fact is more startling
than spacemen roving on the moon,
our imagination is successful
yet coping with reality
we cannot do it differently.

Sure, my dreams have been in touch
with the nature of things,
both my poems and my nightmares
predict and guide me well.
But what when now I am confused?
Only catastrophe
ever altered the human course
to do it differently.

※

A breeze of the evening
and a thrush twittering
  in the sudden quiet.
  My pulse has begun to beat

slower at last.
A long freight train is rumbling past,

I wanly wave and cheerfully
the engineer toots at me.

☙

A friend of mine is in a Federal prison
but I had a heart attack and am under house arrest.
It's better to do time here in my garden
where they who love me care for my small needs
than to live at the mercy of brutal wardens
among few flowers and scared and sullen fellows.
On the other hand, my eyes are narrow with suspicion
that my closest mate my body may instantly betray me.

☙

So as I grow old I philosophically compare
the various bleak conditions of mankind,
the refugees of Bengal mother and infant,
the son dead young as mine is dead.
But I cannot, cannot yet, combine in one
vision the universal panorama
all flesh is as the grass and very good
with the ever unique woes that people suffer.

☙

Six revolutions.
Four dynasties abolished.
    Feng stood like a fort.

✼

Well, now I don't have
to take Daisy on her first
    roller-coaster ride.

✼

Since anyway I have been struck
and I must stop all work,
    I am lucky not to be in New York
    but here where I can slowly walk

from the orange lilies to the purple mallows
and putter among the green tomatoes
    and crawl, with help, down the small hill
    to the river flowing at its own sweet will.

✼

Heart aching for the North Country
ill as I am is my will to live
until at least again the spring.

The view is heavy wherever I look
with those who were and will not be
on the meadows along the river

five lovers who have drifted
to other country and my own
flesh and blood that is dead.

Today I buried as I promised
Alice's ashes next to her nephew
in the village graveyard up the hill.

She liked it here. My son had plans
how *he* would farm it when it was his.
Here is a red leaf on the lawn.

I am obsessed by the plain facts:
writing them literally down
is all the poetry I can.

※

   Twice a week I bring in bunches of blossoms, berries,
or colored leaves, and arrange them in a white
china pitcher against the yellow wall. Then I find myself
staring there for minutes at a time.

   I won't name them, each one more beautiful than the
others, from the choke-cherries that smell like cat piss
to white asters among the first reddening leaves. Whatever
it is, I never want to change it. But in a couple of days
all begin to wither.

   But I mention this habit of mine, that millions of
mankind have practiced, because suddenly, at sixty years
of age, I understand why painters have painted flowers in
vases, which had seemed to me to be a rather stupid exercise.
It is a desperate effort to catch this obvious
beauty that they do not wish to lose, to salvage something
from it, if only an image in a frame.

   The year drifts and I bring it inside once a week.

   In the fall I find dry stalks, husks, strawflowers.
In the white pitcher is a bunch of stalks of evening
primrose and great mullein, husks of milkweed
and steeplebush, and cat-tails and pearly everlasting,
and a branch of pallid violet maple leaves. This bunch
too is beautiful, more beautiful than the others. And

68

it lasts. Soon I no longer stare at it against the yellow
wall, but I do not want to remove it. And what would
replace it?

※

Tireless to excel,
blameless because I did well,
    abandoned, I was competent
    in order to be independent,

I had to be: all this taxed
my heart that finally cracked.
    Now be my nurse and care for me
    while I whimper, or I will die.

※

A fleeting moment ago I wished I were dead
and past the pain and fear and the long effort
to limit the pain and allay my fear,
the gloom of enforced inactivity
and my heaviness because the meadow is beautiful,
my grief for Matty that is always there
and I give no joy at all to anybody.

But now I think of others who are bed-rid,
not even bed-rid, sick by the roadside
or where it is bleak and ugly—not like here,
not cared for and it is too hot or too cold
and the food, if there is food, is not delicious.
I would like to comfort them out of my store
but I cannot comfort myself.

O God, have mercy on us creatures.
To me give what I most lack, courage

to get my second wind. Yes, I believe
the Lord will save me live until He won't
—why must I watch this? And there are other
beautiful places than the North Country,
I have seen some, I am a traveled man.

❧

The V of birds in the blue
   points south. Do not be sad,
start out, you too.

The falling star in the black
   is luck, as it burns out
at the end of its track.

LITTLE PRAYERS

1. Creator Spirit, who dost lightly hover
   whence I know not, and why to me I never
   questioned, come. Do visit thy lover
   after Thy long absence. I turn over

   awaking in the morning: Thou art not
   there to my touch nor is a substitute
   there, but nothing nothing at all to talk
   to and make love when I awake.

2. O spirit wise, somewhere shine!
   so I can squander me again.
   I ask it, if ever I tried hard
   to eke me out a livelihood

   from my grudging city, and if ever
   I have been patient to preserve
   opportunity my sweet
   muse, my darling, my flirt.

3. The tons of trucks that thunder by
   perturb not me who thread my way.
   The sun is roaring through the smoke
   by grace on me who stand and look.

I do not know if happiness
will show before me like a face
    or rise within me like a song,
    deliberately I move along.

4. The flashing shadow of the sun
   in the bloody window made me turn
     and face his face, and I saw
     over his shoulder You.

   Everywhere I look about
   are there outlines of truth and art
     breeding in the dark of this
     moment at the edge of the abyss.

5. Novices of art
   understate
     what has them by the throat
     the climax; You speak out

   for me, spirit who affright
   me in the lonely night,
     nor do I know till I express it
     the message boiling in my breast.

❧

THE EMPIRE CITY

6. Thee God we praise for this complete
   book that overwork and doubt
     and pain could mar but not prevent
     because Thy spirit still was sent.

   Such as it is, this now belongs
   also among the created things

whilst I relapse, Thy dying fact
more spent, more sullen, and more racked.

꽃

THE YOUNG DISCIPLE

7. Guarantor of the harvest, who
    to Noah pledged if he would sow
      and delve some good would come of it
      and sent him Rainbow your spirit

    —though not yet have you promised me
    that the laborer will enjoy—
      I offer you this play
      wistfully waiting for my pay.

8. In how few hours I
    have put myself awry
      and live again in fear
      till I escape from here.

    Askew and queer is my
    existence in the only
      world I make, impatient,
      arrogant, ignorant.

9. Father, guide and lead me stray
    for I stumble forward straight my way
      undeviating, I do not
      notice the pleasant bypaths that

    make us this world surprising nor
    the precipice that sinks before.
      O give me ground for next a step
      to stagger walking in my sleep.

10. By trials too hard for me beset
     with awkward courage toward my death
         I stagger; every usual
         task I perform and, as I fail,

     fashion the art-works to me given;
     but lust is mercifully riven
         from me with hope, for ever our
         task is measured to our power.

11. Help, Angel Courage! for I wooed
     confusion and willingly betrayed
         my blind intelligence in ord-
         er to visit with the Lord,

     but now in the too early dusk
     I panicky have gotten lost
         and cannot make it. Give O ang-
         el Courage me thy hand.

12. O God of fire and the secret mus-
     cles of the world, restore my lust
         and happy power as I used,
         for somewhere now I have got lost

     and am confused and impotent,
     yes, gazing with bewilderment
         in such a face as how Thy dea-
         rest angel looks, looks up at me.

13. Heavy silence, Lord, dim eyes,
     dull ears, and dubious a guess,
         I offer Thee as that which is.
         My tithe is this blind daze

     as I to work return
     without reward for past work done

and for the work I do begin
without desire or hope. Amen.

14. Like Adam firmly walking to
the farm-work that he knew to do
in deep confusion, for the grim
news of everyday to him

happened each thing by surprise
like a fist between the eyes
—so let me day to day work on
in this thick cloud that has sunk down.

15. On the highroad to death
trudging, not eager to get
to that city, yet the way is
still too long for my patience

—teach me a travel song,
Master, to march along
as we boys used to shout
when I was a young scout.

16. Blessed is the landscape that around
the turning will come at a joyous bound
into view! for God who holds my hand
is a wise explorer as our way we wend.

And He explains to me in simple English
the geology and botany that flash
on my new soul, and cities in turmoil
where He points out what is still practical.

17. Your kingdom is within me sure
but I do not inhabit there

with You and me. But searching for
myself among the strange and poor

and violent I go because
my gentle gifts I despise.
    And yet one day I shall be known
    for a native son.

18. At last I know—for friends have said—
    my shameless public ways have made
        me scorned and fail and lonely in
        this teeming city. Lord, between

    us, I would not do otherwise
    for Thy name's sake among these
        Babylonians, although I long
        for the people of whom I am one.

19. Jail and blows, being a coward,
    I dread, but I am inured
        to be misunderstood,
        because the common reason, God,

    communes with me. Let them refute
    the propositions I have put
        with nail and hammer on the door
        where people pass, upon the square.

20. My friends are ruined, I am in dismay,
    the blow will reach also to me;
        fearful, desperate, and resourceless
        we are, and heavy is our loss

    already. Heaven help us therefore
    because our strength and prudence are

unable to the traps and foes
that men have strewn, and we arouse.

21. "Child, resent it not; by grave
    offenses you yourself have
       armed against you every creature." No,
       Father; if today I throw

    beaten my armor down,
    it is to go lighter. Sound Thy dawn
       bugle and collect us bright
       hundreds who are few but right.

22. My anger has become
    a settled rage. I am calm
       but I no longer wish to touch
       human flesh with tender lust.

    Lord, give me back my lust to touch
    human flesh, or else teach
       me some otherwise to make sense
       of my experience.

23. Now dare I anything, O Warden
    of the drunk and careless, guard me!
       for the reins that stay my course
       and hinder me are loose;

    as forth I go, and forth I shall,
    my blond and black horses gallop
       toward a wreck that I forecast
       with little interest.

24. Creator of the worlds, O joy
    of speed! and when the powers that lie

latent into being break
I shall confront the onward wreck

because I am in love with
the nature of things unto death
    and as they loom, say, "Lo!"
    Lord rescue me, this road I go.

25. When hope and hate are so
    much mixed, how shall I know?
        shall I rage or shall I rest?
        —Thou therefore urge upon what is best,

    I will perform it, for Thy word misleads
    all my researches savage into reasons
        ever springing alive, and Thy voice
        in my amazement is still peace.

26. Upon his loyal son
    my father did look down
        and made him brave a few days
        to say the truth he knows.

    Now thou Creator Spirit
    him do not desert
        when he announces news
        he does not know he knows.

27. Rest well thy weary head and heart
    and work no more, my sorely hurt;
        thee God when in the pit of night
        thy sight is sealed can new create.

    Each breath, I know, is almost more,
    poor child of lust, than life can bear

and forethought has betrayed thy foot.
Let help come if it will or not.

28. Manlike my God I make, nor fear
    to be an idol's fool, for
      so hard I think of man the thought
      crumbles into absolute

    un-Nature. Oh, and He will save
    me in the little work and love
      I lust in day by day until
      my name He elects to call.

29. Saved! as I have faith
    and probable proof.
      But O God, am I weary
      of living in purgatory,

    in pain and fire tedious
    waiting for the voice
      of love that summons
      and the voice that responds.

30. My world, my only! as I see
    soberly the necessity
      that so I fail, and my hurts
      are measured to my just deserts:

    fine! as every truth is fine.
    But that I change I do not find
      nor that I triumph by embrac-
      ing my fate, nor that I suffer less.

31. Lord Nemesis and Reviver, who
    bless the past with its curse—I do

therefore cling like death
to what I might forget,

may now this newborn that
I rescued (although late
and gracelessly) at least
not torment me from the past.

32. As blasted by a frost in May
the lofty butternut to me
no countryman looked dead, and shall
I chop it down? I thought. But while

I thought of it, sprouted a leaf
and now my whole tree is rife
with singing green, though I shall bear
—forgive me, Lord—no fruit this year.

33. Patience! for my only one
my world is turning like the sun
toward me her condescending face.
And now behold! there is a race

between the runners, long-awaited
Fame and Death, which I am fated
to watch with fascination deep
as toward the finish-line they leap.

34. Lord, at the moment still and beating
like the mighty heart of the great city
asleep at dawn—when he and I
standing outside our frantic folly

aware of each other clung together,
I thanked Thee! And now another

time in memory
and poetry I thank Thee!

35. God of the Fullness who in hours
hast after my starving years
    filled my bowl and with garlands
    laden my outstretched hands,

  teach me again what it is
  I want, that I by long disuse
    and disappointment did forget,
    and now my brain is slow with surfeit.

36. All men are mad some way: O Lord
Thou takest it not hard
    but when the rage is in me most
    by healing death deliverest.

  I shall not fear, my strongest will
  cannot deliver me to hell
    forever, for an Angel with
    a lamp appears in my death.

37. God, do you make me happier,
for by my doing I am here
    and the outlook is even worse
    as I grow old. I have been cautious

  not prudent, and unusually thoughtful
  not wise. But indefatigable
    has been my love whether I could
    or not, which you count highly, God.

38. Dull, miserable, and ailing
my way of life to which I clung

stubbornly and often I
disapproving proved my way

cannot work, it is not viable,
I am foredoomed to terrible
years I cannot remedy.
Life-saver, rescue me.

39. I never did, Lord, believe
that me you have preserved alive
for any remarkable day
or use—much as my country

needs brains and bravery.
But to be staring stupidly!
to be drifting toward disgrace!
to call for help too spiritless!

40. Stop keeping the home-things alive,
my balky body, their grudging love,
so forth: let them die if they want.
I grew this avocado plant

that never throve and survives skinny
—it has ceased to be a symbol for me,
let it dry! And yet I pour
for pity's sake a glass of water.

41. Whether I am close to death
or not, God of Breath,
I do not know, nor what,
dark God, to do with that.

But my palms are wet and cold
and a pure fear has taken hold

of my heart. This I know,
O simple God and true.

42. Lost—God help me—in a waste
    where the dusk has fallen fast
        I cannot breathe and my cowardice
        is what it always was.

    No light, no guide, but now thank God
    my wet tears are welling hot
        and I can breathe in the black night
        and look about as I wait.

43. Fear with me walks abroad and where
    I live I am afraid. I am aware
        of many real dangers. Others
        are imaginary fears.

    Yet I seek neither, Lord, your peace
    nor the momentary happiness
        that I used to seek to ward
        off terror, Lord.

44. I have thought of my aunt singing
    when I was a child the air of Puccini,
        she is long dead who vividly
        returns to me in a memory

    and I, O God, shall be dead
    like her: is it this certitude
        that has destroyed my hope and joy
        and when I see beautiful things I cry?

45. The flashing summer we forecast,
    the bright beach, the dark forest,

and to tour the famous sights
of Europe, prospects of delight

—but Lord, our name is Joyless, we have
dry voices and our looks are heavy.
  Rescue us, we are immersed
  in the sin of waste, which is the worst.

46. By murder and arrest
  my frantic night is tossed,
    awaking I look forward
    either to peace, Lord,

  or doom, in doubt which,
  bound home from far. And such
    is my travel prayer
    to the Savior.

47. As if my purpose was to drown
  the shining ship I did abandon
    that was not sinking, rapidly
    she stood away, I did not try

  to swim, yet was about to cry
  help when I awoke and thereby
    helped myself, though I was wistful
    of the depths of the whirlpool.

48. Surceaser of foreboding! I gave up
  myself to You to shatter and reshape
    in the plastic order of Your world,
    stranger than the world controlled

  by my rage. And You have bade
  me lay my plans in solitude

with what initiative I can
muster when my heart is broken.

49. God, I prayed, to me restore
some kind of thing to hope for
that, only, creates energy
from nothing for another day,

but You instead have sent Your angel
Indignation with his bugle
to waken the Americans at midnight.
Give me health and I will fight.

50. Not on our knees do we
ask but hear our plea,
Author of liberty.
America our country

has been leased out. We must and will
reclaim her at our own peril,
but do You faithfully ignite
on the hilltop freedom's light.

51. Creator spirit, please let your
soft lamp the soul of our poor
land illumine and its am-
ber comfort us. I am

familiar with your grace when you
call me to look out the window
and quiet with its stars is heaven
and men are doing what they can.

52. If I undertake to say
the conscience of my country,

I only do my duty.
But, Lord, it was not I

who chose it, but the hungry heart
and level look that you allotted
    to me when you did burden
    with different gifts different men.

53. God bless my small home that
I by habit decorate;
    avert the fire, fill the space
    if not by joy at least by use;

make my daughter safe from the pest
and my wife bear if that be best
    and many friends for many years
    learn to climb our steep stairs.

54. I do not much collaborate
not out of spite, but they are not
    my peers, I disregard
    their claims. It is too bad.

But God He is my master and
apprentice I wait His command.
    He asks me what I think of it
    and Him I tell my best thought.

55. I talk to You because I have no one
else, the two or three are gone
    to whom I told my murky thought
    because they cared for that.

I said thanks to them, Lord, also
more than I ever do to You:
    You are as close to my touch
    but I do not know Your love as much.

56. I waited in the parlor, Lord,
    in panic for the messenger Your word
        for whom I had, as both we knew,
        no answer or excuse. But You,

    You, as often, Lord! had stolen
    through the back door into the kitchen
        and seated at the table quietly
        were pouring coffee for Yourself and me.

凶

FOUR LITTLE PRAYERS

57. My island by another week
    has drifted like a rusty wreck
        without a steersman. From the beach
        with hopeless eyes I watch

    her go. I would swim out
    to her but You have also put
        chains on my ankles. What,
        Father, do You mean by that?

58. Yes, weariness and grief
    is a fair description of my life
        —I wonder if
        others are better off.

    I have also written,
    like now, these facts down
        and this has given me
        pride if not much joy.

59. How wistfully I envy
    without hostility

the young who race and breathe
without thinking of death.

I used to try to know them
and made advances to them
   who now seem like a different
   species in the environment.

60. In a panic and compelled
   as when once a devil held
      the knife to my heart and I
      had no choice but to obey.

   I was a child, I could not run away,
   my palms were cold and wet. Today
      but, Father of fugitives, I am old
      though my palms are wet and cold.

❧

FOUR SENSELESS LITTLE PRAYERS
OF CONVALESCENCE

61. On all, the wicked and the innocent,
   blows the beautiful west wind
      and the warm sun sheds his light.
      But from them gather joy and benefit

   only those at ease in the Lord
   to whom all good turns to good,
      and hungrily we convalescents
      who face into the gentle elements.

62. Crazy for crazy, I believe
   that You will make the dead alive

and from these evil things that seem
I shall awake as in a dream

—none hinders me, though I am in
prison among men,
    to say the senseless sentence that
    saying makes me glad.

63. Often have I dreaming frightened
into puzzlement awakened,
    and most days have proved to be
    milder than my anxiety.

On this analogy I'll say
recklessly what pleases me,
    that one day I shall wake to my surprise
    and sweet confidence in paradise.

64. Since daily without hope I go
daily forth my task to do
    —though wistful—and yet somehow
    despite despair I do go:

this is the fact in which I write
without belief the consoling thought
    that when I stand out of the way
    I shall stand in the sun happy.

※

A PRAYER TO SAINT HARMONY

65. In anguish I started from sleep:
those I love I cannot keep

from fire and polluted airs
steep rocks and swirling waters.

To mushroom and rabid animal
my beloved are vulnerable
   and man and his machines may slay
   me or them I love today.

The life is so precarious,
Lord, that You parcelled out to us,
   many to a speedier death
   rush to have it over with,

and I my dreams paint with fright
in the horror of the night
   and cower in the dawn
   writing it all down.

It means that I am raging
within my soul sick and aging
   against my own and You the most.
   But blessed be the Holy Ghost

in whom I know and say,
and to Saint Harmony I pray
   who still makes my nightmares
   into music and calms my fears.

66. I am willing, God, to say
   just how it is with me,
      the prayer best I can.
      But look, again and again

   to say that we are dying
   —this message is boring.
      "No, you do not need
      to write that down," He said.

67. I have no further grief in me.
    I can imagine, no, foresee
        the losses I will suffer yet,
        but my eyes do not get wet.

    When once the brass is burnished, Sire,
    there is no use of further fire,
        it is a mirror. But it can be melted,
        Sire, and destroyed.

68. My Bible text, when I grew
    old enough to be a Jew,
        was God to Abraham did say
        Lech lcha, "Go away!"

    I was thrilled, being a boy,
    at this portentous destiny,
        but to me You did not give
        a hundred fifty years to live.

    Hush. Where shall I go,
    Tour-Guide? Show, show
        me the map and circle
        the place with Your pencil.

69. This is a day the Lord hath made,
    rejoice in it and be glad.
        Our friends from foreign countries come
        because we have been true to them.

    The food we set upon the table
    is rich and good, as we are able.
        —Into the declining sun
        I softly walked away alone.

LITTLE TE DEUM

70. I'm not in pain, I owe no debts,
     far as I know nobody hates
          enough to harm me, no disgrace
          tomorrow stares me in the face.

     Far as I know no new disaster
     is threatening my near and dear,
          and I am less by nameless fears
          beset than in my younger years.

     Thee God for this I therefore praise
     interim of undesperate days
          although it will not long endure.
          I do not live the various hour

     as the happy do or say:
     of homespun of oatmeal gray
          without a blazon is the flag
          that I hold up and do not wag.

LINES, AND LITTLE PRAYER

     Anybody could be shipwrecked,
     who ventures, on a desert island
     like me and waste away lonely.
     I don't reproach me my bad luck
     (I'm wretched enough as it is.)
     I light fires. No one comes.
     But anybody could be shipwrecked
     like me on a desert island,
     I don't reproach me my bad luck.

I light fires I light fires
I light fires. No one comes.

71. Sometimes my sorrow is, God,
    so heavy my heart swells hard
        and I can go no further.
        Then let me sleep, Mother,

    and rave delirious
    in your embrace.
        Though you are anxious, you
        hold me stolidly the night through.

THE GUINEA PIG, AND A LITTLE PRAYER

    I lightly woke to sweet and clear
    chanting, the warbling of the guinea pig
    loud in the dark, not like I used to hear him
    squeaking across the floor, oh his voice
    was really beautiful last night, he sang a tune.
    I smiled as I dozed off.
                    Now it is morning
    and he is still and stiff—at 2 A.M.
    dead in the playful jaws of the big dog.

    Freddy, do not beat your dog in anger
    and stick her nose in it, what does she know
    of dying? Neither did I recognize
    sighs of fright in the night,
    sighs of mortal fright in the night, Freddy.

72. Who know my face wet with tears,
    Lord, where no one else is,

93

and what I sing in the night
is very earnest and sometimes sweet,

but nobody seems to care for this
though I am frightened, and my voice
    will afterwards be much admired
    by the English scholars, Lord.

73. No, neither with my eyes closed and You
    a presence warm that near I know,
        nor in the busy world and wide
        where I am Your friend open-eyed,

but vaguely peering out to see
a small room and I am drowsy
    and You seem to be everywhere
    in the room, if You are.

🌿

THREE LITTLE PRAYERS
ON THE DEATH OF MY SISTER

74. Lord, being sixty winters old
    I am not a child
        and ought not to need this or that person,
        but as an independent person

do Your service in the city.
But Lord, it is not so with me
    as I slowly turn and blink
    at where it is again forever blank

and reach. New nothing is new bars.
If I survive until the ground thaws

in April, I shall put these ashes
next to where my sister's nephew is.

75. Too many now are dead and alive
for us to rise up from the grave
at the last trumpet.
We can no longer picture it,

it is unmathematical.
When the village was small
and our ancestors a couple of dozen,
we used to dream of our reunion.

76. You teach quick and very hard
in Your school, Lord.
To me it is not always clear
what the lessons are.

I was unusually docile
when I was in grade school,
but I don't think I can pass
in this upper class.

77. You notice, Lord, I am half pleased
being sixty to be so confused
and still not know how to cushion the pain
of unlucky love. But it is again

because the case is mathematical,
God of games, like the Chinese puzzle
that used to tease me when I was
a child who could not do puzzles.

78. But woeful with the sin of waste
which is the worst,

Creator of the only world,
I cut the knot with my sword,

the nervous solution for a stupid
problem that Alexander did,
    and still I don't know any better way
    just to live on another day.

79. Maybe because of the rout we made
or some fool tried to feed them bread,
    the phoebes left our porch where
    they laid their eggs year after year,

and when I saw that empty nest
very ashamed I saw the waste
    and raging of my days that drove
    away their sweet domestic love.

But Merciful! they have flown
no further than the attached barn
    through the wide door always open
    where now the two dart out and in

with bugs for their gaping brood
top of the birch post I made
    to firm the loft and left a ledge
    very apt to put a nest.

A PRAYER SLEEPLESS

80. I am sleepless every night.
    Is there—but I don't know what—
        I have not done and I must do
        so You will let me go?

If I could sleep, Lord, maybe
I'll dream of what I cannot see?
   —This offer is too sly,
   naturally You do not buy.

Is there a horror
waiting for me behind the door
   and therefore I dare not pass through?
   I don't know. I don't know.

It is beautiful on this Hawaiian
beach where my age is thrown
   and I watch with tired eyes
   the brilliant sun rise,

but it may be that the joys
of this world and new days
   are not for me—I know them too well
   (though I never had but a stingy sample)

and so I do not fall asleep
because I hanker after a longer sleep
   and this requires preparation,
   meditation, hesitation.

Come out! come out!
evil spirit
   who me possess.
   I cannot yet guess

who you are
but that you are
   whom by dim light
   I hunt in the night.

81. Sometimes I said I was marooned
    sometimes that I was imprisoned

or was in exile from my land
or I was born on the wrong planet.

But my daily fact, Lord,
is that awake I am a coward
    and in my dreams that say the cause
    I have lost the address, I'm confused.

82. Page after page I have lived Your world
    in the narrative manner, Lord,
        in my own voice I tell Your story.
        Needless to say, I envy

    people who dramatically
    act the scenes of Your Play.
        Even so, the narrative manner
        is my *misère et grandeur*.

    It is our use
    that some of us
        insist on how
        it is from our point of view.

83. Save when my sight was narrowed
    by sleepless pain, Lord,
        my experience has generally
        been roomy enough for me

    and I haven't wanted to do
    or learn anything very new.
        But now my life is daily narrowed
        to sleepless pain, Lord,

    and I must learn to do
    something very new
        just to live on. "Ah, but do you
        really want to?"

—that question, God, is wicked,
it is suicide
    which I have no choice
    but, Conserver, to dismiss.

Since to write I undertake
I will say my heart will break,
    censoring nothing; even so
    Creator Spirit, come thou new.

Oh, it is poorly between me
and my closest friend my body
    who will instantly betray
    our marriage stormy till today.

84. What is the Buddha? "Drat!
pass the salt," the sage spat.
    I understand. I understand
    but I am not enlightened.

Am I enlightened? How would I know?

85. If from the bottom of sleep would summon
me forth mysterious some dream,
    or if these golden suns that break
    on the purple water would say "Awake

and choose to live."—Neither has happened.
But my wife and neighbors tend
    me kindly and from far away
    they phone good wishes night and day.

Maybe it is enough to heal my wound
just because the world turns around.
    I never did understand my meaning.
    I rarely have looked forward to the morning.

86. How blue it is! between the water
    and the sky stretches taut
        the silken thread of the horizon
        and the sun's corona

    wraps me around. Maybe my heart
    won't crack a little while yet
        and I can take a swim on this
        practical hypothesis.

87. When I think of the subtile balances
    of chances and circumstances
        that kill or make men thrive,
        O Lord of Moments give

    me onward a few happy years
    as You can—if my desires
        are modest and they do not much
        the great Frame of the Likely wrench.

88. I shall not die, for I shall live
    and say His works. He did not give
        me unto death, though Me he hurt.
        Open up to me the gate.

89. I ask the Lord, "Who are You?"
    though I know His name is "Spoken to."
        Hoping but I am not sure
        His name might be "I am who answer."

    With certain faith let me continue
    my dialogue with Spoken-To.
        Hope has always been my curse,
        it never yet came to pass.

The crazy man that you meet
talking to himself on the street
    is I, please gently lead him home.
    Creator Spirit come.

LINES AND LITTLE PRAYER

If I told you, child,
I heard Johanna Gadski
singing Brunhilde;
naturally I couldn't judge
if she was any good
as well as old and cracked,
but it was the first I ever heard
the Rhine Journey and I was astounded,
in the top balcony, way on the side.
The intervening half a century?
was empty, nothing happened.
What *were* the heat and passion
I worked up in my politics
and in my jealous fits?

90. The day is cloudy but toward evening
the sky is clearing
    and the sunset is vivid.
    Swiftly what is hid

behind the colors the one dark night
will show herself to brave men, but as yet
    not to me who dare not
    seek her and go out.

91. I am too old to be fastidious
    of idols any more, what difference
        does it make?—I could be stupider
        than I am but it's a bore.

    Bring me a drum to beat.
    After sixty Confucius did
        what he pleased, and Lao-tze
        was born at seventy.

92. My genius, God, as an author
    has been to bring it all together
        and show that even this
        unlikely combination can exist,

    and now this mess of poems too.
    Maybe—but I cannot know—
        the whole adds up to more
        than the parts of my disorder.

SENTENCES FOR MATTHEW READY, SERIES I

꿈

1. "Ready" is the password before Aim.
   My past is ready not to intervene
   if I stand out of the way. And in the Garden
   the animals stand ready to be named.
   So like a drunkard father
   with admirable precepts,
   I hereby name my son
   for that which I am not.

2. Ready to say "Here am I!"
   like faithful Abraham in the night
   and ready like at last the Prince
   for poison and rapier-points.
   "Here am I! here am I!"
   : has anybody called?
   But nothing seems to offer
   and now the chance is past.

3. Fatherless I was, nobody offered
   me to the muses, I imposed on them.
   I had no father to rebel against
   and I have lived by making trouble.
   I had no guidance, there were anyway
   no choices, but I staggered from need to need.
   Now I am like a father to these boys,
   why should they be loyal?

4. They pay me as a good mechanic
   of other people's troubles
   and this is what I do: I stay
   and stay, and if they run away
   I still am there in front, and when
   at last they stand and fight I stay.
   This is the therapeutic art
   that I, an abandoned one, invented.

5. The more important before the less important
   and the necessary is the more important
   and the existing is the necessary.
   Choose it. It has the privilege
   of the force and grace by which a thing
   has broken into being and continues.
   Let any gods that come to meet you
   come at *their* ease, not yours.

6. Again and again into the coming combers
   the fisher cast his gleaming lure
   and wound it in. Watching in the salt wind
   I drowsed and Age, the old man of the sea,
   was standing to his waist in hiss and foam
   and shook his oozy head forbidding me
   to fish these waters any more, the unfathomable
   silken swells where there are schools of fish.

7. Meeting in horror in the gloom of the deep
   —as when the flashlight shone
   on the lovers in the brush—
   we quick ones lash out and eat.
   O angler! angel of death,
   which is the iron meal?
   draw us up gasping at last
   into a breath of air.

8. Awaking choking from a nightmare
   to the real that has me by the throat
   "*déserte et effroyable*

and if we ask our neighbor, he knows
no better than ourselves"
: this is hilarious
my teeth are grinning palisades
I will not taste of it.

9. Disbelieving truths I know
   because they are to my advantage
   is the storm-window between
   my dreams and my waking wishes.
   I say "all men" and do not mean myself,
   not by exception but I do not feel
   my substance, as Minerva stole
   Paris from the deadly broil.

10. Once I made the mistake of staking
    my interest on what was possible
    instead of looking for love
    only where it can't be found.
    Another day I did my level best
    and, failing, had nowherewithal
    to reproach myself in order to live on
    : in a single year two signal blunders!

11. I saw no prospect forward, so I turned.
    And I remembered how a lusty boy
    I did not feel the ordinary flush
    at naked images and such descriptions,
    but if I heard the causes of these things
    my penis rose inquiring for more,
    I was one keen to analyze
    and subdivide, and by this wreak my joy.

12. Among the fogs and storms and eddies
    of Lake Interior
    and my scattered isles were drifting
    further limb from limb,
    still I was superior
    to my dismay, as Captain Aeneas

watched crying from the poop
the Trojan flotsam pass.

13. So . . . I have made a Copernican Revolution
in how I see between the world and me:
the wily scholarship I use
to save the facts and save my face
and put you off and forestall fate,
I use it first unwarily
to fool myself, my only dupe
for other men and fate are shrewd.

14. Of the millions, I know, who have gone to the grave
displeased, ungratified, and malcontent,
as one count me, for now it is too late
ever to unmake it and chance has become fate.
Yet in this crowd of every kind of sorrow
still am I signal for a fool and coward,
for few, I think, have seen so fine as I
the remediable faults, and been unable.

15. The herd of beeves driven along the road
to Dublin to their slaughter trots
willingly but bewildered by the traffic.
At the red light a black and curly beef
turns off and wants to go the other way.
Prod him with a stick, he is balky.
He does not seem to know which way to go
as the herd trots into Dublin to their slaughter.

16. I keep a good watch, nothing but
what I avoid escapes my notice.
Wiser than Socrates, I paste
myself together knowable.
All we Americans are blest
by the commodities we have
and it's plain and simple grief
for loss loss, to face too fierce.

17. ¡Freedom!—I force my midriff to shriek it
    like Florestan, but the word comes upside down,
    for my secret is to pin you down
    and have you in my iron hooks,
    to eat my fill and cram, oh rich!
    the hole that you tore from my breast;
    and finally my countrymen
    will make of me a statue in the park.

18. Has sprung the trap: in terror darts
    across the floor without the bait.
    Now he is quivering in the wall,
    his terror permeates the house.
    But hunger soon will lure him forth
    into the kitchen that is also poisoned.
    So Gaius sick with lust comes daily forth
    upon the streets of the United States.

19. In such a stink of filth
    I wade and don't even wallow
    in torment for this torpid woman
    stupid as a stone
    my one my only world
    who fills up all the foreground
    of the shuddering scene that I confront
    like a basilisk looking at a basilisk.

20. From Canton to Pittsburgh
    as I fled through the night
    in my black heart I heard
    the echo of the vengeance
    that the son of Hamilcar swore;
    and I have made a honey-bait
    of art and thicketed an ambush
    of a second-nature of benevolence.

21. "What's all this worry 'bout this world?
    few lil repairs an' she'll roll along!
    years of use in a job like that!

Look, I'll sell her to you cheap."
Chum, you can take that jalopy and shove it.
My last one let me down in Olean
where used to was oil and now is nuthin.
They had to fetch the part from Buffalo.

22. On a careful count I have had six
    happy days in my life
    and I do not know what it is
    to be pleased and not unsafe,
    so I do not find the world of fact
    much worth talking about
    but spitefully I fantasize
    a not dissimilar paradise.

23. Implacable! there is no uglier.
    —who can succeed who hunts
    implacably to be pleased?
    The unicorn that wants to be enticed
    with a mirror and sunbeams, I hunt sullenly
    in the dusky wood. Now I have slain
    something and am standing dumbly
    knife in hand, blind with tears.

24. Why am I bawling? d'ye think I know?
    bawling because the coffee's spilling in the saucer,
    it keeps spilling over—d'ye think I know?
    If I make a swan's neck I can hardly swallow.
    No more! no more! can't take it down
    —bawling because the doughnut's on the floor.
    If I look up—d'ye think I know?—
    can't keep it down if I look up.

25. I dreamt that the face of the President's wife
    was tattooed on my forearm, my ideal
    and military service; I awoke
    to this fool and his drunkard, these baboon
    sailors waging an ignorant war,
    my nerveless hands and tears flowing down my cheeks.

But I would not be a coward if I wore,
Lady (if I know), your colors proud.

26. Twist it and turn it, the fact remains
    where the Marconi wireless station
    broadcasted first across the ocean
    is the anti-aircraft firing range.
    "Army Reserve, No Trespassing."
    where instantaneously the gigantic
    wave across the rough Atlantic
    united the sending and the receiving.

27. You see how these young fellows
    forfeit the cardinal numbers
    big on their hockey-sweaters
    2, 5 and 7, and 11
    the City Island Gophers
    and the Black Corona Hawks
    to end up with a serial dog-tag
    between a million and a billion.

28. When I think how I kicked and hated
    my bicycles with flat tires
    and my cars that wouldn't start
    my wives who wouldn't (I didn't kick)
    these sailors in the Coral Bar
    (I am afraid to kick)—O get me
    a repair-man! for I am unskilled
    in the mechanics of this world.

29. Hard, risky, and in vain I tried.
    Now if my friend described as much
    I'd say, "Desist! for it is you
    who structure the bad luck into the world."
    But what shall *I* do with this good advice
    I do not proffer to me as a friend,
    when what I want is a rabbit's foot and Ponce's
    fountain to refresh my faded face.

30. Awhile we clung to each other abandoned
    in a city infested by
    the violent and the cowed.
    I taught him useless secrets
    that are the art of life
    among men, but not here.
    They were too simple for him
    once he was well again.

31. Scattered! to Pascagoula and Mobile
    and Lexington and Bloomington and Erie
    and thousands of miles across land and sea
    and I myself—I myself soon north
    like the thousands the innumerable starlings
    that northward wing at the March equinox
    and we stand gaping up at them, and here
    is still another fluttering troop and here
    are three or four stragglers, and here is one.

32. "Useful" is the name
    of the bread I bake,
    "Inspiriting" the beer
    that I know how to brew,
    but I ran away
    with comedians
    and the roles I play
    are "Wasted" and "Weary."

33. Throwing me away by the handfuls
    fucking Sally to give her a baby
    and loving Johnny just to keep him happy
    flying to wake up the colleges
    and writing sermons for the Americans
    because if I do not, who will do it?
    My body will not last, my muse has left me,
    why is God throwing me away by the handfuls?

34. The sky gray and the January sun
    is another letter and its red seal

I come impatiently downstairs
to rip and read the message of Messiah
who puts me off—not till next week—
I'm like a comical collegian
peering with a pout of wild dismay
in the envelope where isn't papa's cheque.

35. At my dark windblown face I looked
in the barroom mirror while the juke-box howled
and strong and passionate I looked
but my hair was gray, and sunken to the bone
were the wrinkles of attentiveness
who gave what strength he had away
but none of him takes care, no not
if he is tottering at the grave.

36. Come, a 12-inch board is plenty of footing!
why are you afraid to cross these rooves
to where the fun is looking here?
But that's just it! because Opportunity
is looking, I am sick and dizzy,
my knees are knocking and so help me
I'll topple.—O.K., let's go down,
but a 12-inch board is plenty of footing.

37. Lucky for you we artists deluded
endlessly give you the relic. For us
by way of art is never enough
to be fulfilled as we devour,
fabricators of the meaning of life
that happiness *has* in the heavens and earth
—yet most men miserably need,
it seems, our lying second-creations.

38. Like the cut rosebud blooming one great day!
if you look close, the muscles of her petals
are too relaxed, yet she is broad of face,
apparent! a soliloquy
the communal soliloquy of fame

forced on the multitudes immortally.
Such vengeance is a stratagem of love
:"This lovely monument has all of him."

39. The tide's in at last, the bathers dive
    into the waves, the dories are afloat
    and put to sea into the long sun setting
    at Saint Malô. Soon will the cool night
    calm the feverish long afternoon
    that I survived, as one by one the scattered
    beacons light up: Granville and Regnéville
    Agon and the islands of Chausey and Jersey.

40. Rarely the garden rose but the despised
    weeds of the field, poppies and purple thistles
    are the emblems of the States of the world,
    and we who make up songs while we live
    our raw and scandalous careers are honored
    with statues in the public squares; therefore
    my heart is aching among the meadowflowers
    and I have broken into a cold sweat.

41. Neither the daring nor the prudent choice
    I made but, like inspired,
    some unsafe way that didn't work.
    The measure of my happiness
    has been according to my wisdom.
    Naturally here I am at fifty
    fundamentally the same man
    beaten, but full of finished works.

42. How will I be esteemed by the happy and great
    when mankind comes to be?
    They'll say my behavior was beneath contempt
    and my need was too much trouble for compassion.
    I am not crushed by what they not unkindly
    will say without reproach, but I feel humble
    and wistfully, the while the heavy sun
    pours tirelessly down, imagine paradise.

43. Often achieving, often defeated,
    and highly achieving; and bitterly defeated!
    my aging crowned with praises
    and more, and more often, impotent:
    surely there must be a philosophy
    to suffer this inevitable course
    that will end in my inevitable death
    and likely fame, more calmly than I do.

44. When I was on my way forever
    then came my loyal friends my beauties
    human ones and sundry dogs
    to fare me well and one last fuck
    as we were formerly companionable;
    and this was so sweet, to draw the parting out
    I clung to life which otherwise
    did not much recommend itself.

45. Much-experienced and water-stained
    drowned Palinurus, he that used to be
    our sharp-eyed steersman, lies high on the beach
    cast by the long comber, among squid.
    Others are still flotsam in the swell.
    I walk the waterfront because
    we who chose the barren sea and built
    no houses loiter there to die.

46. My big, experienced, and heavy penis
    dumb Adam sad—the skinny old biddy
    with adoration holds him in her hands.
    I watch it from about a mile away.
    I wish that I were sullen like a fool
    and vent my rage that I am not in love,
    but serviceably just because I can
    I'll fuck her good and make one creature glad.

47. There was a first time, strange as it may seem,
    that soberly preluded the throaty horn
    this public but not vulgar melancholy

wailed to the surprised ears of the world
as if defeated yearning never yet
had a voice, but Peter Ilyitch
simply picked it up
the melody that everybody knows.

48. Like the ocean of springtide air
coming slowly from the land of flowers,
presaged by thunderstorms
wisdom is overwhelming toward me.
Lightning plays on the forehead
of the lowering of March
and he is drowning to his shoulders
in the torrents of the spring.

49. What's new?
the news is Day
the news of the day is Day.
Out of a dark doorway
surprised I came my way
into suddenly
the light of common day
and it is light as day.

50. Once lounging by a roadside in the grass
and I was unbeknownst to myself
elegant as the kudu or the kob
for I am lean and pied and striped in spirit,
yet my thoughts were ignominious
I tortured me with horror and despite
—till my hilarious friends came passing by
and praised my silly beauty till I blushed.

51. When Rosy my cock sprang a button
and out of my bulging jeans broke free
I cried, "Why, you're a lovely
come out to snuffle the sun!"
The others of that company,
however, were severely

uninterested, it beats all!
I always say love me and love my dog.

52. O poor beat cock my soldierly
and duteous spokesman,
aching with fatigue and bruised
and shriveled to the size of a pea,
and yet I am in love and you
stand like a soldier at attention
or a herald of the olden times
announcing an important news.

53. For grandeur yonder of this world,
not a presumptuous rival
of Creation but its next Six Days,
who yearns for this come be my friend,
or say, and let me join the crew.
And now is our truth-worthy Argo
manned with us accomplices.
Truth-worthy does not founder on facts.

54. Hot as the nick of time and bloody
as my lucky break you loom in triumph.
For His holidaylight strewn with a large hand
I am thankful to the creator of the world.
Never again let it be said our flowers
are blighted nor the generous despair,
for beauty has made hell burst into tears
and bravery has dealt out astonishment.

55. Like coming into shade on a hot day
I didn't know I was crazy with the heat,
I suddenly remember how I wrote
that God is love and can afford to lose
and so He lets us triumph in our spite.
Because I see it there in front of me
I often know the truth and write it down,
but rarely does it charm me as this hour.

SENTENCES FOR MATTHEW READY,[1] SERIES II

≚

56. Agree to give it up
    and do yourself without:
    of course a world-for-you is lost
    but you can't cope anyway;
    likely another world
    will come to be and be exciting
    —you can't *know*, but you think so;
    why don't you act accordingly?

57. Because the good die young
    and the wages of sin is death
    I steer a middle course,
    alive to tell the tale;
    so have I and my world
    matured on speaking terms,
    measuring from time to time
    each other with a glance.

58. People who know me tend to like me
    nor am I shy to pick up friends;
    that I am usually unhappy
    is only mathematical:
    rarely is anyone both beautiful and available.
    I am aggressive, modest, and cowardly,
    a congeries not doomed to prosper,
    but pious and grateful unto thee, O Luck.

59. Will it occur to me? and when will it occur?
the imprecise answer to a question
I haven't learned to formulate.
I listen to sentences of Mozart
that gracious condescending spirit
but there is no answer here for me,
I did not have a lucky father
and I did not rebel just when.

60. An eagle on a rock
lighting with wings outspread
and in his beak a writhing snake,
freedom of the spirit
has corrupted me
into an indignant
citizen who cannot sleep,
I drop the snake and scream.

61. Whoever the soldier was who stole
these Vaphio cups, he was a judge of gold
wiser than soldiers I have met,
maybe he was a farmer who knew bulls
entangled in ropes. We others but
who have no gods or burial deposits
wander from Eleusis to Delphi
gathering meanings that do not add up.

62. Let me praise rapid speech
that says how a thing is
in my dear English tongue
that I learned from a child;
forty years and more
carefully I have copied
the meters of my breathing
and pruned out words not mine.

63. One is running away
one is running after
one is running dreaming

of the Olympic games
—across the lush lawn
bordered by eucalyptus.
One is just running,
him my eyes follow.

64. This sequoia is three thousand years old,
    fire, lightning, drouth, and earthquakes
    have been the drama of its world,
    millennia ago it overtopped
    the competition of the undergrowth.
    Only in this decade is it threatened
    by the feet of our hordes trampling
    the roots, who come to gaze with awe.

65. The earth and sky so carried on this month
    as if the poor earth never could recover,
    whipped by hurricanes and drowned by floods
    and stung all night by lightning,
    my only world. Some are dead,
    the newspapers are rich with marvelous
    and pathetic pictures and reports.
    But today she has on her sunny clothes.

66. Last night the moon came close.
    What was picture has become
    shore where men will land.
    Astronomers and engineers
    wide-eyed on steppe and beach
    mount their guns and fire
    fraught with future
    in single-minded darkness.

67. From first base on the left
    on a clockwise diamond
    he threw me toward home plate
    a pure white bounding ball
    I did not field, for heaven
    above his ebony head

broke silver through the cloud:
I saw it all.

68. I let the ball bound by
to field the sun appearing
out of the storm-cloud
silvery and pouring
light, light—oh how
how to get out of this
fool ball-game that I
no longer want to play?

69. He had five sons, Reaper and Thresher,
Mechanic, Wayward, and Daring,
they were his pride and easy to praise
(like himself). He was ingenuous
and did not see how people envied him,
and they were glad he fell into misfortune
and that his beautiful boys hung their heads
in the bitter world where they walked.

70. Like the drowsy child who can't untie
his knotted shoelace, he is cross,
why doesn't he fall over
and slide to sleep with one shoe on
like Willy Winkle my son John?
—my being is noticeable to few
and good or necessary to nobody,
why do I bother? what does it matter?

71. I know it was
but I can't find anywhere
that photo of my face
age of eleven
with a gappy grin
and eyes frankly leering
out of what window
looking at what beach?

72. Daybreak I look into the cloudy sky
    for a telegram from the Messiah
    and disappointed I go back to bed
    and brood about the Way.
    Impatiently I listen for the knock
    that didn't happen fifty years ago
    and devise for the advantage of you all
    spiteful utopias, some practical.

73. They closed my bar, revoked the license,
    and Teddy, Bobby Edmonds, and Bill Brown
    and other harmless hustlers and mad queens
    are scattered up and down Eighth Avenue.
    They were a bore—it was a lousy bar—
    but it was ours; they gave me tips
    that kept me out of trouble up to now.
    Now here I stand staring at a padlock.

74. What are they doing? Making a thread
    of sand to sew the shards together.
    Won't that at least keep them busy?
    No, frustration leads to aggression.
    What are you doing? As you see,
    we are giving a press conference.
    Don't you get frustrated too?
    Yes, but we are pacifists.

75. You ask what is the bay with the statue
    down there and the new bridge across the Narrows:
    I call it "Splendid." And the phalanx
    of Manhattan's warrior skyscrapers,
    I call them "Towering." But these fleecy clouds
    are "Sweet" our plane is slowly nosing
    into the blue, we leave the haze
    at nine, according to the pilot, thousand feet.

76. Out of sight of home I was soon frightened,
    much was unfinished, I could never enough
    in the hurried conditions that I contrived,

on my lonely voyage I worried over
an unlikely danger I foresaw in flashes,
I reread for safety something I wrote
busying myself making small corrections,
and I wrote something new to ward off the unknown.

77. In this black cloud it is confused
though above the cloud clear and bright.
It chooses me to stay confused
in this black cloud in gusts of wet
among erratic slow long bolts
of lightning and I am afraid
of falling down. It is not blue
and rose and pearl where I fly.

78. The engingines
of the ailingplane
are st-tuttering
I hope they won't
beginnnn
to stammer:
30,000 feet
is too high for speech defects.

79. Most ancient dreams and fables
are poorly realized
but this big aeroplane
is very like the Roc
and so softly descends
with clumsy grace and lands us
alas in St. Louis
nor am I Sindbad.

80. In error, incompetent:
I could not stop (perhaps I sped)
his onward wreck;
his wits were wild and mine were blank;
he screamed for help and my marrow froze;
I could not quit him without hurting him

but when I stayed I could not come across.
I was incompetent.

81. A grounder to short and out at first
is our sharp fate. We are not heavy hitters.
The reapers grin at us across the infield.
As I was powerless to help my friend
I shall be powerless to help myself.
We two were lovers, but the field we played
did not look like this world—the grass was ragged,
the players shouted out encouragement.

82. When I was a child, my mother threatened
to abandon me, or did. But my world
my only never made that threat;
although she was a wall she was there
even when I whimpered for my earache
and screamed for what I needed and couldn't have.
Lately, however, I have fallen ill
and my only world is making the old threat.

83. My head is low with my horrible luck
my icy eyes starkly staring
hasty and wholly hand and hoping
I freely offered, it was never enough
men doubted I meant it. But it doesn't matter
for my strength is slight my will too weak
to win anyway even though earnest
so my world is waste. But my work is well.

84. Woeful was the winter
my politics proved futile,
despite me John went mad,
and my sister started to die;
nevertheless, though tattered
in my self-esteem,
I deserve to have survived
to this sunny Tuesday.

85. I have outlived last winter!
    April! I am not dead!
    it is the ancient exclamation
    of Eleusis. Dead do not
    cry out anything, nor bring
    sheaves to Demeter.
    The dead did not outlive last winter
    but I have outlived last winter.

86. "Forward cars for Baltimore and Washington!
    B. and W. way up ahead!"
    they really have impressed that message on me
    but no one offers to tote my heavy heart
    that hankers to go home where Daisy is
    learning to speak and she cries "Cow! cow!"
    also when it's a horse. The Capitol,
    though it is white, will not shine as bright.

87. Oh yes, I'd write more poetry
    about my little daughter Daisy
    except she is so live and sweet
    and pretty that she doesn't fit
    the black mood and painful breath
    of my present thoughts about death
    and the sarcasm of my
    present thoughts about my country.

88. God damn! a hundred people on a train,
    not one worth groping. What do you do
    for four hours? "Sit quiet in your seat
    and twiddle your thumbs like everybody else,
    studiously read the *New York Times*."
    Is that what others do? I don't believe it.
    I look and so it is, I am dumbfounded.
    —This keeps me occupied as far as Trenton.

89. There's never a sexy kid
    on a train to Washington
    nor do the elder statesmen

have humane wrinkles and good eyes.
Sometimes I meet a foreign scholar
and we speak each other's language badly,
as wearily I return
to my little flat under the Capitol.

90. Sunrise and a friendly sailor
made waiting worthwhile,
it was only looks averted quick
and lots of fright was in his eyes
but his prick swelled and so did mine
and thank God for a sign of life
in January, 8 A.M.
at Dulles International Airport.

91. If he grinds his back teeth like a paranoiac
that's one thing, but if he is swallowing
and his trouser's fly begins to bulge
that's quite another; some play with a knife
and some make a fist to warn you off.
Others feign sleep and languorously stretch
their lanky legs out long and lick their lips;
but I, if I feign sleep, fall asleep.

92. Riding to Washington on a mission congenial
to my nature, to be a disinterested judge,
I am well pleased with me today and rapidly
sketching a little book important for the nation:
and every hour flashes in my mind
when I shall have come away at last
to my pretty farm on the Connecticut
and you arriving on your motorcycle.

93. I am looking forward to going away
and how far shall I go?
to my pretty home in New Hampshire
where trout leap in the ragged river?
to prison where the powers that be

will pen me up to hush my voice?
or shall I drift as far as death
into fog on the Grand Banks?

94. My brow is glued to the window watching my land recede
Rockaway the Moriches and Fire Island twinkle
in rifts in the cloud, and I am biting my lips
because for me there has been little pride
in my only country where my son is hounded
by the police and I and all my friends cry out
in rebel anger. So we come above the ceiling
eastward into blue heaven toward the advancing night.

95. Waxing and waning with the seasons, fifty years
I've walked this ten-thousand mile trail
along the shore to here, that's a long hike.
No wonder I plod heavily along
and climb the rocky spots unsteadily.
Yet never till June 1961
have I studied with such winter-starved eyes
the rhododendron thick on the cliffside.

96. All day along the shore to Alpine
they have been line-fishing and trapping crabs,
I hunting cock, that's an unlicensed sport.
The dusk is dull and few of us have any
game to boast, except the afternoon
and the endless largo of the Hudson
and the sun with his hairs on end in fright
as down he sinks behind the Palisades.

97. With drooping groping toes
and black tips of bobbing bills
the gulls touch the water
and hover in the wind and scream:
it's a game—no one catches a fish—
or an obsession, touch and go—
high a thousand yards
they soar into the silent sky.

98. "O Devil who find work
for idle hands, find me
something, for I am jobless
to grind my teeth and spit out porcelain."
So carelessly I prayed
and out of the Bureau of Hell
called "Work for Idle Hands"
they sent me you to grope.

99. You said my lust was like the insistent
mosquitoes in the barn-loft where we slept,
this broke my heart—do you know?—
because I loved you very much
and you found a telling metaphor.
I could not remedy that fault
not since my bleak childhood
unsure, abandoned, hungry.

100. There's a way of rejecting that endears, lad
—you make me know I have the right to it
and you would make me happy but you can't.
But this fellow is still glowering at me
across the camp a hundred yards away.
Believe me, I am not the threat he fears
to his conceited cock, and just as pleased
if he takes down his tent and scrams.

101. Lovely in the distance
are dull at the approach
but you were like a doll
and loomed like heaven near;
your hair was chocolate
your deep blue eyes were frank
and you were taken by
the rapture on my face.

102. Given six or seven
the beauty of them likes me, beauty's kind.
The rest don't see it and get angry

with their tight mouths and squinty eyes
unmagnanimous animals.
The face that has the golden glow
smiles me welcome. People say otherwise,
but lust is the magnet of beauty.

103. His beauty sparkles, his big eyes blaze,
his moist teeth gleam and his wide smile
turns up a lamp that was aglow,
his laughing-wrinkles crackle like a campfire,
the flush across his neck
is like the slowly burning ruby
I drowned in swimming for tomorrow
west into the blushing sea.

104. Now only praise makes me cry,
when David Hume praises Alfred
I read it through a shine of tears,
and if a poet praises loud
—naturally loud is praise—some ancient
hero who never lived in this world,
then my heart breaks and I bawl
for joy in this land of loss.

105. Aligned at last the bass-drummer
picked up his drum and the leader
twirled his baton and forward all
they stepped and big the brasses blared.
My heart leaped up, I laughed for joy,
because I am the Muses' boy
and never people are so fair
as making music loud and clear.

106. I wish we could already fly
to the moon or another planet
of lesser gravity so you and I
could make love unencumbered
by our heavy bodies. Weight is sweet

but it's nicer to hold on lighter;
not—God forbid—that I'm complaining
of what we have, very good.

107. After I'd stared awhile, I heard a voice:
"I see that your primeval dream,
your Easter Island face,
has come to classic lines
—you like your soup weak," Eros jeered,
"your punch is weak too. Nothing comes from nothing."
I turned, and there the face of horror was,
but I at this one also idly stared.

108. "Great Tao is a ship adrift"—awakes
at sunrise asking, where am I?
and deviates forward slowly to nowhere.
What does he know? to front afraid the gale
and painfully climb the next oncoming wave.
It is by an inevitable mistake
that the ten thousand cheer and shake their flags
lining the shore in the indifferent port.

109. Though little of what I try succeeds
most of what I try means something.
God keeps after me
in his pedagogic way.
I was accepted long ago
into this university,
listen to my tone of voice
and you will know an upper-classman.

110. One school was at a ford
and the other at a bridge,
dry foot or wet feet went their way.
But where I studied, we couldn't cross.
Some of us swam and drowned.
I plough my acre on the shore.
I am a pupil of Lao-tze,
my friends were Nietzscheans.

111. "Man, I'm shook to see you in a commercial,
     I thought you was opposed to advertising."
     This is news-casting, dammit, these *are* good,
     National Biscuits Triscuits—crunch crunch—
     not so good as nooky or Vivaldi
     but—crunch crunch—better than Ingmar Bergman
     or the academic friends that I—crunch crunch
     crunch crunch—made at the University of Wisconsin.

112. Of things I use and that use me
     you my modest old black car
     cause me little cursing
     unlike my wife or son or dog
     or soul or body. I have often marveled
     how you started at a touch
     climbed the hill picking up speed
     and gently taxied into Groveton.

113. We drove the old red car to Kailua
     to replace a leaky brakeline.
     "When they get down to brass tacks," David said,
     "they'll find the whole thing is a heap of rust
     and fall apart."
     "Well, you see what old age is," said I.
     But no, they by-passed this and passed by that
     and to my surprise we drove it home.

114. I use my spoon and do not spill
     spear with my fork and do not miss
     my sentences progress to periods
     and I am toilet-trained.
     Much beyond this—although this is
     already much—I am confused
     not like a wild animal
     but like a senile imbecile.

115. He stands there like a gently taut bow
     from which his anger may fly hard
     or like the live strings of a violin

with many songs in it if rightly touched,
so light and straight he stands there on the corner
in the yellow afternoon—his eyes are blue
his name is Possible. I can hardly remember
how my heart used to pound when I too could.

116. Isn't somebody calling "Paul Goodman"
past my cabin—it is midnight—
running through the rain? But who
in all the world without a lot of trouble
could find me out here on the far north coast
of Oahu at this hour? It must be bad news.
Who of mine is stricken in the night
that half around the world they call me in the night?

117. It is nothing new, no, nothing new
that as people grow older
their friends and sisters die off
and they are left bleaker alone.
The probability of it
increases geometrically.
But oh God it's monotonous
to *keep* one's face screwed up with woe.

118. Thirty-foot waves cross-colliding
on the north coast in the Kona wind
—beyond the foam and spray the gray
sea is flat to the horizon:
it is enough to swirl Alice
Matty and mama and many more
confounded in the nature of things.
I sat there till I became calmer.

119. Good for her, Nancy Morris knew it was lantana
the pink and peach I stopped the car to cull.
They leave me at a loss in this exotic climate
these people who can't name their wildflowers,
maybe because there are so many showy blooms,
but naturally I study the flowers by the wayside

and in the field without a gardener
as in the North Country where my son and sister lie.

120. Were I still more industrious and didn't get sick and tired,
instead of half a column my obit in the *Times*
would run a column, with an anecdote
and a quotation from *Growing Up Absurd*.
But there is nothing, nothing that I could ever do
to warrant a brass band when I get off the plane,
for some cats have it and some dogs don't,
roosters cock-a-doodle, hogs only grunt.

121. The driver is testy because of the traffic,
the rider in a rage because of the meter,
but we agree the primaries are bullshit
—in my native city where from time to time
I visit, the folk are apprehensive
(I am not radiating joy myself)
but we aren't brainwashed and we aren't robots
as we chatter the vernacular.

122. Hm. You thought I meant Immanuel Kant
a sexless philosopher from Koenigsberg,
but I really dedicated *that* book
to Chaim Yankel Kant my daughter-in-law's
beagle who was run over by a Buick
at Columbus Avenue and 83rd Street.
He had such brown liquid eyes.
I don't even have a daughter-in-law.

123. People are watching a fellow climbing a ladder
because it is an interesting thing,
and I am watching them and that beauty
doing his interesting thing.
Everybody seems to be happier than I
but I have this poem to write about us all.
He is painting the railing of the West Side Highway
and I go under to the dirty river.

NORTH PERCY

1. Playing too happily
   on the slippery mountainside
   my only son fell down and died.
   I taught him to talk honestly
   and without stalling come across
   but I could not teach him the cowardice
   and ambiguity
   to live a longer life unhappily.

   You see, girl, you ought not to
   center your affections so,
   little short of idolatry.
   A young man is untrustworthy.
   In the morning satisfied
   he gets up from your bed
   and in the evening he is dead.

2. His mother and I did our best, Lord,
      for Matt, and it was pretty good,
         and he for twenty years gave us
            the chance, without our disappointment or remorse.

   But now this leaves us nothing
   to blame or regret—only this bawling
      and the bright image that
         around the grave his friends confabulate.

3. Our prudent Master has begun
      us at last to disburden
         of our long cares, Sally, too
         heavy often for me and you

      but we did not quit them. Oh
      as these things fall away we go
         lighter to our own graves, who are
         burdened also with each other.

4. Where I swim on the gravelly beach
         along the smoothly flowing river
      the purple joe-pyeweed smells sweet,
         the enclosing mountain lowers over,

      and I am small and safe with my grief.
         Everything is lovely in my home
      today when we have little grip on life.
         My little dog stands waiting for me to come.

5. God of choice, in your real
      we two are wandering in hell.
         You know we chose to rear that boy
         rather than to live another way,

      when now the corpse blocks the view
      what are we supposed to do?
         Too much of us is now a failure
         for us to have a future.

                  "Nothing yet awhile."
                  Then—mark time march?
                  "No, just nothing."
                  Company, halt.

                  Shall we break ranks, Captain?
                  "Yes, for food and sleep."

Shall we go back home?
"Do not yet go back home."

6. What does it mean when I moan
I want to go back home?
By "go back home" I mean to die
and this is why I cry.
It means that I am not at home
not where I am nor where I come
nor anywhere I sail or fly
and this is why I cry.
But I say "back" as if I knew
and once had such a place. Who
took me away and when was that?
I don't know and it is too late.
Do I imagine when I die
—and maybe this is why I cry—
that I will then see my son Ready
whom I saw on the stretcher bloody?

※

FOR MY BIRTHDAY, 1967

7. O God who wear a heavy veil,
I do not need to know what is real,
yet lead me further where the real is
although that way is rough. Your mysteries

are probably too hard to live with
at least for me who draw my breath
short by art and my perverse ideas,
and now it has been six and fifty years.

8. I figure this bad world is purgatory,
I am not damned but suffer and do learn.

Annoyed by flies when I would simply turn
face to the wall and rest, or if I bravely
lose another war to set men free,
I gather meaning from it and I earn
merit as I grow gray—though age is a stern
teacher more than my capacity.

"Is there paradise?" No, no,
I have not heard of anything to hope.
"Purgatory without paradise
has no meaning." But I have no choice,
I do not need to carry my task through,
neither am I free to give it up.

9. God, you did exempt me from original sin
   and your spirit with me often does commune
       but you have plunged me into purgatory
           where faith and hope have little substance any more.

   I look in the mirror guiltless at my haggard face
   and I know that you hear my direct address
       but I don't know how to pray or what to pray for
       and my eyesight is growing dim, your creature.

10.   On the wooden bridge
    the snake slipped between the boards
        and dropped. It was dusk.

    Out of the thicket
    before the man sadly came,
        I knew he was dead.

    Although this happened
    a long time ago the scene
        does not pass away.

PAGAN RITES

11. Creator Spirit come
    by whom
        I'll say what is real
        and so away I'll steal.

    When my only son
    fell down and died on Percy mountain
        I began
        to practice magic like a pagan.

    Around the open grave we ate
    the blueberries that he brought
        from the cloud, and then we
        buried his bag with his body.

    Upon the covered grave
    I laid the hawkweed that I love
        that withered fast
        where the mowers passed.

    I brought also a tiny yellow
    flower whose name I do not know
        to share my ignorance
        with my son. (But since

    then I find in the book
    it is a kind of shamrock
        Oxalis corniculata,
        Matty, sorrel of the lady.)

    Blue-eyed grass with its gold hexagon
        beautiful as the gold and blue
        double in Albireo
    that we used to gaze on

when Matty was alive
I laid on Matty's grave
   where two robins were
   hopping here and there;

and gold and bluer than that blue
or the double in Albireo
   bittersweet nightshade
   the deadly alkaloid
     I brought for no other reason
     than because it was poison.

Mostly, though, I brought some weed
beautiful but disesteemed,
   plantain or milkweed,
   because we die by the wayside.

(And if spring comes again
I will bring a dandelion,
   because he was a common weed
   and also he was splendid.)

But when I laid my own forehead
on the withering sod
   to go the journey deep,
   I could not fall asleep.

I cannot dream, I cannot quit
the one scene in the twilight
   that is no longer new yet does
   not pass into what was.

Last night the Pastoral Symphony
of Handel in the key of C
   I played on our piano
   out of tune shrill and slow

because the shepherds were at night
in the field in the starlight

when music loud and clear
sang from nowhere.

Will magic and the weeks placate
the soul that in tumbling fright
    fled on August eighth?
    The first flock is flying south

and a black-eyed susan
is livid in the autumn rain
    dripping without haste or strain
    on the oblong larger than a man.

Creator Spirit come
by whom
    I say that which is real
    and softly away I steal.

THAT OTHER MAN AND I

12. He as wandering he walks
    up the hill to the mailbox
imagines, his mind lapsing,
    that my son is living.
We are among the steeplebush, I do not dare
    reach to him there,
bereaved are touchy. But I intend
    to leave him there behind
with his botany and try what it's like
    on a longer hike.

That man would rather go on
    mourning than his son be gone
for good. This is impractical
    even in dull

Stratford Hollow. I'll go roaming
    among the screaming
cars in the city, carefully
    threading my way.
Let him go crazy
    back there without me.

A day will come when I am dying
    that we two again
may meet. And when we look like strangers
    into each other's
sullen eyes, what shall I say
    and he to me?
when once for all we join
    in absolute bawling,
blinding tears that blot
    the world out?

13. Going mad with melancholy
    I write down words that make me cry
        —yet let me speak no ill of the
        Creator Spirit who does not forsake me.

    We do not choose the real, she
    whispers and I obediently
        write it down, often in horror
        of the things that are.

14. This miner like many another musician
    has gradually and now suddenly
    struck a vein of crystals, death.
    Plutonic fire was here. I descend
    unwillingly into the blazing cave.
    My admiration of discovery
    has caught a chill from the circumstances.
    My voice has no spirit as I speak.

139

15. "I will revive Hippolytus,"
    said Aesculapius,
    "but me, me I cannot revive."
    I can revive neither one
    but can, Creator Spirit come,
    twist the non-being of the once alive
    into artificial flowers, and praise
    also the never-to-be rose.

16. My last two books I dedicated
    to men alive, and they were dead
    before the books were published.
    These serious little gifts I make

    I was unable to give
    to A. J. Muste and Mathew Ready
    who both were warriors of peace,
    one was eighty and one was twenty.

    Ten millennia and more
    men have slain one another
    for causes, before I learned
    how it is to lose my son.

    Do not speak to me of violence
    and do not praise to me
    guerilla fighters in Bolivia.

17. "At last," said Po Chu-I, "by thinking
    of the time before she was born,
    by reason I drove the pain away."
    No. I am grateful to the mandarin poet
    who protected the poor and had a practical heart
    for the unhappy; but my son was twenty,
    I cannot think of prior to my son,
    we must walk with the presence of his absence.

BLACK FLAG, APRIL 15, 1967

18. At the spring rally on the Sheep Meadow
    there's a black flag—I am enchanted,
    we anarchists used to be out of date.
    Black it is the colors
    of the sovereignty of none
    but in our land the grass is green
    the rivers they are sparkling clean
    and the children frank and keen.

    Today but in the dirty reign
    of Johnson, here at our black flag
    some solemn students are igniting
    draft cards at a rusty can of fire
    and one young man holds up a sign
    "Twenty Years Unregistered."
    The black flag is a vivid shadow
    at the spring rally on the Sheep Meadow.

    And if the merry day shall come
    again the black flag is my country's spirit,
    lovingly my wife will take it home
    and cut it up to make pants or a shirt.

A GRAVESTONE, AUGUST 8, 1968

19. The Sun and the Ocean
    and Death are unique,
    the limiting conditions
    within which we live.

    And there is one single Night
    (although De Falla sang

of nights in the gardens of Spain).
Freedom too

is indivisible,
its flag is therefore black
not like the other flags
that have armorial bearings.

Come and see, on this granite grout
gravestone is the motto cut
of all the youth of the world:
Twenty Years Unregistered.

Off Route 3 it is,
a few miles north of Groveton,
if you want to know something,
among the orange hawkweed.

20. Ocean, Sexuality, and the Sun,
and Death, and Flora are the gods for real
that sway my soul, so I freeze or smile
or am awestruck. Secretly I often
salute them when I meet them. But this ruin
of my lifetime for the commonweal,
I do it as my duty and I feel
nothing but weariness and indignation.

The Holy Ghost is also my acquaintance
whom I when I encounter sing and dance
with the musicians. But there is one god
for whom I have the others all betrayed,
Adam—wasting me for fifty-six
winters in waiting and peace politics.

‰

CHICAGO 1968

21. My son would have voted for the President
this year his first time, being twenty-one,
if he were not in jail or a refugee
in Canada, and if he were not dead
like the Republic: we are seeing scenes
reminiscent of Caligula.
How shall honest men respond to it?
Mathew would have known to tell me.
I was a champion of the resisting young,
I usually vainly tried to guide them,
more often guided. But my liaison
is lost. Now they are right to call me senile.

22. So they sentenced David Harris to three years.
He always did remind me of Matty
who was bound that way too, until he died.
Dave is a talker, Matty was quieter
though not shy. Both of them were stubborn.
They do not grow many as beautiful
among the Americans as those two shaggy boys,
I am pleased and sad for the women who loved them.
But what shall I say to my country
that has no better use for David Harris?

‰

WINTER SOLSTICE

23. Thee God we praise for the short days
of winter and the instant pause
of the sun concealed this morning
in the unbroken cloud. It is raining
gently on the northeast and we

have brought a dripping Christmas tree
   in, and put the golden star
   on top as every other year

—the golden star and oh the blue
that Matty used to pin below
   to represent Albireo
   the double in Cygnus. There are few
things as beautiful in your creation,
Lord, as this thing that my son
   sought out with his telescope
   and used to pin on our treetop.

NOAH'S SONG

24. What is that lovely rainbow that abides
     upon the dripping moments till it fades?
        God promised me, though I am old,
        if I will work this new-washed field

    while my future vanishes past,
    something will come of it at last.
        This is the rainbow that abides
        on the dripping moments—till it fades.

25. I doubt, though it is possible,
     that when I die will be so bad
     and I may yet go mad,
     which they say is horrible;
     but probably the worst that can befall
     is past me now Matty being dead.

    If he were here he would have hoed
    this field where my shoulders fail,
    except that he would be in jail

which he and we would cope with as we could.
He was a quiet one but stood
conspicuous and did not quail.

It is one year—I wish that August 8th
were blotted from the diary—
by now he glitters like a wraith
of mist on the mountain at mid-day,
and my sadness is joining with
the other sadness of humanity.

26. The beauty of the world
    —I still am hungry for it—
    to me was always poignant
    being in exile,
    I see it through a gleam of tears
    —it does not nourish much.

    Sally and I are living on
    —I see it in her eyes—
    it is a kind of bond between us
    sure, where much is false.
    And what a thing it is
    to be living on.

    I picked a sprig of dogwood
    blossoms from the grove
    to bring to my pretty home
    where we have many flowers,
    they are a kind of bond between us
    —I pick them where I wander—

    and then we hold each other close
    sometimes for an hour
    that has no words,
    looking at the withering
    dogwood from the grove
    in our pretty home.

27. I love lilacs, their violet and ivory wood.
   Walt Whitman said their name in a good poem.
   But my son disliked their smell, they are tabu,
   I will not bring them in, though it is May.
   So religiously I live on in rituals
   among non-beings, for so long as it lasts.
   Yes, others manage happier
   but my way is conservative and pious.

28. In the variations of the Arietta
   molto semplice e cantabile
   Beethoven seemed to find it hard to bid
   good-bye good-bye to the pianoforte
   sent him from London, he kept improvising
   rather than leaving off to go about
   some other business of dying. He
   had had such a long friendship with pianos
   and this one was unusually good,
   its minor seconds were harmonious.

29. The young man played it, really, very well—
   passionately—and quite out of his mind—
   except that it was marked by Beethoven
   molto semplice e cantabile,
   and how do you play *that* molto semplice?
   I'll tell you. It is done by walking along
   quietly and quite out of your mind,
   quite out of your mind cantabile.

❦

FOUR LITTLE PRAYERS

30. I can't control, daily less,
   any of my circumstances,

it doesn't happen as I forethought,
I am trapped where I would not.
But if I let be, as You counsel,
Lord, it is unbearable,
   Matty dead, Daisy ill,
   worse I don't will than when I will.

No, it is not amazing, Lord,
that the young I desperately wooed
   and me they paid no regard,
   now greedily around me crowd
to pick at my exhausted love
for wisdom that I do not have
   and still pay no regard to me
   though I am sick, plain to see.

What never was, what cannot be,
what is no longer, are the three
   themes that men invent; and I
   too live on by writing poetry,
talking to You who are
deaf or do not choose to answer.
   Yet I prefer this conversation
   to that of men or women.

Doggedly I daily write
the whispers of the holy spirit
   I hope I do not much distort
   by my misery distraught.
Others have nothing but their sorrow
—perhaps—how would I know?—
   but dry and brief is the phrase
   that I say, Lord, Thy praise.

31. Eating alone
      apart from the company
because no one
     is interesting to me

and walking alone
	every day
because no one
	will walk my way.

It is no use
	to withhold criticism,
I cannot choose
	to be stupider than I am.

And now a year of woe
	since my son died
merges with "I too
	shall die" that did abide

and this mortal grief
	mixing with
my lonesome life
	and sex-starved youth

I am crying because
	the woods are lovely
in this world that was
	not made for me.

(Nevertheless
	it is good for exile
to live in a place
	that is beautiful.)

Bitterly because I
	jealously murdered
like the Moor in the play
	her who only murmured

—I walk along here dazed,
	crying because
I am more confused
	than I ever was

until I hear in my grief
        again the flawless sound
        of the child abandoned
that does not deceive.
        The red fall has come
and tomorrow I will leave
        for still another home

and there renew my grip
        on life and make do as I do
by making up
        sarcastic hokku:

                "I abandoned me
        and then took me wailing in
                to my foster home.

                "Having exiled me
        I now champion my rights
                as a citizen.

                "Turning my spirit
        away from You, I have faith
                I am justified."

Yes! when this veil of
        the world is stripped away
I will again fall in love.
        Not today.

A man so little
        in touch with folks
ought not to meddle
        in politics.

The peace my trouble
        is thirsty for
is too universal.

It is no wonder
I do not want power

and victory
    that sits with joy
    on a naive boy
is hateful to me.
    For me there is no way
    but magnanimity.

32. Surely the destiny
    that seems mathematical
    to a mind like mine
    must be an illusion.
    Full of false promise
    first weeks away from home
    fly by, only later
    they drag till I return.
    The first year of my exile
    dragged, the next went swifter;
    though the gnawing pain never ceases
    now I have grown inured
    to being a second-class
    citizen without franchise
    who has a foreign accent:
    I say what is the case.
    Oh the first life I shall have lived
    in this world has a red sunset,
    I shall be reborn
    as a braver hunter,
    as one whose only son
    does not fall down North Percy mountain
    and bash his brain on a rock.
    People will call me Lucky
    when we two carry on
    the manly conversation
    between the father and the son
    that we just began.

When Matty was a boy
he used to quarrel and vie,
but I learned much truth
from the quiet youth.

33. The Northern Crown, nearby Arcturus
    in the meadows of the Bear,
    for this abstract of stars
    in the cold latitudes
    affirming what is not
    I gave my life—see how she shines
    in the clamorous night
    around my famous head
    as staggering I walk
    sightless with tears away
    from me and my little boy.
    I never made this crazy contract
    willingly, God.

BALLADS

✤

BALLAD OF JOHNNY RISTOW
ESCAPED FROM RIKER'S ISLAND
ON DECEMBER 30TH

for Judith

He got the grease in the workhouse laundry
    and he slip through a hole no biggern a dime—
there is a lad who wants out bad
    he is tired o doin time.

A mile an a half in the icy river
    from Riker's Island to Astoria Queens,
he swam by night in that moonlight
    an he wasnt wearin blue jeans.

Johnny was in for indecent exposure
    ninety days for showin off his cock—
there is a lad wants to go unclad
    an now he got out in the dark.

Naked he dove an naked he rose
    till he stole some pants from a barge clothesline,
he was wearin these when the harbor police
    caught him under Pier Ninety-Nine.

Shit! why did they catch Johnny Ristow
    yellow with grease an blue with pleurisy,

Johnny was tired o doin time
  but got no furthern Astoria.

Jesus, am I tired o doin time
  in this lousy jail! but what's the use?
he's cover with ice an the harbor police
  are draggin him back to the workhouse.

"I jump into that pitch-black river
  cause I was tired o doin time,"
he said. O Johnny, I wish you
  were loose an be a pal o mine.

Indecent exposure! indecent exposure!
  Johnny Ristow, arent you ashame?
a man could catch his death December thirtieth
  goin like that for a swim.

※

THE BALLAD OF SANTIAGO AND RICARDO

San Antonio in Texas
  was once a Spanish town
and many people there
  cling to the Catholic faith.

A Spanish boy of twelve
  let us call him Ricardo
(I do not know his name)
  loved stories about Jesus.

He told them over and over
  till he had them by heart
and he taught them to a child
  whose name was Santiago Lopez.

153

The child was only three
  and both were orphan boys
who had no mothers of their own
  and lived in an asylum.

Both of the boys were dark
  and had brown eyes like dogs.
Ricardo felt important
  having the other in charge.

"Repeat it after me,"
  he'd say to Santiago
and the child looked up brown-eyed
  and did the best he could.

The lesson was Lazarus
  stinking in the grave,
the eleventh chapter of John.
  They came to the sentence, "Jesus wept."

"Repeat it after me,"
  he said to Santiago,
"Jesus wept." The child
  repeated, "Jesus swept."

"Not Jesus swept! He wept!"
  Ricardo shouts with laughter,
imagine Jesus swept!
  "Not swept! Jesus wept!"

Dutifully Santiago
  repeated, "Jesus swept,"
laughing at the fun
  and that was part of it

he didn't understand,
  nor did he understand the stories,
not as we understand.
  But he understands enough

how a big boy Ricardo
    pays attention to him
and holds his hand and smiles,
    and neither one is lonely,

and also in a crowd
    how Ricardo's proud
when Santiago loud
    repeats the Bible story.

The both are orphan boys
    and live in an asylum,
the child is all mixed up,
    the boy is more experienced.

A somber thought has darkened
    the dark face of Ricardo:
"Repeat it! Jesus wept."
    The other, "Jesus swept."

A piercing thought has stabbed
    the dark soul of Ricardo
that cannot bear frustration;
    he'll teach him to tease.

Ricardo's grip has tightened
    hard on the child's arm:
"Get it right! Jesus wept."
    "Ow! Jesus swept—

"leggo my arm, Ricardo!"
    "Get it right! Jesus wept!"
The child can only whimper
    and wail, "Jesus swept."

The lesson is Lazarus
    stinking in the grave,
the eleventh chapter of John,
    the sentence, "Jesus wept."

"You're saying it on purpose
    for spite!" hisses Ricardo,
"I'll give you one more chance."
    The child can only bawl.

He has no words any more
    not even "Jesus swept."
His friend is hurting him
    and he can only bawl.

And suddenly this bawling
    engulfs Ricardo's world
as when the hurricane
    smashes to bits the houses

and all the people are drowned.
    The safety of his stories
is washed away in the flood
    like sticks like little sticks,

and again Ricardo's earnest love
    that tries so hard as best he can
has smashed against the other one;
    but Santiago is tiny,

he has thrown him on the ground
    and is kicking sense into him,
kicking him in the belly and head,
    the child will die of it,

there is unbelief in his eyes,
    the folk of the asylum,
kids and nuns, are crowding
    to the place where both are screaming.

BALLAD OF THE HURRICANE

When you was little, man, your mama
    threw out the baby with the bath,
man, you ain't got the equipment
    to beat your feet an laugh.

So sit down there an drink your beer
    an don't be botherin
the people dancin with their friends
    so gay and good-lookin.

Don't snap out of it, buddy,
    stay with it till it hurts,
because you only live once
    you may as well know the worst.

Listen, he said, my situation
    is delicate! he frowned,
I gotta be here in the center
    o these winds rushin around,

a hundred twenty miles an hour
    round the edges, knock you silly,
but here I'm just as calm as calm
    an the sky is sunny.

They wouldn listen, an a mile an hour
    he drifted out the door northwest
by the compass that he wore
    danglin from his vest.

That was the blast that wrecked my house
    and knocked the spire off Old North Church,
it drowned a man in Providence
    and left New London in the lurch.

Mighty trees with dirty roots
    came floating down Narragansett Bay
with chickens roosting in the leaves
    at the break of day.

After that flood at daybreak
    our town was dirty and washed
and we walked the streets in wonder
    to look at what was smashed.

   ✻

THE BALLAD OF CLOSING TIME

With unerring finger he put
    a bullet in C-sharp,
the piano sank to its knees
    with wiry cries of its harp,

it laid its chin on the floor
    and sank its teeth in his calf,
ending with a grin
    the tune that started with a laugh.

So often near closing time
    the shaky jigger overbrims
and a man comes off inside his head
    instead of in his limbs.

He had a lovely wife named Lou
    but she made him impotent with guilt.
"Why do you fuss where my cock was,
    when now it's in you to the hilt?

"What skin is it off your ass, honey,
    if I been here and there?
all of that was a dress rehearsal
    for the grand affair."

Dress rehearsal! dress rehearsal!
    warming up at a dress rehearsal.
What time is this to commence a quiz
    when a man's nuts are irreversible?

"Dress rehearsal, is it? well
    this ain't the opening night.
Theater's dark," and she switched off
    the pink boudoir light.

She opened a space between them
    as if he was a copperhead,
she dug a chasm down the middle
    as if they had twin beds.

Twin beds! twin beds!
    it's cold in them twin beds,
but the worst is a chasm down the middle
    as if you had twin beds.

Another word she wouldn't say
    and fell asleep, not he,
but when the dawn in the window shone
    he was in a settled fury.

All night she leaves you weak with guilt,
    by dawn you won't or can't put out.
"I used to truly love you, Lou,
    now all I want is out.

"I used to have a feeling, Lou,
    alive where my legs meet
my belly, but you took a bite
    and left me feeling weak."

Oh it's a miserable frame of mind
    when a man can't get it up,
because she makes you weak with guilt
    you can't or won't get it up.

O sing a song and down a cup
   for the fellows who can't get it up
before we close up for the night,
   to all who cannot get it up!

Closing time! closing time!
   the streets are full at closing time.
Women, if they need a man,
   walk the streets at 4 A.M.

At 4 A.M. at closing time,
   some men go reeling home,
but some fall flat upon the street
   who have no home to go.

❧

BALLAD OF DAVID AND MICHAL
2 Samuel vi, 14–23

When David danced before the Ark
   hauled in a wagon to his home town
he danced War and Weeping sore
   and Lust, and played the pretty Clown.

King David he was crazy
   for the presence of the Lord
wheeled into Jerusalem
   after years abroad.

He threw away his golden crown
   and fought his battles up and down,
the Battle of the Barley Field
   when Philistines were overthrown.

He threw away his angry sword
   and melted into grief,

to gloomy thought before the Lord,
   he bawled and tore his clothing off.

He put his clothing off and made
   love like a Canaanitish quean
to the austere Lord Jehovah,
   his gesture was obscene.

At last the King became a child
   and grinned and played the pretty clown
to tease an unwilling smile
   from Father's awful frown.

This dance was last and was the best:
   a ray of sunshine fell
out of the gloomy overcast
   on David who danced well.

Now Michal was his wife and watched him
   out of a window dance and sing.
Cold disgust her heart possessed,
   she said, "Is this a King?

"They married me unto a fool
   who dances naked in the street.
Behind their fans the royal queens
   of Babylonia bare their teeth."

Now David strong with dance and song
   wanted to put it in his wife,
she turned away, "Some other day!"
   her voice was like a knife.

His orbits flashed a mild surprise.
   "Why Michal, what's the matter, what
good is a wife who won't put out
   when music it has got me hot?"

"Go! go!" she sneered, "among your slaves
   and naked in the yard carouse!

there, there take a whore
  and use her whom you choose,

"while the people dine on meat and wine
  and stand around in a ring.
As for me, my privacy
  is for a man and a king!"

"Madam," said the King of Judah,
  "let me tell *you* some news—"
The flaming scorn of the poet wronged
  around her like a fire rose

that withers in a gale the prairie
  and scorches the house of frame.
(King David is my patron!
  I sing in David's royal name!)

"I fought a giant as a boy
  naked of armor, the better to leap;
ten thousand Philistines did I destroy
  that you might sleep.

"When Saul was mad and hunted me
  I held his skirt out on my spear.
To offer sacrifice to Him Who Is
  I quake but dare.

"There is no risk to compare
  with the song before the folk
when I sing and dance with all my might
  and never know what will be spoke,

"when I have thrown away the book
  and unrehearsed the speech I share
with the folk my darling pours
  out of my mouth, the while I stare.

"I will be stupider than I am!
  ashamed in my own sight!

but the common folk of whom you spoke,
 to them I shall be honor bright."

King David spoke but would not touch her,
 no, not from that day forth,
so Michal never had a child
 unto the day of her death.

BALLAD OF THE GAMELAN OF BALI

The hammers on the xylophones
 a busy clamor make,
the drummers are like monkeys
 chattering in the canebrake.

We keep our noses down and play,
 look neither left nor right;
a fellow who has seen a ghost
 his eyes are round, his face is white.

Nobody will raise his eyes
 to look at what is not,
but try try by keeping busy
 not to think a thought!

It's hard to be happy like monkeys
 for one of our playmates is late.
Do monkeys have bad memories?
 we had a definite date.

The gamelan of *my* town
 is famous overseas,
the rich Americans have heard
 the music of the Balinese.

The gamelan of *my* town
   is famous on Broadway.
Play louder, Bali, drown me out
   the speech I have to say.

The gamelan of *my* town
   returned with dollars in our hands.
O ghost who haunt this gamelan,
   have you come to dance?

Look up! look up, musicians!
   look up and never fear,
it's only the ghost of Master Hu
   come to dance for us here.

Waiting for the first drumbeats
   and smiling softly at you—
a dancer waiting for his cue—
   don't you remember Master Hu?

He only died last night and did
   you think he would so soon forget?
He has come to the rehearsal
   because we had a date.

When to America we came
   the fame of Hu was loud,
we did not envy him his fame
   who shared it and were proud.

Proud! proud of my Bali!
   when to their astonishment
he danced the clever dances
   our simple villages invent.

That which is deathless cannot die,
   why is your pounding heart?
he was the pride of our countryside,
   why do you stare at him and start?

He is dancing the dance of reaching out
  that used to end in bed,
he whispers "Come!" and disappears
  —he is a ghost and he is dead.

He is a ghost, he comes and goes,
  through him I see your circle eyes
with a ring of white around the night.
  He is bigger than lifesize.

Ow! he is bigger than lifesize
  and he is reaching out—for what?
Last night our darling was alive,
  today we have him not.

It is hard to be happy like monkeys!
  One of our playmates is late!
Do monkeys have bad memories?
  We had a date, we had a date.

Now what is the drummer on the right
  muttering upon his drum?
"Why must he flaunt his golden watches
  before the men at home?"

And what is the drummer on the left
  tapping with impatient thumb?
"Is loot of America a license
  to lord it over men at home?"

What is the noble terompong
  hammering on angry gongs?
"Tell me, gamelan, to whom
  the Island of Bali belongs?"

Now all the gamelan is clanging
  the alarm that wakes from trance.
"The gamelan is everybody's!
  Little children clap their hands!

"The women shout cha cha cha cha!
    The monkeys chatter too!
The villages of Bali
    do not belong to Master Hu.

"The clanging of our gamelan
    can put to flight, can put to flight
this ghost that we are staring at
    with dark eyes ringed with white."

We shout, and it is still
    and there is no ghost in truth,
only out of the silence softly
    the sorry solo of a flute,

the sorry solo of my flute
    is murmuring as my tears flow,
"Where, O musician of Bali,
    where is the chosen of Dario?

"Of Bali dancers," says my flute,
    "was no one in my recollection
like the disciple of Dario
    who bettered the instruction;

"now where is he, whose boyish beauty
    could quiet lust for seven days
and when a man he grew to be
    his performance was beyond praise?"

If him you seek go down to where
    the waves are shining, never fear,
you will find him there his throat
    cut from ear to ear.

"O fellows of the gamelan,
    which of you on the shining shore
waylaid him as he lightly came
    and left him in his gore?"

This will no one ever know.
    Four men we chose to meet him there
as he danced along his way
    on his way to nowhere.

One from the drums, one from the gongs,
    one from the xylophones,
and one from the melodious flutes
    to meet him where he comes.

Along the shore the moonlight
    was shining on the sea,
"Who is there?" he cries in fear,
    for we have barred his way.

He thinks that we are robbers
    who rudely bar the way.
"Here, take my golden watches!"
    but we four nothing say.

"Musicians of the gamelan!
    what do you wish of me?"
His voice is sweet with relief.
    But we four nothing say.

"Don't you know me in the night?
    is this a game you play?"
Terror has caught him by the throat.
    But we four nothing say.

"I am the dancer of Bali!
    the chosen of Dario!
Hu Nga of Bliatan!
    On my way let me go."

Our dances were not meant to sell
    for gold and power, young man,
but for the Villages of Bali
    to prosper, safe from the Evil One.

BALLAD OF JENNY AND THE FIREMEN

When all that's left is dirty glasses
  and the butts are cold upon the floor
is a melancholy moment, chum,
    but it's worse if the party is next door.

When she went to complain about the din
  she caught them necking in the hall
but nobody invited her in.
    Drinking alone is worse than none at all.

But how do you bear the unearthly silence
  when the last laugh is swallowed in the gloom?
Did they all leave? Maybe Roberts
    is stretched out dead in the bathroom.

She's got to scream, she can't help it
  —splits your ears a scream like that,
it pins you cold sober
    echoing in the night.

"I'll turn in a fire alarm!"
  —that's a happy notion!
"I'll have a lot of company
    in the hullaballoo and commotion.

"Firemen are gentlemen,
  they smash the furniture professionally,
not like drunken bums." She giggles
    at such a vigorous idea.

Softly shines the orange globe
  of the firebox on Eighty-first
where the park is closed after dark
    because of muggers and perverts.

Mysterious at 3 A.M.
    under the lamp on the corner of the street
while Jenny waits for the engingines
    to come in about a minute.

The residential neighborhood is quiet.
    The siren sounds far away.
There's time to light a cigarette
    while a beagle lifts his leg to pee.

(Between the act and its effect
    I fell into a revery
that I could never recollect
    when the clang awakened me.)

"Where's the fire?" "This way, men!"
    She leads the huskies with the pole and axe
graciously to her apartment
    where beer is in the icebox.

The hook-and-ladder fills the block.
    Sleepy people look out the windows.
The chief arrives in his red coupé.
    The firemen unroll the hose.

They smash the furniture. "Hey, what goes on?"
    cries Roberts, rushing to the scene
without shoes. "No!" says Jenny,
    "*that* one is drunk, don't let *him* in."

Five firemen with rubber coats
    can crowd a spacious living room.
Their ways are rough, their muddy boots
    are like the peony in bloom.

THE BALLAD OF ST. PATRICK

I tell St. Patrick about the condition of Ireland

Patrick, it's a sorry story
    of the emerald isle in the West
depopulated by the plot
    of your thin-lipped priest

and Greedy Witch the Irish mother,
    these two have made the blight,
although from Cork to Donegal
    the daffodils are bright.

Says Thin Lips, "If a lad and lass
    go walking, it's a mortal sin,
they'll burn in hell for it," he gloats
    and oh his lips are thin.

And Greedy screeches, "Shame on you,
    ungrateful whore, your filthy tricks!
Stay home and take care of your mother,
    time enough when you're thirty-six."

Was it for this you set ablaze
    the bonfire on Tara
and shamrock spread where'er you trod
    from Meath to Connemara?

From Glendalough to Connemara
    the lakes of Ireland are blue
yet what can a lively fellow do
    but skulk in a pub and stew

and brag of what he would do
    if he ever did anything,
and the old reminisce about nothing
    on a scratchy string?

Till the roaring rage of it all,
   how the lustless spring is sped,
catches them by the throat
   and some of them break each other's head,

but most become resigned
   and passionately then
they wager on lovely horses
   ridden by other men.

The Saint tells how he rested from his labors

Mea culpa! Patrick moans,
   I meant it for the best.
I was a fool old and blind.
   He smites on his embroidered breast.

I labored to introduce a little
   learning and civility
—little I had—the manners
   of Rome across the sea

to dirty barbarian pirates
   that kidnaped me as a boy,
repaying like a Christian
   love for injury with joy.

(And pride and joy I've had to praise
   John Scot's mind and Tom Moore's voice,
and bitterness when Dublin brays
   at John Synge and Jamie Joyce.)

With a gentle winning nature
   and wrath only for cruelty
I brought peace to that brawling race
   and I was satisfied with me.

I built a house in Armagh
   for the gifts I got in Rome

and there I rested my worn-out eyes
    waiting to go home.

The fire of the Resurrection
    on Tara blazed and in Kildare
the fire of fertile Brigit,
    now wasn't that a grand pair!

The Saint falls a prey to the ever watchful Devil

Woe! and you'll laugh when you hear
    —no laughing matter—how poor old Pat
did a disservice to Ireland
    and fell in the Devil's trap.

Arrogance was my vice,
    it drove a saint to make mistakes:
"I'll build an earthly paradise,"
    I said, "and ban the snakes!"

The innocent snakes that slither
    in black holes out of the sun
with as much right as me to bite
    what interferes with fun,
the old fool swore with a great furor
    he'd root out every one.

"Ha ha!" howled the Adversary
    and he bounded out of Chaos
—God bless him, he keeps us wary—
    "The snakes is it? my arse!

"old Pat is blind as a bat
    he wouldn't know the difference
between a you-know-what
    and a snake or other indecence.

"I'll make up as his deacon
    and help him on his rounds."

God save me! groaned St. Patrick,
   I banished out of bounds

every young lively cock
   in Ireland from that black
Friday in 457
   until of Doom the crack!

St. Patrick and the Devil prepare to ban the snakes from Ireland

Lad, help me with my amice and alb.
   That Devil tucked me in.
When he touched my pectoral cross
   I did not see him turning green

My chasuble of lace and jewel
   I labored under like a horse,
I was a fat and pompous fool,
   he pushed my mitre on my nose.

Give me my crozier in my hand
   that knocked the idol of Cromm Cruach down
in County Cavan! said I grand,
   Pig-ears the cowboy on the town.

And look ye, bring the magic book
   that has the words and no mistakes.
Rat-a-tat-tat! here comes Pat!
   where are these Irish snakes?

"Your Grace looks like a million dollars,"
   he flattered me, "that damnèd brood
will hang their tails between their legs,
   so to speak, when we say the word.

"Ah, here is the form: *Every worm*
   over five inches, make it six,
that lifts its head and starts to squirm
   and especially if it spits,

"Come out into the April sun!
  one fond farewell and begone!
retire underground
  or quit this island on the run!"

So armed with staff and words
  we came into the Irish spring,
the fishes were leaping in Lough Neagh,
  the swallows darting on the wing,

the dandelions in the grass
  a-riot. And every rosy cock
was also snuffling the air
  as by we came with bell and book.

It never used to rain so much,
  aye, and the sun was closer to us
those days we smiled on growing things
  and we let nature take her course.

Tricked by the Devil, the Saint makes a disastrous mistake

Sang out that damnèd spirit, "Look!
  here rears a monstrous serpent. You!
reveal yourself to Father Pat!
  a foot long, give an inch or two."

It was an Irish fisherboy
  holding his patient line
and thoughtfully playing with himself
  in the hot sunshine.

With blushing pride the innocent youth
  took it out for show,
glad for God and the public world
  his bravery to know.

His prick looked up with dumb inquiry
  like a puppy to be petted, oh

I could not see the charming sight.
   "Go!" cried I, "monstrous serpent, go!

"quit the sod of Ireland!
   no longer tempt Mother Eve!"
I said it like a Jesuit
   who would have believe?

because I never found, not I,
   when I was young and incontinent,
that my reservoir ran dry
   or it kept me from becoming a saint

—the contrary! the more you come
   the more you can. Period.
Attend to lowly things, my lad,
   and you'll attain the glory of God.

The blind Saint makes another mistake

Now that Devil ran ahead of me
   disguised in a low-cut gown
and a wriggle of the behind
   but never the tail shown,

to entice a simple cowboy
   lying dreaming on the lawn
(he was a damned entrapper
   like cops in a California town),

and when in hope the lad stood up
   and his moist eyes were a benison
for this lovely saint from heaven sent,
   the entrapper shouted, "Another one!

"Pat, grab it!" "Ouch!" I cried, "this one
   is hot as blazes and hard as wood.
Lord, Lord! who ever heard
   of a rigid reptile with warm blood?"

"Those are the worst! here is the book:
    Hot-blooded snakes, they prowl by night
and day and accost young ladies
    or anybody else in sight.

"*Of these the so-called rigid species*
    has an indiscriminate appetite,
be wary of him, he is hard
    and hungry and about to bite."

"Be banished!" I release my grip
    in horror of the risk I run.
"O father," says the boy, "a minute more
    I would have got my gun."

And many many more mistakes

"For heaven's sake! a Jewish snake
    with a big nose I see!"
"Suppressed, suppressed like all the rest!
    Ireland sober is Ireland free!"

Ireland sober is Ireland free—
    did y'ever hear such idiocy?
Ireland free is Ireland sober,
    Ireland free o'the likes of me!

A well-assorted pair we were
    who walked through Ireland on April First,
I scattered blessings on every hand
    and everything I blessed I cursed,

I and my entrapper,
    a devil with a false book
and a fat fool with a mitre
    abusing his shepherd's crook.

Oh and the pitiful result
    of my misguided enterprise

176

is a million copies of Shawn Keough
    holding their fists in front o' their flies.

The length and breadth of Ireland
    fine women keened, their hair they tore
as rat-a-tat-tat there went Pat
    from Parknasilla to Bangor,

old Pat blind as a bat
    from County Down to County Clare,
I never got my sandals wet
    so the Aran Islands are still there.

"The fire of fertile Brigit
    is going out!" the women keened,
but I paid no mind as I inclined
    to the dogma of the Fiend.

Only the Laughing Laddy of Lough Neagh escapes the curse

One likely laddy and one alone,
    whose name I dare not tell
(for government of Ireland
    is still a fief of hell)

escaped because he loved me:
    he figured, "That's not Pat
led like a bear by the nose
    under that ridiculous hat.

"Pat reads the book himself
    not far from common sense.
Now my sex is as neat as the next
    but this is no time for romance;

"in the wildwood and with madmen
    trust the wisdom of your toes."
With a last laugh into Lough Neagh
    he deftly dove and the bubbles rose.

And there he waits immortal
    for truth and nature never wane,
he sticks his head up every morning
    to see if the people are yet sane.

That laughing Laddy of Lough Neagh
    has a head on his shoulders broad
instead of a block, and a rosy cock
    that he'll protect by force or fraud,

O Laddy of Lough Neagh, would
    that I could call, Come out! begin!
begin the reign of sense again!
    purge St. Patrick of his sin!
Darling! take your Irish bride!
    Nay, as it is, Stay in! stay in!

Saint Pat is standing on the shore
    and tears are flowing down my beard,
my longing arms are stretched toward hope—
    Lord, must not such a prayer be heard?

The Moral of it all is that First Things are First

Well, whether I drave the snakes away
    I do not know, I doubt it,
but this I know, our boys are slow
    and in a pinch they do without it.

Seamas cowers when Mama lowers
    and hides his prick between his legs,
while Timothy goes over the sea
    leaving Ireland to the bogs.

And isn't it a shame? I love
    their freckles and their brogue and blarney,
their speech is lilting music still
    and even their jokes are pretty funny,

but there is no use or future
    of a lad won't take his penis out
or when he does can't get it up
    or if he gets it up can't shoot.

The fire of fertile Brigit
    is going out: there's a thought
to freeze your testicles but good!
    Forbid it, God! Man, look to't!

For to have lovely children
    takes patience, intellect, and luck,
and God's grace, and affection,
    but first you have to f.

※

BALLAD OF THE GREAT BOOKS, 1935

Now let me teach this Dialogue,
    the little hand is touching eight
—my throat is tickled by the fog—
    the man from Newark is always late,

he'll neatly pull his rubbers off,
    and sit down next to Mrs. Brooks.
By way of starting I will cough.
    Do all the desks have open books?

And what will Plato do for us,
    for Mrs. Kraus whose heart is weak
—too bad, she is so studious;
    for Troy who cycles like a streak

because his soul is ill at ease?
    What if tonight I did not break
the Great Books Tuesday Evening peace
    but listened to the ticking clock?

No, I'll chatter soon enough
  —I often am in doubt this way—
once I start, once I cough,
  I get lost in what I say.

The mole that Dr. Davidson
  above his golden eyebrow wears
is what I'll fix my eyes upon
  and hear my voice go down the stairs.

And what will it be like when I
  have said what Proclus said he said?
The ancient learning will not die,
  young Blake will toss upon his bed

thinking of the Upward Way
  among other fantasies of sex,
Miss Simkovich will learn to say
  the while her father's business wrecks,

"The soul departs before the body,"
  and when the khaki sentry tires
and drops to his knees, McGillicuddy
  will close his eyes before he fires.

ꙮ

THE BALLAD OF THE PENTAGON

Staughton Lynd he said
  to the Secretary of War,
"If on my little son
  This can of gasoline I pour,

"can you light a match to him?
  do you dare?"

The master of the Pentagon
 said nothing but sat there.

"Then how do you command
 your soldiers to rain down
blazing gasoline
 on little yellow children?"

This happened in America
 in 1965
that people talked about
 burning children alive.

Now Norman Morrison
 heard this conversation
and he took his stand in front of
 the frowning Pentagon.

He had his baby in his arms
 but in his mind I know not what
for he also said nothing
 but he whispered to the tot:

"Let me show you all the things,
 babe that I adore,
this is the United States
 and here sits the Secretary of War.

"Here is the broad blue sky
 with the sun at my right hand,
and far far far down there
 are people and the sea and land."

He poured the gasoline upon
 himself and the baby,
he lit the human torch
 but he threw the baby out of harm's way.

How long can this continue,
 how long can this go on,

these crazy incidents
   in front of the Pentagon?

My country falling to pieces
   —frantic demonstrations—
people jumping up and down
   with signs in frustration—

our public men machines—
   Norman Morrison
afire with determination
   in front of the Pentagon.

THE BALLAD OF THE CORAL BAR

He was a good mechanic
   till she cut him down to size,
now he walks the street and haunts
   the Coral Bar with yellow eyes.

His rosy cock was quick to rise
   and he was one to have his way,
she did not move, she did not moan,
   she turned a stony face away.

Twice a week for fifteen years
   adds up to fifteen hundred tries
—the rate is Martin Luther's—
   she cut them all down to size.

"Wife, you have won the game,
   to play games I did not marry.
Don't expect me to forgive
   your grand victory."

He tried no more. She took a lover
   who flattered her a Friday night
and she was giddy all over
   and had the fulness of delight.

For it is easier to love
   a lover than your daily mate
—some of it's fear and some is pride
   and some is nothing but spite.

There are no kids to interrupt
   when you fuck with your lover
and you can feed on fantasies
   like a cow in clover.

"Husband," she taunted, "how is this?
   I had it like I never had."
Oh, they'll do it every time,
   insult to injury to add.

"Fifteen years," she wept, "I wasted
   the best years of my youth!"
She said no more for with his paw
   he slapped her on the mouth.

He threw in her disdainful teeth
   the years of insult to his hard-on,
the gift he used to offer
   as if begging her pardon.

Making of the strength he had
   this miserable use
he left her lying on the floor
   bleeding from the eyes and nose.

And he was right but she was right
   and you and I, no doubt, are right,
and with that and thirty cents

you can take a subway ride
—unless the fare has gone up,
  which it does overnight.

Farewell to glory! to the wheels
  farewell that were towed in
but out they rolled upon their own
  while he watched with a grin.

Farewell to courage! to the prick
  that rose ten thousand times again,
but New York City gives no medals
  to such a citizen.

Lover, rescue her you likened
  to the Venus of the Medicis,
but you have gone away, I hear,
  to Los Angeles.

This is a tale I heard or told
  Saturday night in the Coral Bar,
I can't remember which it was
  but it rang familiar.

THE BALLAD OF A TRUCK BY THE RIVER

No, ah cain't afford to get a hard-on, boss,
  it cost a nigger money to screw
an ah cain't make a livin in dis town
  count o dis yere Jim Crow.

So ah sits here out o mischief in de sun
  singin an meditatin dis an dat
jes' avoidin any lil fancy
  as is liable to get my nuts hot.

But if yo wanna fuck me, sho,
    ah likes to feel a white man's push
as got a job an ain't ascairt
    to dirty yo pants cause yo can wash.

To make me feel dat ah belong
    white man's cock is better'n pot
an it usually don' cos' nuthin
    which usually is what ah got.

De river's bright today, ain't it?
    it hot in de back o dis yere truck.
Jes' shove it in. Ah recollec'
    when ah was a kid ah had a big cock.

My mammy when her knees was spread
    an she solid wi' dat man   °
she said dat she at rest in Jesus
    like a turnip in de groun'.

An when yo push it in an out,
    boss o New York town,
ah be so happy an belongin
    like dat turnip in de groun'.

Lyin yere grinnin an watchin de river
    fo company while ah gets fuck
is jes' like home where I was born,
    some niggers dey got all de luck.

SONNETS, I

※

1. A new thing with heavenly motion made by us
flies in the sky, it is passing every hour
signalling in our language. What a power
of thought and skill has launched this marvelous
man-made moon! and from this day the gorgeous
abyss lies open, as you spring a door
to enter and visit where no man before
ever came.   It is a mysterious
moment that one crosses a threshold
and "Have I been invited?" is my doubt.
Yes, for our wish and wonder from of old
and how we patiently have puzzled out
the laws of entry warrant we have come
into the great hall as a man comes home.

※

1959 (FOR HAROLD ROSENBERG)

2. Their theater! their businesses! their State!
it is the Whore of Babylon again

falser than Rome, and fewer are the men
not turned to swine. Her streets asphyxiate
honor and literature is lying prostrate
in the mud of Madison Avenue that "fen
of stagnant waters," while the denizen
hoodlums prowl with boot and chain and switchblade.

The witnesses are few. Convenient
allies, thank God, have vanished at midnight
and we are marked for oblivion who dissent.
So they believe. But an uncanny light
is shining on our faces at the faint
dawn bugle when the things fall of their weight.

3. Foster excellence. If I do not
who will do it? The vulgarity
of this country makes my spirit faint, what we
have misdone to our history and what
to the landscape. The tasteless food we eat,
the music, how we waste day after day
child, woman, and man have stunned me to dismay
like an ox bludgeoned, swaying on his feet.

John, rescue me by becoming. I have well
deserved of the Republic, though it has
rewarded me with long oblivion.
Make you me proud and famous as the one
who thought that we could be what Florence was
when angry men made rough rocks beautiful.

4. They say the Florentines, that day the Arno
flowed over and stormed into Santa Croce
at fifty miles an hour up to three
meters and more, rushed rather to the rescue
of statues and old manuscripts than to
their homes and wives and children. Naturally,
because these were not things, they were their city

where climbing on the amazing rocks they grew
and thought whatever they thought as they stared
at Perseus lifting the Medusa's head.
There was an hour the tombs of Machiavelli
and Dante and Galileo Galilei
stood in ten feet of water in the mud,
until the water started to recede.

❧

THE RUSSIANS RESUME BOMB-TESTING, OCTOBER 1961

5. My poisoned one, my world! we stubborn few
    physicians work with worried brows and speak
    in low voices; in the epidemic
    our quiet will is only what to do.
    The time is Indian summer and the blue
    heaven is cloudless, but the rains will reek
    with poison and the coming spring be sick,
    if fire has not blasted us in the snow.

    The virtue of physicians is compassion:
    we do deny that you are as you are
    and will to make you otherwise. Creator
    spirit come, and join our consultation;
    we do not have the leisure to despair,
    but we cannot without new inspiration.

❧

THE AMERICANS RESUME BOMB-TESTING, APRIL 1962

6. My countrymen have now become too base,
    I give them up. I cannot speak with men

not my equals, I was an American.
Where now to drag my days out and erase
this awful memory of the United States?
how can I work? I hired out my pen
to make my country practical, but I can
no longer serve these people, they are worthless.

"Resign! resign!" the word rings in my soul
—is it for me? or shall I make a sign
and picket the White House blindly in the rain,
or hold it up on Madison Avenue
a silent vigil, or trudge to and fro
gloomily in front of the public school?

O'HARE AIRPORT

7. For wearing out the spirit with dull size
O'Hare's the worst, it is a fitting gate
to come into Chicago, if your feet
can drag their shoes and if your weary eyes
survive the miles of Stygian blue. Be wise,
lovers of wit and art and you sedate
humanists, tribe of Erasmus, to evade
this labyrinth upon your winged ways.
Our number is grown small, our patience
these days is frayed; though we are sweet and bland
by disposition, we are known to kill
and die of grief meeting the imbecile.
And through these corridors they pipe a canned
music that is neither song nor dance.

ADLAI STEVENSON

8. We told the old ambassador to quit:
   "These brutal lies you have to tell defame
   us and you." "No, I am on the team,"
   he said, and was unhappy saying it.
   Now he has dropped down in a London street
   and every one is weeping over him.
   He said, "It's not the way we play the game,
   to quit to make a point."
                              The flag is at
   half-mast in Springfield. A bombardier reasons
   loudly for us in Asia. Our sons
   will be commanded to the senseless war
   —but many will not go—that does not cease
   generation after generation: this
   has been no worse, but there may be no more.

A DOCUMENTARY FILM OF CHURCHILL

9. These images are a remarkable
   recapitulation, to again
   watch the wars and listen to the men
   not making sense. Wilson and Churchill
   and Roosevelt, resolute and even noble
   in their delusions, until on the screen
   victory fades into the next war, and vain
   policy bursts quietly a bubble.

   What is it with this race that does not learn?
   I am weary for meaning and they tire
   my soul with great deeds. Yet I cannot turn
   my eyes from the stupid story in despair:
   since I have undertaken to be born,
   Adam, Adam is my one desire.

FOR A.J. MUSTE AND
FRANK TANNENBAUM, 1965

10. I don't much eulogize dead men,
    but when I think of the admirable old
    friends that I have, my style that is cold
    and critical otherwise can't but awaken
    to generous tribute for the veteran
    of peace, A. J., of whom I lately told
    the pleasant truth, and lightly I extolled
    Frank Tannenbaum touching threescore and ten.

    About my own next years dismay has strained
    my voice, and my only world falling apart;
    but these old heroes prove they know the art
    of living since alive they have remained
    —though not without surprises—all of a piece
    in the vast wreck of common sense and justice.

"WE WON'T GO"

11. How many years of history it needed
    and stupid choices by how many men
    to manufacture that grotesque machine
    the sovereign State that yesterday decided
    to hurt a simple student who has wanted
    little but good in this world and has shown
    much good sense although young, my only son
    Mathew gentle with animals.
                    Demented
  are they, and because we live with them
  they drive us mad too, in this beautiful
  country they have turned into a slum
  with dirty waters and no place where people

are let be, nay they sail across the seas
ten thousand miles to slaughter Vietnamese.

ツ

FLAGS, 1967

12. How well they flew together side by side
the Stars and Stripes my red and white and blue
and my Black Flag the sovereignty of no
man or law! They were the flags of pride
and nature and advanced with equal stride
across the age when Jefferson long ago
saluted both and said, "Let Shays' men go.
If you discourage mutiny and riot
what check is there on government?"
                                        Today

the gaudy flag is very grand on earth
and they have sewed on it a golden border,
but I will not salute it. At our rally
I see a small black rag of little worth
and touch it wistfully. Chaos is Order.

ツ

A DEMONSTRATION AT BERKELEY,
SPRING 1969

I.

13–15. I can't remain and listen to the hatred
in those young voices, I stalk off alone
my spirit sunk. But this is the spawn
of their elders decade after decade

ruining my country—sometimes I protested
and sometimes only winced in Washington—
and now the offspring bawl like the ill-born
that they are, and their faces are distorted.

It's quieter as I withdraw away
from the campus by the square of the distance
—at least that law is lovely—and I stray
into an historical revery:
I cannot recollect for years an instance
that our chief men showed magnanimity.

II.

Gifts of the Holy Ghost in memory
the great learning, and the mutual
aid and fierce independence that we call
the commonweal: these were the policy
I spoke for. Such a howling hit me
as if I were a policeman and they all
were smashing windows at the capital
to inaugurate the reign of liberty.

I stood there a couple of hours more
and answered a question and gave a reason
and showed the history was otherwise.
After a while one youth with grateful eyes
perked up and listened to me, but another
—I didn't intend it—now hates me like poison.

III.

Under the forsythia's yellow blossoms
into the blue heaven I sprawl here
meditating, no longer much disturbed by it,
their fanatical hostility last night
was mainly, I conclude, because I say my say,
not identically theirs, in simple sentences.
—A sprinkler is spraying a hundred parabolas
into the sunshine.—During my long lifetime

by and large what I have blabbed arousing resistance
recklessly has proved to be what I intend.
But these grown up in a world too meaningless to listen to
now resent that they have learned very little.

IV.

I know myself, if I made out
with one or two of them,
I'd be quicker to hear
the signals of distress,
attentive hanging around
to what they mean but cannot say;
but they come on so ugly
I don't even try.

V.

I didn't grow up among the atom bombs
like these, and my career such as it was
was never built on sand. A stupid maze
has been the pattern of my dreams,
but I do not hanker till the explosion comes
and still the holy spirit—why, who knows?—
sometimes speaks to me.
                        So I morose
go back where they are beating their tom-toms
and shouting "Shut it down!" They do not sound
like Isaac Newton, more a mob of monkeys;
but they are Adam the next time around
and what I hope. I see it doesn't please
them either that I stand here as I am.
Let them put up with me as I with them.

16. To what a world—like a dream of mine—
    You rough artisan of nature and history
    in Colorado Springs allotted me
    whether by sloppy work or by design:
    to sit next to but far away by nine

inches from a blond animal incredibly
beautiful with a torn shirt where I
must not nor dared kiss his creamy skin;
nevertheless, now dazed and suffering
—he has gone away—I praise God who created
with Pike's Peak in the background such a being
and showed me him as a true souvenir
of paradise when I felt alienated
visiting the campuses this year.

    Some happy folk their faith
    and some their calling doth
        justify, but Lord,
        I am justified

    by the beauty of
    the world and my love
        of Your animals, though I
        may not be happy thereby.

KENT STATE, MAY 4, 1970

17. Ran out of tear gas and became panicky,
    inept kids, and therefore they poured lead
    into the other kids and shot them dead,
    and now myself and the whole country
    are weeping. It's not a matter of degree,
    not less not more than the Indo-Chinese slaughtered,
    it is the same. But folk are shattered
    by home truths—as I know who lost my boy.

    I am not willing to go on this week
    with business as usual, this month this year
    let cars slow down and stop and builders break
    off building and close up the theater.

See, the children that we massacre
are our own children. Call the soldiers back.

ON THE RESIGNATION OF JUSTICE BLACK

18. Sad news, age and its ills have made him quit,
    curator of our curious document
    the bastard of the French Enlightenment
    and English history. We cannot trust it
    to the others, for they do not have the spirit
    (good Lord, I hate to think of his replacement!)
    conservative precisely of the ferment
    that surprisingly is seething in it yet
    —sometimes.
    　　　　　　When some bureaucrat
    bugs me to affirm the Constitution,
    I am indignant at his asinine
    inquisition, but I sometimes sign
    "providing it is the interpretation
    of the Constitution by Hugo Black."

SONNETS, II

Sonnets, II

༯

FOR MY BIRTHDAY, 1939

19. I walking on my birthday met a young
    Enterprise, Hope and Animal Spirits' boy,
    and I had the crazy thought again to try.
    He was like a banjo, bright and high-strung
    and jazzy with, no doubt, a wicked tongue,
    and so I fell in step with him and "Why
    do you avoid me? don't you like to play?"
    I hinted and my heart was hammering.
    "You're middle-aged!" "Only twenty-eight.
    There are lots of older poets, Enterprise."
    "But you have given hostages to fate,
    that sky-blue car, your cat, your daughter, these
    multiply accidents you don't create,
    collisions, wild dogs, and disease."

20. In the Universe of Correspondences
    —my longing and the things, my longing and
    my reaching, my longing and their presences—
    this is the rule: where I stretch my hand,
    darlings dissipate to absences,
    my call is terrible and my command
    exacts unerringly their disobedience,
    and like Lot's wife where I stand, I stand.

Except my gentle Peace—I do not seek—
comes freely to me. Quietly we speak.
She says, "You pious man, you pay your debt
to the Creator of the heavens and the earth."
And I reply, "A little longer yet
attending to these things of little worth."

※

FOR SALLY, WITH A PIANO

21. This old piano with a sweeter treble
    and a strong deep voice to you we brothers give;
    no longer inconsolably grieve,
    Sally, that Scarlatti's brilliant ripple
    and Haydn's *Variations* are unplayable.
    This quaint old box of strings will not deceive
    your touch but courteously come alive,
    the action is brand new and serviceable.

    I came upon you weeping in despair
    seated at a bad piano in
    the accidents of life. God knows how far
    beyond me each day is, and physical pain
    doubles my bafflement; and yet we in-
    novate this detail and that detail repair.

※

FOR MY BIRTHDAY, 1956

22. I missed the boat. She is a half a mile
    standing down-river, and such friends aboard
    as I apparently can do without
    or I'd be on her (a shit-eating smile)

on the excursion to the Joyous Isle
where they give prizes, and Some One had bought
a ticket for me. Now she's a small spot
in the open bay. (My tears begin to boil.)

It's slow and sunny on the wooden dock.
The crabman has hauled in his wire cage
crawling with claws. A flying fishhook
is stuck in his boy's calf. I set him free.
There are startling reflections on the oily sea
the forty-fourth confused year of my age.

23. Among vistas and panoramas fair
and vivid recognizing is the great
Cape Cod Canal, and notably where in state
he rounds the turning and the ships of war
recede toward Newport. Shall I stop my car
one day and watch, before it is too late,
enough to slake my thirsty eyesight at
this Boundary that makes me glad?
                                        So far
I glimpse him only as I speed away
looking back from empty summers on
the withering Cape across to Buzzards Bay;
or alternately sanguine in June
salute him as I hurry on my way
toward joy I shall not find in Provincetown.

24. Wherever I go, city or country place,
every scene reminds me of my blighted life:
sick wanting what I couldn't have, or grief
losing what I never had in peace,
shouting my anger in a desert space
or fleeing from a shore where shame was rife,
sweet villages where I lived as a thief.
With awful thoughts I look at my worn face
remembering what has been.

                                                And of these all
the pier at Provincetown in early fall
is the worst, the sea-gulls crying and boys diving,
crossing to Boston in wartime in the rain.
But I wrote it down in pages more than pain
poignant and more beautiful than living.

꠸

READING *ADONAIS*

25. Sternly my eyebrows meet as murmuring
    the measured verses I read Shelley's lust
    to die ill-hidden in this rapturous
    paean to eternity the beckoning
    Hesperus on the water. How they sting,
    the sentences that life holds out to us
    nothing, and never did, though I discuss
    my memories back to the early spring,
    but disappointed days, which as my grim
    autumn sets in have at last downed me.
                                        So

    about the other English poet dead
    in this dead poet's book whose stanzas glow
    incandescent with his even hymn
    to blinding light before he sailed, I read.

꠸

FIVE SONNETS

26–30. Grief how into useless age away
       ebbed youth and I was unhappy all those years
       I also do not feel, for now new fears
       possess me and I steel myself today
       today's pain to endure, so I can die

without a reckoning and weep no tears
for promises deceived. Maybe my peers
or my disciples will this tribute pay.

Oh, when He bound my arms behind my back
and threw me in the sea, I heard Him call
"Swim! swim!" and so I have swum to this hour
breathless in the cold water rough and black
where many have already drowned and all
shall drown in the swells that sink and tower.

Almost everything lovely in my eyes
is banned to me by law or circumstance
or impractical people. Sometimes a long chance
and hard labor won for me a prize,
but grace ought to be easy, a surprise
when need is met halfway in its advance.
Fighting to wrest my inheritance
I have stayed alive not in paradise.
I am not cheerful, I who always taught
my students with good humor to beguile
gloomy bogey-man, am myself caught
in mid-career with a freezing smile.
I see the streets around me with distaste.
I look at common daylight as a waste.

One thing, thank God, I learned, the grisly face
of Hope to abhor, her eyes bloodshot with dreams,
her hair unkempt with fury. Lying streams
out of her mouth and men drink it. Alas,
if you look ever in a looking-glass
and see an ugly Hope in hungry flames
devouring you, so the unreal seems
real and the impossible to come to pass
possible, see, when you look again
Disappointment! But *this* face of pain
is mine, which I and all my family have,
my mother wears it in her southern grave,
my sister grown old woman has it, and
my brother building buildings rich and grand.

I start awake at night afraid of death,
gasping for air, exclaiming O my God!
and sit up. My heart is beating hard.
But when I school my thoughts and catch my breath
and recollect myself my forty-fourth
discouraged year in a loveless bed
in this cold-moonlit lonely countryside
in America where my use has no worth,
why, it would be comfortable to be dead.
Death is like sleep that I often woo,
and cease to nag myself to start anew
when I have no resources. Why do I
fight to wake up in panic, cry with dread,
and clutch at the bedclothes afraid to die?

Despairing to be happy any more,
on the other hand I am not much in pain,
I can work, and sometimes from my pen
such lovely sentences of English pour
as I am proud of for their casual grandeur
nor will, when I am dead, they be forgotten;
I look about and I am as most men
as happy.   Yet my spirit is still sore
with disappointment of the paradise
lost that I could not enter; a hard question
haunts me, "Is life worth it as it is?"
A baffled man looking for the direction
from side to side I shake my head, but oh
my toes are tense to go, to go, to go.

❦

WORLD, ELEPHANT, AND TORTOISE

31. I firm enough on my two roughshod feet
    with a heavy pail hanging from either hand

walk slowly forward over solid ground.
I *understand* the World rests her weight
quietly upon the broad sedate
back of an Elephant whose legs around
like Norman towers on the buckler stand
of an ancient Tortoise that was never fleet,
now budges not at all.
                    So have I faith
to falter another step along my path
and bravely stagger onward. Yes! these three,
World, Elephant, and Tortoise, are my strength
to hold myself erect along the length
of my moorings from nothing to the sky.

32. Taylor, these unreasonable days
    gentle it is how we have been for each
    other practical and very sweet
    friends. I am not bashful to praise
    how we in spite of persons and bad laws
    and the envious opinion of the street
    enjoyed our simple sex without deceit
    that others fear and hide for no good cause.

    Exactly of a continent the span
    divides us now: you where upon the rocks
    the seals play outside the Golden Gate,
    I watch the stormier Atlantic that
    ceaselessly on Fire Island knocks,
    who only yesterday were hand in hand.

33. For Donnie who taught to me the secrets of
    pleasure in a thicket of guilts and fears,
    this sonnet—niggardly for thirty years
    withholden—written in a flush of love!
    For I saw a boy as you were wont to go
    soberly eager, and glad songs and cheers

rippled from his progress to my ears
all the way up Greenwich Avenue.

Such ordinary joy as is the day
when once we dare to stand out of the way
I felt; my hunger did not sicken to
disappointment nor my misery
darken the day with spite. I yawned and grew
heavy and fell into this revery.

34. Lord! have I known until these faded days
beauties! the complaining in my mouth
uncalled for, it is greedy and uncouth,
that rightly should be saying such smug praise
as angels used to the best, astonished cries
at speed and power, character and truth,
and brave and gentle gestures, and so forth,
that no one undeservedly enjoys
—for I tried with an everlasting hard-on
humbly lavishing my best attention,
slow to be bored to tears and quick to pardon,
several times rewarded, let me mention
my center-fielder and my scholar lad
and her who wore black velvet and Maxwelton plaid.

35. The way I teach is, in the space before us
I hold the thing up and invite you to
its beauty, and attend to you.
But this one! I am training like a horse
remorselessly and harsh for the racecourse;
I shame or fuck, whichever is to do,
and peevishly demand his love on cue,
and ridicule his manners and his clothes.

I guess he's my disciple; naturally
noisy refractory material
—what else would you expect of Master Paul

.

who does it the hard way? What is the prize
we seek with sweat and effort, I and he,
looking trusting in each other's eyes?

36. God damn and blast and to a fist of dust
reduce me the contemptible I am
if I again hinder for guilt or shame
the blooming of my tenderness to lust
like a red rose; I have my cock traduced
to which I should be loyal. None to blame
but me myself that I consort with them
who dread to rouse me onward and distrust
what has a future.
               Let me bawl hot tears
for thee my lonely and dishonored sex
in this fool world where now for forty years
thou beg'st and beg'st and again thou beg'st
because this is the only world there is,
my rose in rags among these human wrecks.

ༀ

MARCH APRIL MAY AND JUNE

37. The March loves that Braggadocio
is boasting about won't last till spring,
outside it's sleeting and that whistling
gale is not blowing here from Mexico.
But the friendship under seven feet of snow
that we two husbandmen are nourishing
prudent of seasons, diffidently holding
hands for warmth until the morning—Oh!
I'll wheel my motorcycle from the hall
into April, and we two cruise behind
our flapping banner in a southern wind
into May.

Yet will the dogwood stun
again to anguish my defeated soul
alone among the meadowflowers in June.

※

ADAM

I.

38–39. Adam awoke and boundless was his surprise
to see, to see his own flesh red,
to see the nameless zoo parade,
the sunset flaming and the white moon rise.
He was astonished when before his eyes
sat Eve; and afterwards both shame and dread
were news to him and with uplifted blade
Michael at the door of Paradise.

Everything that Adam fell was new.
When like the setting sun himself he shone
red on the horizon and saw Cain his son
and Abel on the field whom Cain slew,
he was amazed that him the quiet one
did not acknowledge as he used to do.

II.

For Adam the sun
forty-six degrees of arc
was one minute far,

he stood in the gale
of the corona without
intermedium,

not filtering out
the pearly and rupose and
ultraviolet.

Later, he made this
golden disk to gaze at here
in the museum.

III.

With little learning and no history
yet Adam was a good farmer for he noticed.
Having fine senses and no preconceptions
what plants were weeds oh he did not uproot
what love us well and flourish where they are.
Except for treats he planted nothing,
but he cut back what choked the useful
so his acre of jungle became a garden.

IV.

Weary was my ancestor in exile
Adam when at dusk he plodded
firmly from the field and when at last he was dead
like Mathew my son and like his son Abel.
The people who were multiplying meanwhile
carried on in this world they never made
like at home, a child with a crayon scribbled
on the wall and a boy broke a bottle
on the sidewalk.
                        Now they are moving out
and going to the Moon with their baggage,
leaving behind a barrelful of garbage.
But I wish them well. What is it to me
as I dutifully go about
my business in this foreign country?

40. Giggling, bashful, and immensely flustered
    like a squealing tickled girl or like a child
    tossed overhead and laughing high and wild,
    sits in majestic weakness the unmastered
    Buddha in the universe, lovingly pestered
    by the thousand things and thrown by the firm mild

power of the playfully frowning world
that has struck millions dead.
                        The sage has fostered
greatness and greatness turns on him with fierce
affection, he is blushing to his ears
scarlet like the flamingo on one leg
in the Everglades bright-eyed for the quick fish,
or like the sunrise through the masking fog
ruby when the morning wind is fresh.

⁂

VENUS AND MARS

41. Though other names I call the gods and call
    them not gods, yet must I in secrecy
    own their enormous transient souls to be
    my tides—the masts are bobbing, rise and fall.
    For the Mother of Love has her inscrutable
    favor irradiated over me,
    I poisoned smile her smile and I see
    her smiling while I sicken.
                        And the squall
    of Mars' cornet reels me into the wars
    nostrils aflare as if I were the horse
    War-horse that Whirlwind to the Sufferer
    among his horrible sores and losses did
    describe, so he forgot the things that were
    and might be, and his hairs on end stood.

⁂

DIESES IST DAS TIER DAS ES NICHT GIBT.
Rilke

42. Lose yourself of thoughts and fears.
    Your face will fade out of the looking-glass.

You breathe a mist of sighs, they slowly pass,
your heart is empty when the mirror clears.
What's *in* there? what's to come? what of art?
—this void no natural animal can breathe.
Stifle the clouds that from your nostrils wreathe
now eagerly.

        Ah! the light-curtains part,
appears the Unicorn with his light step
and the breath of roses curling from his teeth.
He wants to speak. *"I am not fed on corn
but on the chance of being."* His white horn
silently shatters the barrier with its tip
and he emerges between life and death.

※

MIRIAM WITH TAMBOURINE

43. She jangles on her ankle the way we spurn
    the common lot and slaps her hip the lust
    to flaunt her ass at you because we must.
    In front she shakes her jingles as we yearn
    and bangs upon her head the tambourine
    our mental joy, and on her elbow brusque
    beats brutally our way we thrust
    to whither there is no return.

    My Miriam! leads us by no straight path.
    Unerringly we whirling dancers de-
    viate to vengeance the astounding truth:
    "The horse, the horse's rider hath He tost
    into the sea!"—she *raps* it on her knee,
    she jingle-jangles to the sky our boast.

44. Transfigured both the fucked and the fucker's face
    no longer beautiful, terrible, austere,

more alike than people otherwise appear,
every breath draws nearer the animal race
drowning in uproar, as in the witch-grass
of Easter Island the strange heads uprear,
pre-classical, with lips like a nightmare,
high up the hillside in that lonely place

—how came they there? to our surprise
as our new ship approaches in the sunrise.

The ocean is around a thousand miles,
the noisy surf is battering the gunwale,
the statues are not wearing human smiles,
the sculptors did not speak a known tongue.

45. Continually the interminable
hurrah of the assembled universe
shakes its banner and we shut our ears
to it in vain—audible still
as the instant fades and bursts like a bubble
is the silence of the music of the spheres
and humming in their holes the anti-matters
that are dark.
             Raucous and amiable
is the noise of opening daffodils, the scratching
and booming of their yellow muscles stretching.
Angry men hear the grinding of their jaws.
Lonely maniacs hear their names called out.
The boyish hero listens for applause.
"Help!" the drowning do not cease to shout.

ꙮ

IN LYDIA

46. I am touring high on the Meander River
the scenery ever varying. The land

is Lydia, the wheat rich, the climate bland,
and very sweet the modus of the zither.
Our queen is Omphale, for never never
cut was the curving cord in which we end
—when shall we arrive? I round a bend,
the view is changed, and forward is another.

That's not a woman in the palace yard
spinning! unwillingly—breathing hard—
Hercules! here, for pity's sake
the thread is long enough, it leaves the wheel
and tangles, and the world is areel.
My hands have hold upon it; shall I break?

THESEUS

47. "There is no Minotaur after all,"
   he ended, and he paused in the blank square,
   "now to wind up the spool." Why does he stare?
   his hair rise in the silence and the blade fall
   from his hero hand weaker than a girl?
   "*I* am the Minotaur!"—met dare for dare
   in the labyrinthine heart. And everywhere.

   Where can you flee? O Theseus, recall
   your blood to you and oh, pick up the knife!
   At last, the second moment in your life
   (the first was long ago, you have forgot)
   you have a rival worthy of Theseus.
   But softly, this is for the surgeon's cut.
   No; better declare an hour's armèd truce.

ORION

48. Me have they left to rust, from my occasion
    bar me! though never was so genial
    a need of me as now to shape and call
    tomorrow in young spirits, as by reason
    and lust I can uniquely, and we blazon
    the ordinary with baronial
    glory, each has his rose. Yet here I stall
    useless and bored, out of season.

    Then such a thirst for grandeur makes me phantasize
    giants! Orion extent in the skies,
    him who blind, like Milton, through the wild
    pursued the clang of hammers to the forge,
    later through sightless eyes astonished large
    drank sunbeams that renewed his vision mild.

HENRY HUDSON

49. I like to think because my Captain proved
    there was no Passage, mind and body lost
    in ice and darkness, *therefore* all the rest
    directed south their prows and thrived
    on the possible, rewarded for they braved
    the possible with pineapples and rust-
    colored wives. I envy them, yet must
    continue as my great Captain believed:
    There is a shorter Passage.
                                We have learned
    nothing. We have steered into ludicrous
    inlets and explored them to the marsh.
    We have sat bawling studying the charts.

The fog no longer lifts where we cruise
and flecks of snow shine on our chest and beard.

❧

READING *WEEPERS TOWER*

50. Thousands of days later, now the words
I wrote in horror in calm print I read
rich, famous, and with weariness half dead.
Was that I? Screaming harbor birds
were circling as among the shells and shards
I thought of crazy Hudson and thought led
to me. I see his bushy beard is flecked
with white as snow falls thick and idly towards
mid-winter. *Is that I?*
                              There is no northwest
Passage among these icebergs, Captain. Best
to put about. Our spars against the sky
are crosses. But he's crazy and no longer
even consults the charts. *Will that be I?*
Day after day I am not growing younger.

❧

UNEXPECTED SUNFLOWERS

51. O radiant you sunflowers abound
on Thirtieth Street and Tenth Avenue
spectacular where no one would expect you,
but *I* know, my birthday comes around,
to look there for you lush on barren ground
with hairy leaves. The buds are cut like beau-
tiful emeralds.
            Let me pick a few
of these wildflowers native among abandoned

trucks and empty freightcars and warehouses
and bring them home and put them in a vase.

I cannot look away. Their symmetry
is Mediterranean and their energy
Northern, and each has the majesty
of the sun alone in the blue sky.

※

MY SISTER

52. Of us three who fifty years and more
have worked too hard, Alice has always been
unassertively a kind of captain
of our attentive course, she, noted for
kindness. Now age is driving us ashore
toward death's rocks and our sister is again
the first among us, to be gravely stricken
and guide us nowhere.
                            But outside the door
of the infirmary the nurse tells us,
"Oh she's a tough old bird and she'll pull through."
The corridor is crowded with her friends
astounded she is ill who never was.
She told them not to let her brothers know
so we would not be bothered while she mends.

※

BEETHOVEN

53. The age of life I am, Beethoven died
unhappier than I and lonelier

than human beings ought to let each other.
He had when he took death for a bride
never known another. Rough and rude
he came in character an awkward lover,
yet she did not rebuff him nor defer
the night.

As for me, I have often cried
when he speaks to me. Everything is plain
between us definite and understood,
but what to do with it I cannot guess.
Many hours we have spent we twain
conversing: what he says is very good
but when he leaves off I am at a loss.

৺

SCHUMANN'S VIOLIN CONCERTO

54. Music and silent death in league
    perfect and kill. Times they go wrong
    —a poor musician ages, Keats died young—
    but mostly, as if fearing to fatigue,
    Music gives up her favorite: once big
    and now delivered, no soul overlong
    is able to live. Tchaikovsky wrote a song
    of adequate gloom and died; the little jig
    at a big question was for Beethoven
    the last he had to say to us; and when
    he scratched these repetitions, Schumann came
    to the madhouse and death. I therefore watch
    my poems morbidly for one in which
    I finally shall recognize my name.

FARADAY

55. Son of a blacksmith and it stood
    the lad in good stead later to devise
    hardware for Davy and to improvise
    his own magnets, for "I never could
    know a fact that I didn't see," he said.
    But then they bound him over as apprentice
    for seven years to a bookbinder.

                                    This

    also happened to be very good:
    All kinds of old books come
    into a shop for new covers, and some
    were natural philosophy. Michael could hardly read
    but stalled a day or two until he copied
    a curious paragraph and diagram,
    and the scholars talked to him he was so sweet.

FREUD

56. First through blooming fields of hell among
    gay jokes and colored dreams and gorgeous
    mistakes our guide had conducted us
    to where desire, the dragon of my song,
    was flaming in his nether parts and tongue.
    Next we were exploring hideous
    deserts of heaven by salt pools of loss
    and spiny cactuses of right and wrong
    even to the Sphinx the wish for death.
    Here we stood awhile to catch our breath
    —when suddenly dead for all our hopes and fears
    is our guide across the sky and deep,
    this morning a surprising flood of tears,
    a friendly dream after I fell asleep.

ꕤ

ON THE SONNET

57. These hand-me-downs of Milton that I wear
    I wear well, we are a family
    baroque, ambitious for abundant joy
    except that we are duteous and severe.
    The fourteen verses of the sonneteer
    are thoughtful about this anomaly.
    In spite of us a passionate outcry
    interrupts.
                Things being what they are,
    mostly we are indignant as we write,
    God did not make the world to be the best
    but man has monstrously insulted it.
    At other times more gently we have witnessed,
    quite surprised, the being of some sweet
    friend like you, David, in the waste.

LA GAYA SCIENZA

for my 61st birthday

🌿

I.

This pretty island in the Pacific
night and day noises of the sea
roaring roaring along the reef
whispering on the beach
the steady trades are blowing
sometimes a storm stirs the whitecaps
to hiss a higher octave
B-flat, B, C
as swifter winds whip the water
shrill in the cocos and puhalas
it will never become quiet
here in Hawaii the unrest of my spirit
wherever I am in the world
I am marooned I might go mad
I will go mad before I die
the ripple is whispering "persist
just persist just persist
a man marooned has one duty
only to have survived"
this is *la gaya scienza.*

II.

It's poignant and gloomy to me who am grounded
to see the young how they race and clamber

tote heavy loads and sing all night
and sleep away and snore.
It's simply boring to hear them repeating
the ideology of nineteen thirty
that was inauthentic also the first time.
They'd lend me a little of their vitality
if I could hang around condoning their politics,
but I lash out and make them dislike me
and teach them nothing, gloomier myself.

I know it's no advantage to be right,
la gaya scienza is nature's way.
What an ugly character I have!
I am able to love only the kid
that I can talk to seriously,
imposing the heavy weight of my attentiveness
that of course neither of us can sustain.

III.

"Knowledge of celestial phenomena,"
says Epicurus, "has no other end
than peace of mind and firm conviction"
—to banish the archangels,
the circling minds that cause us dread.
But an astronomer who loves the stars
passionately gazes from the tower
and studies like a jealous husband.
Science distresses him as much as superstition.
Sometimes he is mad with lust
if she favors him, a moment naked,
and Aristotle says that *this* is happiness.
Blake and Wordsworth bring back angels
and they say *this* is happiness.
Myself, I follow William James,
I am willing to believe
anything that makes me cheerful
these days I am so sad,
but what *is* la gaya scienza?

Neither big bang nor steady state
ever made me happy to believe;
when I was vigorous, however,
creation out of nothing
was an amiable theory
—for what are equations to a man
who has an extra ounce of strength
and the creator spirit
sometimes whispers in his ear?

IV.

It's one thing to cope with a problem
and get the damned car to go,
and quite another to know the truth
to understand mechanics
and who am I: where am I bound?

Wouldn't knowing the truth
help me cope with the problem?
No, I wander off
on foot into the woods,
interested in the ferns,

and English sentences
are my gaya scienza:
to say it neat and clear
that indeed I don't know where
and the damned car won't go.

For it sounds as good on paper
if it goes or it doesn't go
and I know where I am bound,
to the last line of this stanza
like a tip-top mechanic.

V.

> Best is on the floor
> and can't fall any further
> except fast asleep.

VI.

The others can sit in their chairs listening to the long lecture,
I go to the rear of the hall and lie on my back on the floor
and the voice more pleasantly drifts to me
like wind in the aspen trees. It comes and goes.
Is it only I who need to be comfortable?
—granting I am not well—are all the others well?
I don't understand them. The ceiling doesn't fall.
I'm not despised as if I had bad manners.
Most people pay no mind how people please themselves
and I try not to discommode anybody.
But when I fall asleep, I hope that I don't snore.

VII.

Whether I'm a nice guy—equals thoughtful,
patient, useful—or abrupt, self-centered,
depends entirely if I feel bad or worse.
God damn my years have come to this!

I'd ask you, kid, to come two thousand miles
to see me as you seem to want,
and then be breathless to be rid of you
in order to lie down—alone.

And how in hell can I get better
unless I have a little sex?
and how can I have sex
until I feel a little better?

Come anyway! Forgive me when
instead of making love to you
I can muster only strength
to try and satisfy myself.

The blue Pacific Ocean speaks
for itself, it speaks for itself
and I have a polyurethane kayak
to paddle to the reef.

David, he repaired it
when it blew up in the sun
and we painted it turquoise
with a border of maroon.

The taut horizon wavers
like a line drawn by Ingres
between the light blue and the dark blue
from Makapuu to Mokapu.

VIII.

I sit in my old car
as in my body and we go well.
I do not sit as confidently
in my body and we go erratically.

If I were a mechanic and could hear
the misses and rattles of my old car
as I know the signs and portents of my body,
I wouldn't drive so fast to Honolulu.

I wouldn't speed so happily by Koko
and glance delighted at the wine-blue sea
toward Molokai, as if I were hearty,
as if my old car never yet broke down.

I'll stop for this dark fellow by the road
who wants a ride. How beautiful he is

still wet from the big surf at Sandy Beach,
even if he is the angel of death.

Yes, it is better not to live in fear
for "Of all things," the Zendavesta says,
"the fear of them is worse than the things themselves
—only hell is worse than the fear of it."

IX.

Think away Jupiter, Neptune, Pluto
—that band of brothers gives me the creeps—
remain the Sky, Ocean, and Death
my limits.

Sun and the grass and flowers
that reappear in the North in April
and lust, these are my gods.

And the little mouse in the kitchen
and the woodchuck wary by his hole
are my fellows, I am married
to the startled deer—these have warm blood.

JUNE AND JULY

※

I.

I say "I love you" more than I do—not lying,
it's an hypothesis I hope will be surprisingly confirmed.

But there's no rime or reason for you to love me too
—I don't expect *you* to say anything.

I like to announce my intentions with a fanfare of six trumpets.
I'm tickled when I sound like an old book.

II.

Rightly he defers to me
because I am royalty,
he knows my ancient power
obeys and does not cower.

And he is bigger stronger
and more skillful and younger,
if he is masterful
I will meekly do his will.

Freedom pours like lust
out of us for we are just.

We wonder at the spite
we notice left and right.

III.

Just as it shouldn't be
I have the hot ideas of youth
without the energy
and the responsibility
of age without the satisfaction
—so I claim the right of property
namely, to exclude.
Oh these nights I dream only the truth:
I fumble the ball—I lose my baggage.

Yet the objective view
from long experience
is interesting too,
as I ride by Lake Winnipesaukee
on the public bus
going on a mission
about which I couldn't care less.

IV.

It was because of need, Lord,
that I myself deluded
   an unlikely thing could be
   and stubbornly did it, and I'm not sorry
just sad. I gave of myself
a lot and did not get enough,
   too bad for me. But I did
   not do him more harm than good.

Then O You dry fountain of actions and passions
abounding beyond the equations
   of the conservation of energy,
   therefore smile again at me
as distraught I go

among the flowers of the meadow
  the innumerable daisies
  and tangled vetch loud with bees.

v.

  Daisies we trod down
weren't lopped by the mower,
  see, some have survived.

  As it turns out, lad,
we could have been more careless.
  Oh another time.

  Modest the flowers
missed by the mower, and those
  along the margins.

  Being a poet
I notice small; the great cows
  will eat the big bales.

VI.

For great pebbles the beach at Middle Cove
Newfoundland! they fitted the palm
like baseballs, you hurled them into the sea.
Many maroon, most were gray,
green when I wet them with my tongue
crawling on hands and knees to lick the stones,
and God were they smooth. I am desperately
in love with this tangible, as I grow old,
belly balls and buttocks world, David.

VII.

Like an angel: the piano light
  glinting in his aureole hair

sticking out the tip of his tongue
   he picks on his guitar

—one is no longer supposed to see
   these pre-Raphael images
but watching him through the window
   so it is, so it is.

Be precise. The wonder lasts
   only an hour in the woe
and storm of nineteen-seventy
   but it is so, it has been so.

I am pleased with myself tonight
   a veteran I am not shot
when he fucked me it felt sweet
   and my own hard-on was hot.

Therefore in Victorian stanzas
   riming the second with the fourth
I will praise the nature of things
   in my pretty home in the north.

That lute song of the sixteenth century
   though Spanish was international
like the famous fight between the fleets
   —men make war too in international style.

VIII.

Clear to loneliness on his hilltop
shines the deviating Way,
in the valley my divided heart is darkly
boiling. My voice is bottled up
and though I'm only half blind my hands grope
as if I were quite blind. Is this for me
therefore the floundering Way? mind murky
and to fumble is to cope?

—a harvest grows rich under my inept care,
my children are beautiful and one is dead,
I don't know if you care for me or not,
and the Americans after their love affair
hate me again and nobody will read
my next book that I don't intend to write.

IX.

The least effort made him drowsy.
Needless to say the sex
with him was second rate.
I turn over and he's asleep.
It's mathematical!
—I never did have luck—
queer has fewer chances,
likes of me hardly any.

> I must be thirsty,
> man, to make love to such a
> long drink of water.

X.

How soon my relief from the chore of being with you
is less than how I miss your onerous presence!
I had hardly the morning to say "Oof, he's gone!"
before I began to be unhappy.

It's wiser for lovers to quarrel before they part
and you and I know how to pick a fight,
but last night we were mournfully affectionate
even though I didn't have a hard on.

Should I after all have driven away
like the lady with the raggle-taggle gypsy
in his panel truck, where by now
we are glowering at each other?

228

But he alas, lonely and dismayed,
is rolling across Canada
while I go swimming in the cold stream
without my Scottish laddy.

XI.

Haunted by presence, harsh with your absence
this room flashes sunset in the mirror.
Do you think ever of me there
as I think often of you here?
It is humbling to be old and needy.

XII.

You are lithe like the doe I do not see
    any more along the road
    to Maidstone Lake, and it is hard
to remember how my hands were free

with your shoulders. Surely
    I did not make simple love
    to your smooth belly enough
as you let me kindly.

And now she is deep somewhere
    in the woods or to another mountain fled
    or taken (God forbid)
by an out-of-season hunter.

XIII.

His truck he drives in day and night,
he painted the inside orange and white,
he hangs up his clothes and keeps everything neat,
and he sleeps alone and it's not home.

I ought like a father to him
because I love him a lot

to bring him home and let him alone,
but I'd never be content with that
and my wife won't care for that.

So variations of Frescobaldi
he plays on his cracked guitar,
sweet and earnest does he play
but he throws the song away.

O God, there must be some way
that he and I (and many another)
can be a little happier.
Whisper it to me in my ear.

XIV.

"I wasn't disappointed being here—"
was his only compliment in seven weeks,
referring maybe to the food (which I cooked)
or a cool swim in the Connecticut.
Meantime he ground his molars as they do
when they are doing what they call thinking.
Chewing over what to answer.
Forty thousands years elapse.
Often they believe they said something
or that he took my hand—
"I don't have the image of myself holding hands,"
he offered after ruminating.
The image! this turned me off but good.
In the welter of the facts of life
where men cannot afford to clutch at straws!
I felt contempt and my cock fell
and there it was:
if he didn't talk I was exasperated
and if he did talk I got angry.

XV.

"I woke up and I had the bed all to myself!
there's something nice about unlimited space."
I didn't dig that. But there *is* something nice
since I'm going to be lonely anyway
to have no one to reach at wistfully,
but go about my own sorry business.
It has a sharp taste like the prussic acid
in peach pits. *One* cannot will for *two*.

XVI.

The two babes lost in the wood
is the emblem of the kind of love I have,
clinging to one another
among the hooting and howling
and there is nothing to eat.
Yet it's rather peaceful
in the center here
kissing away our tears
and then just kissing and kissing.
Obviously two grown men
cannot live on this way.
Can we not!

XVII.

Afterwards, if I *felt* fucked,
I wanted only to hold close
and we were all the space there is;
to say nothing or maybe once his name
as his face looms great,
we kiss each other slowly

—such a good hour I never knew
with you, David, even so
I'm proud of us how we have coped
and kept our thing going

as if it had a morrow.
Isn't this the essence of love?
God, are we threadbare!
people will smile hearing about us.

XVIII.

Being a man of strong ideas
I lay with you sometimes without ideas
and because of such an empty hour
I sometimes say what has substance.

And it is lovely for an aging man
to be able to make poems,
I am grateful for them to you,
David, however it was.

Goethe said he lived what he would write.
Not that he made love to write about it
but it's the same: we will the world
to have a meaning even if she won't.

Accept this gift, it has a classic plot:
break and grief, memory and making poems.
It must be interesting for a young man
to have a wise old fool for a lover.

XIX.

"Both ways," I cried out, "I defy
You, Father, because it is necessary:
    first I will what cannot be,
    now what might be I destroy."

So saying I fell dizzy down
on the ground that reeled around
    and the young man led
    me home unsteady to my bed.

XX. FUGUE IN D-SHARP MINOR

What does Bach say? what does it mean?
for I seek in this song when I am in trouble.
Andante, he is singing at the speed
of a person who is walking along thinking
unflagging. If you attend to the three parts
in their detail it comes out anyway
to a great breadth and whole. And even so
there are moments in it that are sweet.

XXI.

    In twenty poems
I have now finished living
        through June and July.

    By and large I judge
that I am less unhappy
        than I used to be,

    but I'm not carried
away by this surprising
        new dispensation.

A DIARY OF MAKAPUU

from the Oceanic Institute, Fall 1968

🌿

Moving to Hawaii
I didn't mark the equinox,
winter when it blows
won't mean much to me.
But a flower lei and aloha
will also mean not much
to one who needs what is
nowhere a native product.

I.

    Of Makapuu
  drop on drop you cannot hear
    is the roaring surf.

I've come to hate, it is appalling,
Adam I used to love.
In the war between mankind
and the beauty of the world
I am a traitor, my loyalty
does not lie with mankind.
How can I write poetry
my earnest speaking with mankind?

These learned men mean no harm,
just to palaver with the porpoises.

234

My guess is the sagacious animals
won't talk in prison to the wardens
and maybe the language of the ocean
can't communicate except
freedom. Instead, another
has decided not to breathe. O dolphin—

      You who drew by choice
    every breath, yesterday
      chose not to bother.

Yes, if they draw by art each breath
—that we don't draw, it breathes us—
this porpoise did not kill himself
but chose not to live on
like Gandhi when he found
like a child the food tasteless
under the British Raj
and fasted forty days.

      And oh if my next
    poisoned breath must be gulped in
      up there where men are!

II.

At quis custodiet custodem?
—who will watch the watchman on his rounds?
I will, he is a good-looking Samoan,
the scientists have left and he is lonely too.
I watch his wandering flashlight
visit the dark offices and peer
behind the bushes, he has nineteen stations
to punch before at last he wends this way.

When I read of the races of these islands
their histories and grim vicissitudes
and each has prejudices and sore spots
that I can never learn to take into account,

here I will never be able to make love,
the people are not plain. I would be happier
trying to make out with the porpoises
if only I could swim better than I do.

Swept off my feet and
drowning I rode high and dry
with the squid ashore.

My prints on the sand
are more gingerly than when
I passed here before.

Capella! Saturn! and Aldebaran!
among which rises the Hawaiian moon
brilliant on the ocean—"we arrange it
for the tourists, twenty thousand bucks
worth of electricity per annum.
It pays off, I suppose, except these days
the fuckin airlines get the lion's share.
Well, easy come easy go. Aloha."

"The same big old moon
shining on the same old sea,"
says my five-year-old.

In the great wheeling of heaven from the east
the oblong of Orion is rising at 10 o'clock.
When I return at midnight he is glittering
high and his dog shines over Makapuu.
End of October there are many brief
meteorites in the Hawaiian sky
and the steady trade-winds push the ocean
ashore faintly foaming in the starshine.

III.

> Some bits of coral
> have holes to string at leisure
> a savage necklace.

I got a little car real cheap
it clanked and shuddered like a wreck
but I knew it was the universal joint
not a big job, and now my friends
admire me for a mechanic.
No. I drove when I was poor
a car whose universal gave,
I know it well, I know it well.

My little blue car can go up Pali
in high—at thirty miles—
the utmost feat demanded in this little world,
and there you can pause and study the famous view
across the sea. It is the very cliff
where the Oahu warriors
were pushed headlong by Kamehameha
the father of his country.

The bitch Pele and Kamehameha
that ugly son of a bitch, what a couple!
—even the American missionaries
were civil by contrast. What do you expect?
Bully rovers who have ants in their pants
and cross two thousand miles of open ocean
would not be the most elegant
or merry dancers of Tahiti.

At the public school in Waimanalo,
my little girl says, they stand up
at strict attention for the Stars and Stripes,
but for the Bars and Crosses of Hawaii
they lay their little hands upon their hearts.
It's realistic anyway.

So long as there is no idolatrous salute
this father doesn't intend to make a fuss.

A white American New Yorker
talented Jew, I am by birth
the royal family. And since my lust
is democratic and pan-humanist
inevitably I come on *noblesse oblige*
magnanimous and paternalistic,
as the foremost foam of the incoming tide
sinks in the dry sand without a trace.

Otters got loose and people were joyous
shouting Freiheit! like the prisoners in *Fidelio.*
Dammit! in the thorny mesquite
we flushed them out or they would perish
in the salty sea far from Malaysia
or be hit by a car. Moimoi let out
a shriek of rage when we threw him back
and everybody went away depressed.

Dead mongoose, a dead dog,
dead boobie on the highway.
No shame in being dead
so many are, it may happen
to anybody. The atom bomb
of Hiroshima surely shrove
many of guilt and I am made
easier by the dead mongoose.

> Only a mile more,
> as if I am there! but I
> must still go one mile.

IV.

> For no reason I
> hurried back in time to look
> for someone in vain.

Trust natural signs
more than whispered arrangements
in two dialects.

The skinny Chinese boy who sweeps
is sexy and he lies in wait in my way.
My interest is infinitesimal
but I don't say no. Other times
he's mad for money to buy acid
or pay his debts before they take his car.
Sometimes I give him a five-dollar bill.
He's bound to rob me sooner or later.

Copious and dangerous is the visible
beauty of the Hawaiian islands,
but Adam has gone away
and what will become of me?
I wish I could make music but a piano
will never thrive in my damp house
and it's not worth it to learn to strum
the couple of chords of an ukulele.

"You hanker for the Noble Savage,"
said the Dean to me (on the TV).
No, I hanker for Neolithic Man
beginning to be a farmer
circumspectly steering
in the economy of the cosmos
and fashioning a golden disk
to gaze at when the days grow short.

Oh but despite the poisonous flowers
that I cannot identify in this foreign place
—I am mortally sick already anyway,
what difference does it make?—
I'll breathe *in*
this climate wet and windy
that willy nilly I breathe in and out.
How rapidly the days grow shorter here!

Do not try to think
when you have a high fever
do not write hokku.

He has ideas,
he says turn over and he
loses his hard-on.

v.

With unremitting energy
starting from a far storm
whipped by the steady wind
fifty feet high on the rock
the billow forward foamed
already another was looming
—diminishing in the backwash—
the third crashed greatest of all.

The child of Have and Lack is Longing:
I followed with my hungry eyes
the unremitting energy
of the billows as they came
starting from a far storm
whipped by the steady wind,
the far storm is what I have,
the steady wind is what I lack.

A reckless sentence
I wrote is true, a long wave
from the horizon.

Disorganized rage
is best, and the hurt and tired
make a kind of peace

and a little sun
a little rain, said Goethe,
and the grass grows green,

        my poor earth! he said,
    I evermore repeat it,
        every twenty years.

VI.

        The steady trade winds
    blow from east to west the sun
        across the heaven.

        The winds have died and
    the sun rises in the east
        and sets in the west.

So white the sun the sea
so deep blue it is black,
the sky a sheet of lightning
it is like a raging storm.
He rows his kayak
into the canyon of the quiet
and the fish fixed in glass
stare at him from either side.

        The tide is ebbing
    yet will one mischievous wave
        surge and wet your shoes.

        The tide is flooding
    the tide-pools with their quick fish
        become the ocean.

Riding around Koko the old volcano
to my lecture at the University,
before me stood a rainbow
with one foot vivid in Manoa Valley
and through the center of the arch my highway
onward: but when I arrived on campus
there wasn't any pot of gold there
nor did I bring one.

They have no hands and make no cities.
They know death but they don't need
to immortalize themselves with propositions.
Yet the convolution of their brains is like my own,
their sensorium confounds imagination,
and they communicate in several voices.
What do the dolphins *do* with all that?
—It is, of course, our kind of question.

Nothing in nature surely is just wasted,
Dolphin? Sometimes with what looks like pleasure
you circle in your cement prison
and glance with what seems to be a knowing eye
and like to be caressed on your tin skin.
It all adds up to nothing. Let me think:
how would *I* be in my ocean
if I did not do the things I do?

How *is* it that they know death and do not need
to immortalize themselves by making
an objective world that stays
while they swirl in their melodious waters?
The regularities of it
are too trivial for them to mention
compared with the particularities
of play and passion, like poets.

Or if routine, the regularities
we take for granted, is for you foreground,
Dolphin! it is interesting enough
and there occur surprises
as once befell Adam *my* ancestor.
So you are calm. Yes! if I can attend
just to how it is as I go,
wherever I go come into being worlds.

But why doesn't he jump over the barrier
into the other's tank if he's lonely?

No, said Gregory, there are no barriers at sea
and they avoid doorways.
Uncomprehending of walls
some species dash themselves upon the rocks.
But they do make wandering fences:
a swimming mother pens her baby in.

They say these porpoises won't learn
by punishment but only praise,
fish, and petting; try the other
and they mope on the bottom and die:
childlike and lordly. But we also
are noble who can't take it any more
until our only world instead of this
is more like paradise, and we live on.

Like all prisoners and all wardens
what the porpoises and scientists
have in common is their prison
and this is what they talk about.
I useless look and listen
in the solitary cell of my exile
where it is inauthentic to speculate
and it would be inauthentic not to speculate.

Creator Spirit come, by whom
I say that which is real,
nor has this way of being
failed to save me alive
like the indefatigable surfers
on the indefatigable waves,
riding the long froth,
sunk suddenly in error.

VIII.

That ocean changing
colors are many waters
is this ocean green.

Somebody's feelings
I recollect in altered
possible meanings.

I didn't count on it, human nature
abhors a vacuum and I'm in love
with the skinny one. Stupid with troubles
I don't enjoy it but leave that to him
generously adolescent. Even so,
O God of strict and unexpected causes,
thanks be for him as practical a sample
of Adam as any, though not for me.

Anxiously waiting
to make love I fell asleep.
I'm glad that's over.

We crouch, panting, on the river bank.
The Angel is invisible, the willows
are brightening through where he ought to be.
"The day is breaking, let me go,
Angel! you have wrestled me enough."
I hear the waters gurgling as they race
among the mossy rocks. I am in pain,
I notice—limping on my left leg.

I let the Angel go, the day was breaking
and I had wrestled him enough.
I heard the waters gurgling as they raced
among the mossy stones. I built a fire
and made a pot of coffee as I do
before setting forth, after my nightmares,
the beautiful few minutes of the day
when I have new thoughts I soon forget.

IX. CHRISTMAS 1968

Daisy chose and I have cut
a thorny little mesquite

to be our Christmas tree
soon droopy, sad to see,
we trim with a string of tinsel
and a star of aluminum foil
    because our pretty baubles are
    across the ocean far.

Meantime, circling the to us half moon
go the three Christmas spacemen
    whom we with human pride
    wish well as on our way we ride
quit of the mass and the horizon
of Earth at last. Is this the reason
    we are so careless of our trust
    that we are objects of disgust?

X. THE CHIEFS

You ask, What is the use of the chiefs?
Our tabus are so fierce nobody is safe,
if you do or don't you are doomed.
We throw them off the cliff,
we hold their heads under water.
But the naha chiefs have mana
to pardon when they are in the mood.
How can we live without the chiefs?

Needless to say, persons so potent
are afraid of themselves. Since it's death
to let your shadow fall across a chief,
chiefs emerge only at dusk.
High chiefs, they say, under base names
have stolen up into the hills
to mingle with the out-caste.
One grows bananas in Kaneohe.

    Without gravity
    I couldn't drop anything
        nor plod by falling.

245

Listen, as we leave
the clamor lessens by the
    square of the distance.

Of Makapuu
the roaring surf you cannot
    hear is drop on drop.

BALLADES

BALLADE OF DATES

October 10th I gave up hope
  of being happy for this year.
September 17th said "Stop!
    that dog is mad, don't have it here"
    —but I didn't heed my inner ear.
Or first on August 28th
    I shuddered and said, "Good-bye, my dear"
and began to be interested in death.

The fall of '44 down-slope,
  '40 I was in full career,
by '35 I gave me rope
    to say what no one wanted to hear
    and hang myself. Much earlier
in '26 I saw from what beneath
    the water-lily snakes into a star
and began to be convinced by death.

Now neutral, large, and wide in scope
  my grown-up age is void and drear.
My boyhood had the hue and shape
    of Hot-with-Lust and Cold-with-Fear.
    When I was a child long before
I cried myself to sleep with wrath

and every face a face of nightmare
and became a devotee of death.

Physician, like a dying deer
    I stand at bay to catch my breath.
Otherwhen, in the dateless era,
    I shall have been at grips with death.

᯽

BALLADE TO VENUS

Some things I would (if I could) steal
    mine! mine! to hoard and share:
the Tlingit blanket of the Whale,[1]
    the Little Street of Jan Vermeer[2]
    in front of which I hummed a lilting air,
and from the Age of Stone this grand
    Lady of Lespugue stands here[3]
no bigger than a human hand.

Two Unicorns—the oceans roll
    between—I want: one leaping there
with his curly beard in a floral jail,[4]
    the other does a banner bear;[5]
    also that tiny Chapel where[6]
the sailors came in Pisa and
    foreboding offered up a prayer
no bigger than a human hand.

My twitching fingers! I conceal
    deep in my pockets while I stare
past the watchman, and the seal

1. In the Museum of the American Indian, N.Y.
2. Rijksmuseum, Amsterdam   5. Museum of Cluny, Paris
3. Musée de l'Homme, Paris   6. Sta. Maria della Spina
4. The Cloisters, N.Y.

248

drops from my sight: this hall of treasure
  where like a thief I poise in fear
is home where I was born and trained,
  my hand is neither emptier
nor bigger than a human hand.

Mother of peevish hurt Desire
  as you were painted by Rembrandt,[7]
still hold me in your loving-care
  no bigger than a human hand.

※

BALLADE TO JEAN COCTEAU

Martyrs of the crimes of sex,
  Sappho, Hyacinth, and she
who fucked the Bull, and Oedipus Rex,
  these are not by Jean and me
  blotted out of memory
but wept and named, so all may read
  and know them and ourselves and ye.
To heaven was raped Ganymede.

Read, all, and pay respects
  of etiquette to outlawry.
Don't look away, fate protects
  these names from shame: Pasiphaë
  was mounted not for luxury,
the boy drowned in the pool for need,
  and Sappho jumped into the sea.
To heaven was raped Ganymede.

Jean and I meet among wrecks
  cast by froth and cut from tree

7. The Louvre, Paris

and vanishing in the vortex.
    His hair is white prematurely
    and I say to him from what I see,
"O poet of the winter sun indeed!"
    but who am I is yet to be.
To heaven was raped Ganymede.

The clawed and wingèd angel, the
    Eagle, did not make beauty bleed
lifting him over field and sea,
    to heaven was raped Ganymede.

✲

BALLADE OF THE MOMENT BEFORE

"Which in this bar as they stay or go,
is the god in disguise and everything
will otherwise be when I know?
Ah, is it you who staggering
loom in the door as to the dying
king came happy Hercules
and hiccuped and began to sing?"
So joked the god in disguise.

"Maybe it's you who add the row
of numbers and sit listening
or don't listen, yet know—know;
so Klamm sat in the village inn
and dipped a pen, the pen was scratching,
he did not need to lift his eyes,
Franz's heart was thundering—"
So anxiously the god in disguise.

"To Aeneas by the undertow
cast ashore in the morning,
his mother with a Tyrian bow

appeared bare-kneed as the spring
just as this waitress comes to bring
my dinner—I am otherwise
at a loss for a next thing."
So at a loss the god in disguise.

"You unknown god, I feel your wing
close in this tavern, and it is
the instant of its opening!"
cried out and rose the god in disguise.

꙳

BALLADE OF THE MOMENT AFTER

Table and chair were overturned,
bread and wine spilt on the floor,
King Macbeth stared straight in front
and still he saw what was before;
his lady's voice came from afar
over his shoulder wooingly
but not to the point anymore,
the moment after the catastrophe.

In a cloister, by a dried-up font
—di Chirico that cloister saw—
the shadow of a man was burnt
in the pavement and its length was more
than a man is high; beyond the door
a locomotive silently
puffed, and it was half past four,
the moment after the catastrophe.

So little Perseus did confront,
tricycling down the corridor,
the gorgon of his mother's cunt
before his mother could withdraw.

Nothing was said by either or
but from that day he chose to see
the world backward in a mirror,
the moment after the catastrophe.

The wonder that I waited for
suddenly has come to be.
My hands are clenched around neither/nor
the moment after the catastrophe.

ༀ

BALLADE OF DIFFICULT ARRANGEMENTS

He's drunk again and doesn't show,
my wife's home he can't come here,
yesterday the bus was slow,
or let's suppose the coast is clear
deep in slumber lies my dear.
We have our moments even so
and fuck and fondle front and rear,
but happiness is touch and go.

Even though neither one says no,
to get both bodies to appear
has been a science I don't know,
though I a yellow hood can wear
and slashes blue in sleeves that flare.
Yet times we kiss and times we blow
and other times we just sit near,
but happiness is touch and go.

He's off to work, money's low,
my wife's lonely, I love her,
he keeps on terms with Tom and Joe,
at dinner I'm in daddy's chair,

how can you be both here and there?
Nevertheless we whisper slow
sweet talk in each other's ear,
but happiness is touch and go.

Mercury, bring the distant near!
Apollo, make the sun go slow!
Linger longer, fleeting year!
Happiness is touch and go.

※

INTRODUCTION AND BALLADE OF MUSICIANS

Look away, profane! and do not dare
to watch the slow tears on my face.
But why tonight am I ashamed to cry
in front of you for music's sake?
when such a sadness rises for the musicians
both who are dead at rest and us alive
I cannot hold my tears and the theater
is brighter than the stage-lights.
For it is the last act and last scene
of *The Mastersingers,* our red-letter day,
and there is no artist's heart
in madhouses, poverty, and solitude
that is not crying now. Approving love
is the right of every man and child.

Your *applause* is not relevant,
it does not help. We have made good our loss
—too many times.
We have too many times made good our loss.
We have too many times made our loss good.

Too many times made good their loss:
one sang all day though his health was bad

and yet his songs are various
some happy some sad,
he died young. One never had
what he lusted sick with fright
but his songs too are glum and glad.
I wept for both of them tonight.

Another made spontaneous
gay music, yet the instant dread
of death and hell sounds ominous
lest anybody be misled.
And still another one went mad
repeating one poor tune aright
until the tired strings went flat.
I thought of these and wept tonight.

One was deaf. Boisterous
he wrote *prestissimo* "to be played
faster than you can" and hush,
piano subito dismayed,
and then the quiet song he made
that will never finish in despite
of art, but he was not afraid.
I wept for that rough man tonight.

Holy Ghost! I never said
a word against you, come with might.
But I have worked and not been paid
and I wept for me tonight.

BALLADE OF BEAUTIFUL PLACES

The light is preternatural
on the high plateau
though the temples and the game of ball

were abandoned long ago
in Xochicalco
and goats and geese feed on the grasses
among the fallen stones that grow.
There are many beautiful places.

The light is also magical
in Delphi in the mists that come and go
—she on the three-legged stool
sniffing gasses from below
might well have spoken with Apollo—
and sheep are grazing on Parnassus
thyme and oregano.
There are many beautiful places.

But the light is common day and still
in the North Country here and now
where in the graveyard up the hill
my sister lies and I too
will maybe lie—who can know?—
and there are other empty spaces.
Robins hop to and fro.
There are many beautiful places.

Creator of the world, thank you.
My eyes are weak and I wear glasses,
I can witness even so
there are many beautiful places.

IN THE MANNER
OF ANACREON

SOLSTICE

1. Leaping my shadow and Prick my dog
   I took to walk the park
   the streets the bars the wooden dock
     all a hot afternoon.

   My shadow had a lively run
   and stretched out long he came back home,
   but Prick had never a sniff or jump
     the twenty-first of June.

ST. VALENTINE'S

2. "A baby!" groaned my Eros, the contempt
   curling his orange lip and slowly dripped the words;
   "they have a holiday, St. Valentine's,
   and there my picture is on candy-boxes
   pink, like a fucking girl, two years of age!
   with hardly any hair except a curl
   and nothing, nothing at all, between the legs
   but a diaper to shit in, oh! and look—"

Disgust took by the throat
my eleven-year-old wiseacre
and he coughed and broke in a sweat
—"look! a toy bow and arrow! naturally,
that's what goes on, instead of my sharp jokes.
When *I* was Eros," said the boastful boy
and laughed maniacally with zigzag eyes,
"their hot hides used to smart for it, you bet,
they woke up roaring in the dead of night!"

—he paused. His deadly but not tragic bow
dropped from his nerveless hand, and like a hen
his wings outstretched in fright. For at his shoulder
stood his big brother the Homeric love,
the Angel Eros armed with might, played round
by fire, the hilarious Archer.

AN OLD-CLOTHES MAN
mesonuktiois pot' horais —*Anacreonteia, 35*

3. On the first of March when the snows into waters
      were melting and running in the gutters,
   "Hi cash, I clo!" in the street rose up
      from a merchant wearing three hats like the Pope,
   and I, awake from dreamless slumber, thought,
      "It's time to throw my winter garments out.
   Here is a fellow to make it worth my while,"
      I beckoned from the window with a smile.

   But when he came in, I grew ill at ease
      for his whiskers were false and his dark blue eyes
   laughed under the hats, his big hook nose
      was made of putty, and he swam in his clothes.
   "Make schnell mit de garments!" said the Boy
      as if in Yiddish and roared with joy.

Then from my somber closet I laid out
   the mackinaw with matching hat I bought
before I made a pass and lost my job
   —the cuffs were frayed, the hat a hustler robbed;
the sweater long ago that Mary knitted
   was eat by moths like the trust we had;
and when I took my outgrown only suit
   off its hanger, with a scornful hoot
he named it, "Careless love! oh I can smell
   a fool and his prick at half a mile.
Cheer up, the season's on again!" and he drew
   an automatic pistol blunt and blue
—less human than his ancient bow and dart—
   and point-blank leveled it against my heart.
Glass-eyed, beneath that absurd coat I saw
   the rosy flesh of the god of jokers glow,
and he fired, clapped hands, and jumped from the floor
   holding the hats, and made for the door.

I staggered and I broke into a sweat.
   "Wait up!" I begged. He stood there with one foot
downstairs and spun his weapon on his thumb
   insolently. My brain was growing numb.
"Am I going to be very sick?"
   "A shot like that you don't get over quick!"
"Who is it that will leave me there for dead?"
   "Oh these days," he cynically said,
"when March is terrible and April horrible,
   you won't lack to get you into trouble."

❦

A NEW DIRECTIVE FROM THE PENTAGON

4. Cupid was the cunning tailor
   who cut those pants for a sailor,

258

a lad couldn't have a hard-on but it showed
and his behind rippled as he goed.

Now if they ban the bells and jumpers
and "all will look like officers,"
why would anybody join?
and why would anybody toin?

5. "Saturday liberty, the fucking Town
   is on the avenue, I draw a blank—"
   but Cupid cut me short, "O cut the shit!
   who are you kidding? When by accident
   you get something and lead it by the hand
   etcetera, how do you finish up?
   You write a sonnet to her bovine eyes
   or maybe that a pig's ass has two halves.
   Or like tonight, suppose you draw a blank,
   before you go to bed you write a ballad,
   'Damn, I was drunk! I fell before I rose!'
   or 'Curses on the 8-hour working day,
   my amorous piano-mover fell asleep.'
   Pass or fail, you hunt and make verses.
   What must I say? you want to make verses.
   Good! you have the verses. Why d'ye gripe?
   Why do you call on me to help you hunt?
   Call on Calliope, on St. Cecilia."
   "You peanut!" said I, "you ungrateful bastard!
   if Ovid and Anacreon didn't write,
   nobody would bother to make love."

6. For God's sake, sailor, I'd be glad
   to suck your eager cock off,
   but what you say about Nigras
   makes my hair crawl, you're stupid
   and stupidity is graceless.
   Cupid left when you opened your mouth.

Oh if they wouldn't open their mouths,
the beauties whose roses grow
in a tropical garden and God
wove them from wild stuff
—if they wouldn't open their mouths.

But come back, Cupid! by unreason
you bind me to humanity
even with marines, those butchers.
I close my ears and stomach horror
and lust unpardoning.

TWO LIMERICKS

7. Miss Forgetful, how do you do?
   I'm pregnant and cannot guess how.
      Let's walk around the block
      and check up on the stock
   and deduce a cause or two.

   Mademoiselle, let me persuade
   you to *a tergo* be laid,
      so if, Heaven forfend,
      we get stuck in the end,
   we can walk out of here for first aid.

8. With a tube of grease in his pocket
   he walked the avenue to get fucked
   but every queen in town mistook it
   for the hard-on which it looked.

HOMAGE TO HUGO BLACK

9. Thanks to a couple of rational
   decisions by the Court
   that struck down censorship
   and—brrr—its chilling effects,
   I get by mail a gentle stream
   of booklets of poetry
   by young men in love with each other,
   good news I read with pleasure
   though naturally wistfully.
   I used to write the same myself
   a hundred years ago
   —my muse is hard to chill—
   but publishers and line-o-typers
   wouldn't touch it with a tongs,
   much less the post office.
   Hugo Black it was,
   the champion of Cupid,
   and he is dead and gone
   and cannot be replaced.

A SUBURBAN TRAVELER

10. "Like a garden for its lady who
    lavishes cares on it, yellow blue
        and purple blossoms brighten her coming
        out of her house in the morning,

    "so sprinkled in and around New York
    where I have always liked my work
        bloom my beauties Austrian
        French and Irish by origin."

—He rides the morning trains
commuting to White Plains
    that by their nature carry
    never a trick to see

and this in-between half hour
he puts his lists in order
    as a housekeeper careful
    keeps a place half-way cheerful.

❧

LLOYD *(SEPTEMBER 9, 1941)*

11. I never, today, went on the courts except
    to angle sharply tremendous bounces
    and catch the younger men flat. I'm 30.
    But before each play the little Welshman
    was stroking in unconscious meditation
    his swelling prick, this threw me off my game.
    "Hinder!" I claimed when my first serve fell short,
    my second hit him squarely on the spot.
    "Ouch!" he says and lays the offender bare.
    "Looks O.K.," say I with expert eyes.
    "Yes, ain't it a beauty?" whispers Lloydie.
    "I'd better take you home and fix you up"
    —and I toss in the ball, to their relief,
    because today I would have scoured the courts
    like Hector when he set the ships afire.
    This, this was the birthday present
    that Aesculapius and Eros gave me
    and may such a unanimity of joy
    reward all who forgo the victory
    and leave the courts of glory on an errand
    of mercy, and make love instead of war.

※

SUSPICION AND WELCOME

12. Fidgeting under my scrutiny
    as if he had to pee.
    As if to guard his life
    he is opening and closing his jackknife.
    Now beware,
    stare is grinding against stare.
    Then such a smile cerulean spreads
    across his frown of doubts and dreads
    as when suddenly the breeze
    dies down and leaves calm seas.
    Cries of fisherboy and bird
    are ringing in the stillness heard,
    and there floats by the *Argo*
    with heroes as its cargo.

※

IN TRAFFIC

13. All up Eighth Avenue
    in his apple-green pie wagon
    big Jim and I had a party.
    And was that traffic thick!
    honking us like geese
    backed up, I guess, to Wall Street
    while we loitered at a light
    and our thoughts were far away.
    The looming cop was plenty sore,
    "If you'd keep your hands on the wheel
    instead of on his prick—" he said,
    but Jim unstretched his six-foot-four
    and both of them said, "Yeah yeah,"

as we sped away in our cloud
and handily came off
at Columbus Circle.

✻

CLASSICAL QUATRAIN

14. The plane crashed and our darling—O
cursed aeroplane bound for Toronto!
why would any one go to Toronto?
—our darling with the others perished. But

Jeanie boasted, "I! I was the last
he ever fucked upon this earth, of all
maidens and matrons in his travels wide
and also boys were glad to entertain him."

Rosy Eros in the dust was dragging
his noiseless wings that ferry flying dreamers
in color, and he groaned, "I could have spared
Very Important People and celebrities.

Lover, farewell!" And I on my swift hops
from town to town will write him poetry
as the honey-bee secretes, I sip my food
from the meadow-flowers of reality.

15. Rough flight. "So frightened
my wig turned gray."
(Kant.) Take better care
of that valuable horseflesh
maybe a Nobel laureate.
Cupid'd bawl,
said John who works real hard
to keep me young and sexy.

VOYAGE À CYTHÈRE

for Charles Wallis

16. "Boy, let's us two have a serious talk."
    "Oh no," said he and pulled away. I held him
    close by my will: "Here in this book I'm reading,
    see here, there is a traveler to Cythera. . ."
    Eros turned white; I seized the advantage:
    "He sees a sight there, hey? a horror, and
    you know it well, the gallows, the beaked birds,
    and the castrated corpse, and the long retch.
    Hey? hey? let's talk about all that."
                                        But such
    a shuddering was shaking him, his feathers
    turned inside out like leaves before a storm,
    in awful fear I stopped. Eros was ill,
    and what if he should die? I didn't know
    another way to live another day.

    But he, with a wan smile, his feathers closing
    though ruffling nervously, said bold as brass,
    "You think I'm a fool or a fraud,
    an innocent, or perhaps a treacherous
    wizard who aims to hang you there and gloat
    with lips drawn back over my crooked teeth.
    I know these newsy stories. I am Lust.
    Have I ever been a hypocrite?
    concealed the facts of life or whispered hush?
    especially to you who crave unrest
    and blurt it out in your next book anyway.
    Put no faith in a naive remorse
    ignorant of psychoanalysis.
    If you had had a better fuck last night,
    you would not now be guilty."

※

COLD TURKEY

17. A couple of weeks of careless
     love and I'm hooked again,
     shattered when I can't
     score my daily dose.
     Sexy, you have doomed me
     to cold turkey in Washington,
     goose-pimply at the Department
     of Health, Education, and Welfare,
     and biting my nails at Justice.
     I thought I was too old to relapse.
     You, traitor, are young,
     you have lots of fixes,
     you don't live in the capital
     of the Great Society,
     even if your pad is in Brooklyn.

※

A DEPRESSING QUESTION FOR DR. R.H.

18. If I have desperately low
     blood pressure these grim months,
     might not this, Bob, explain
     why I'm so slow to get a hard on,
     although the beach abounds
     from Waimanalo to the Air Force base
     and some of 'em available
     and I sometimes ache like blazes?

19. "Good fun, feeling at peace in the world,
     and knowing other people is what sex
     has given me, I wish I had more of it.
     It made me comrades as if, in so far,

we had a decent city. For the torments
and the super-reality of love
I am too old, I do not need to lose myself,
what I need is health to find myself."
So I explained (God help me) soberly.
And Cupid the physician commented,
"He will have neither health nor love nor sex."

TRANSLATION OF HORACE *ODES* I, 27
Natis in Usum Laetitias Scyphis—

20. Only a Dodger fan would clout you
    with a bottle made for drinkin out,
    don't be a barbarian, stow
    your liquor without makin a row.
    A quiet place with television
    ain't the place for a panzer division,
    so quiet down you fuckin fools
    an' keep your asses on your stools.
    If you want to drink with us
    wipe that growl off your puss.
    Let Joe Massouli tell us what's
    the score, for who's he got the hots?
    No soap? O.K. by me. No soap.
    Next round, Harry, pass me up.
    Whaddye bashful? sure she's nice,
    you're a clean kid without no lice.
    Oh, you don' wanna others to hear?
    whisper it, tell me in my ear.
    —Holy smokes! so that's her name,
    you're a dead cookie, what a shame!
    a nice Catholic boy like you!
    Mother o God, the things we do!
    Sonny, you oughta have your brains picked
    by one o them psychiatrix.

MAKING LOVE, I

※

FOR M.

Your face your profile while we fuck
isn't heavenly it does not float
is like the big pale-golden
pebble I picked up
from a Smoky Mountain freshet
ground by the torrents of the spring
and polished by warm sparkling waters
millions of summer afternoons
until this norm of rural granite

—I showed it to the artist-students
molding abstract shapes:
"No use," I said, "native stones
are the refinement of enormous powers
applied a billion semesters
billions of storms and still in the making,
you can't match it, try at something else—"

Say out you love me, tell me lies,
if necessary tell me lies,
so blotted to you I may wander
somewhere, anywhere, and lose my wits.
Some one once said to me,
"Paul, you have a human face
lined with experience." I was embarrassed.

※

We had a few moments of quiet beauty
in our dark room lit by lamplight through the trees.
They were not in the reliable order of events
nor in the practical order of what I know to do.
I didn't know what to do with it, too close
—it was inside arm's length—to ward it off,
only to murmur "Stay! O thou! last long!"
till I grew uncomfortable in the unbearable
pauses sweet in which *I* could not stay
and soon lapsed into lust and fell asleep.

Those beautiful moments we deserved who tried,
we tried hard, both daring and forbearing,
to preserve the possible into a fact.
Honor and good judgment guarded us
like angels. We were proud of being lucky.

Oh, even while I lay there at a loss
how to cope with this closer than opportunity,
I was in a panic for the shameful waste
—one badly nourished by my only world
I am alive to the sin of waste!

And now these things have left me where I am.
As I did not know what to do with that
I cannot find myself in the world as it is.
I am distraught with longing for paradise
and convinced it is unattainable for me.

※

(MANNER OF SAPPHO)

Such beauty as hurts to behold
and so gentle as salves the wound:

I am shivering though it is not cold,
in the dark though it is noon.

My ears are ringing, fire
has stunned my hands and feet.
I do not feel any desire.
I am at peace as on a height.

This lust that blooms like red the rose
is none of mine but as a song
is given to its author knows
not the next verse yet sings along.

You ask what I am muttering
stupefied, it is a prayer
of thanks that there is such a thing
as you in the world there.

꿏

Because I love you, walking with you
Seventh Avenue is blurry.
You must have stolen my eyeglasses
I am in a panic of surprise
like the President of France assassinated
fumbling for his glasses on his lap
blood spreading on the heart of his shirtfront,
the poor old man who ought to have retired
during the revolutionary situation.

꿏

Clouded with love, a tear drops
from my spirit like the tiny Lake
Tear of the Clouds on Mount Marcy

out of which flows the Hudson River.
These raindrops are as big as eyes
big as hearts; the U-shaped gorge
was cloven by the glacier but it is brimmed
to an open sea where blasts of dawn
lighten the horizon and
the suns bound up. The crazy waves
are rolling from the shoreless to the shoreless
and a rainbow of turbilous, pearl, and dizimal,
the colors of September, stands
across the sky like a granite hope.

❦

Now is the dreadful midnight you
have to do what you want to do

not by your will which is afraid
but by my hand upon you laid.

My hand withheld almost too long
moves by lust, its grip is strong

and callous, it has turned to fire
the arpeggios of a lyre

and we love carelessly
who gravely love Saint Harmony.

Resist not, nor can you resist, the cries
that in your bowels rise

which I to song shall modify
and neither of us will ever die.

❊

Dancing slowly
like the giant
flickering flames
fed on black oil
that devastate
the people's houses
and blight future
green forever
was my disastrous
past, and the present
a blazing ghost
wears on his face
a frightful mask
and his footsteps
are soft and sure.

But being next to you
the hours stand still
nowhere to go
having arrived.
Next to you
or making love
or in my house
are all equally
solemn and final.
The words we speak
are like touching
each other's faces,
and we have gently
fallen asleep
holding hands.

❊

Let me withdraw and grow small and so speak.
In the big quiet there is little to say.

"I love you" is not a wide discourse
nor very useful to you as time flies.
But to me it is panic to be speechless.

Quiet, your great face was a sunshine
suddenly broken warm upon the field
and the bees roared and the grasshoppers jumped.
The shadow of the cloud slipped up the hill.
Pan stepped from behind the boulder lightly.

He had me by the throat. A foreign voice
was ululating ilililileee!
it wasn't mine, that panic poetry.
Therefore shyly, darling, I let sink
like a horse my silent muzzle in your neck.

   🗲

I lustily bestrode my love
   until I saw the dark and poured my seed
   and then I lay in sweetness like one dead
whom angels sing around him and above.

I lay with all my strength embraced
   then swiftly to a quiet grave withdrew
   like a grotto with the sea in view
surging and pounding, till the spell was past.

Since then, my hours are empty of
   everything; beauty touches me
   but is like pain to hear or see;
absent among the tribes of men I move.

✳

O singularly gifted at giving
yourself to me away
you flurry of mere loving
like snowing on a sunny day.

The snowstorm of seconds that crowded
the afternoon is melted
to a trickle of water
in the gutter.

Our love is without substance, yet
it has withstood the months and reasons
and the departure of long since
I and Thou from our untidy bed.

✳

Saint Harmony my patroness
   is slight and she has yellow hair
and she whispers to my loneliness
   in a whiskey voice in my ear.

She moves in an idle way
   putting a foot here and there,
her counsel is nine parts dismay
   but softly ends, "Don't you care."

And people think the morals of
   my pug-nosed muse is carelessness
and so are mine, but we shall prove
   longer lasting than they guess.

A BERYL

Those who search in dirty and dangerous mines
in gas and heat among fern and feather fossils
find (not five times) if they are diligent
an emerald fired in the original
explosion when the world was wrecked.
Cut, that gem has heavy in its heart
a green sun opposite heaven's yellow sun.
So in my dark and slippery passageways
where I am diligent I found
my love for —— ——,
and if this beryl of mine has a crack,
yet do I turn it this way and that way
and study and enjoy its prismatic lights.

We two like to talk
dirty when we fuck,
and afterwards we two
say "Thank you" "thank *you*."

TO DAWN *(MANNER OF SAPPHO)*

Gray-suited Dawn O day
of many voices, ma-
   trix of moments, speak
   to and bring this thing I seek

if I all night for this
hour at the window, whis-

pering many times that
thing I most wish have sat

waiting to greet you first
palely coming yet uncurst
   by acts, therefore yet free
   to grant anything, grant it me

guide it to me, not
by force, but by—O polyglot
   Dawn, for many through the burning
   midnight whisper—yearning.

   ✼

Moments I had of glad delight
with you, when first my eyes caught sight
of you, when you regarded me
and gave my hope a chance to be,
another day you pressed my hand
promising because underhand,
we made love you were not afraid,
we chatted quietly afterward,
agreed to meet another time
we both were there ahead of time
nor shall I soon your face forget
the light of recognition lit.
Once a whole day of joy I knew
riding the neighborhood with you
and noticing to east and west
north and south.
               Not one to rest
content am I; folly and guilt
tear down my house before it's built;
but when I was a time or two
happy, friend, it was with you.

276

His cock is big and red when I am there
and his persistent lips are like port wine.
Then would I stop and breathe his closeness
a long time hungrily, for it is there.
Yet we dress in haste and friendly say good-bye
and do not intend, each for our own good reasons,
to commit ourselves to happiness together.
Our meetings are fortunate and beautiful,
he is chaste and I am temperate,
for I have learned by the unlikely way
of scarcity and excess temperance.

We have a crazy love affair,
it is wanting each other to be happy.
Since nobody else cares for that
we try to see to it ourselves.

Since everybody knows that sex
is part of love, we make love;
when that's over, we return
to shrewdly plotting the other's advantage.

Today you gazed at me, that spell
is like why I choose to live on.
God bless you who remind me simply
of the earth and sky and Adam.

I think of such things more than most
but you remind me simply. Man,
you make me proud to be a workman
of the Six Days, practical.

277

❦

HE FOR GOD ONLY, SHE FOR GOD IN HIM—
Milton

"Thanks, it was sweet. My ready wits
are like myself again. I can forget
how we were lying body along body
and I drunken breathing in your breath,
and now for this General Motors Corporation
that makes the town unlivable, and this
Federal Bureau of Investigation
that makes the country coward, oh today
I'll bring low these insolent giraffes!"
So boasts he, while the white sun blazes
on his forehead in the fresh outdoors.
She with pride and a smile watches him vanish,
still feeling fucked, soon dreamily intent
on the seed in her belly quietly.

❦

JOAN COWAN

Somehow I learned with grander thrusts
  and joy to make love and fearless feeling
—as I never could with Joan Cowan—
  those hours that I watched appealing
the radiant smile of Joan Cowan.

Another fills and fills it well
  of both my arms the warm embrace
—as they never were full of Joan Cowan—
  I never felt but an empty ache
for the body of Joan Cowan.

At the contour of a lovely song
  I weep tears for my thwarted past

—as I wept them for Joan Cowan—
  and when I'm wept enough at last
I'll think with thanks of Joan Cowan.

❧

BUCOLIC

The dark armpits of my unwashed
honey taste acrid but her crotch
musky and delicious with
its primrose of the field
where in summer cows browse
in the hollow and bees buzz.
Her tiny lice, seen up close,
wildly wave their legs like spikes
of alfalfa in the gale.

❧

The undeciphered language of her motions
  and silences, till I interpret I
am lost. I must deduce to its emotions
  that quiet gesture of her hand, her eye

ambiguous. Oh for a Rosetta stone!
  like Jean Champollion upon the Nile
in front of the colossus looking down
  at the French army with a granite smile

and at the Arabians and at the Greeks.
  Many a soldier has stared back his fill
puzzled. What is it everybody seeks
  from objects like these that maybe have no will?

꙳

HAVERFORD

Never did I see so much pretty dogwood
tamed on lawns as yesterday at Haverford
both pink and white, and also Peter Bevin
proud of his pitching and very wide his grin
like the youngster's on the cornflakes box.
To meet "a real writer who wrote books"
he sought me out.
                                He was a troubled boy
late last night among his friends when
long hours leveled my attention at him
at only him. And all the time
we kept looking into each other's eyes,
not catching each other at it by surprise
but as if endlessly drinking, in spite of
himself in love, I willingly in love.

꙳

SWAN RIVER

Hardly of the class of rivers, claimed
    on the one side by swamps or water
    fringed by rushes, on the other
among the brooks or freshets to be named

that have a springtime life, Swan River
    is a tiny river of an hour's row,
    forever turning back the prow
like a swan's neck and forever

rounding a bend. Suddenly between
    the willows and the cattails I behold
    Billy dive with a splash. His body is gold,
his penis taut of age thirteen,

his eyes are lapis, his teeth are square,
   he is laughing. And how to get
   to kiss this river boy? His hair is wet
with the dripping moments. He emerges near.

✲

SALLY'S SMILE

Sara has smiled upon me such a smile
   that caution and resentment both my wardens
are flung into the winds that mile on mile
   pour northward to us from Miami gardens

where dead my mother lies and red the rose
   and the hibiscus bloom, but there is no
memory to me more fair and dear in those
   distances than the presence of Sally-o.

✲

The golden pendent to Deneb
like the two opals that I bought for Sally
set by a silversmith in Taxco
and she was pleased.

✲

DOLCE STIL NUOVO

In Copenhagen one in three
blond or black looks good to me
and since they troop a hundred by
there, give or take a few, are thirty.

Look how now throughout the Western world
the black and blond wear their flowing hair
kempt carelessly almost to the shoulders
—I also ought to write a sweet new style

and call it April. It rains here a lot
but the round sun is rolling in the cloud
silver and is trying to come out
through the great morning fog over Europe.

MAKING LOVE, II

꽃

''N O''

From the swirl of smoke
—a cigarette tip
aglow in its heart—

as the smoke on the draft
wafts toward the door
appear his eyes, hard,

and see themselves mirrored
in the drop of tear
hanging on her cheek.

Small is the one word
let fall, still heard
between their heads.

꽃

1 9 4 3

What sparks and wiry cries shall I
strike first upon the iron strings?

283

for I have got a pick of flint
and I have learnt a skirl of glee.

I'll say the love I had a little
and longing like a block of ice
—never never never again
shall we two meet. My blood stood still

my sparkling hair rose up in fright
as wide between us grew the space
now fixed. Oh brilliant more than fire
is the song of a heart undivided by hope;

my string that sounds again
is twangled with a furious joy.
And next this drizzling war I'll keen
that no man wills and all rush toward.

LOW TIDE

Low tide. A youth, as I pass by
and brake, is on the shell-strewn flat
idly tossing pebbles in the cove.
His bicycle is gleaming in the dune-grass.
And mightn't I be interesting more
than nothing at all? But though I park
and hesitantly drift back toward him
death is in my heart already
because I have in misery grown ugly
and my way is odd because I wish
to please as almost surely will offend
in this unfriendly countryside
uninvited as elsewhere.
He moves a step away
from my indecisive and speechless approach,

I turn and stare at the flat water
giving in to woe and the blinding sunlight.
He confused throws one more stone
and watches the ripples spread from the black center,
then wheels his wheel onto the road
flashing me a look that bodes no good
if ever we should meet again in town.
So better were I not alive
another afternoon I may not give
an innocent and pleasant service
but cause instead pain and fear
and suffer instead fear and pain.

※

Sad little boy sittin by the road
    with a long face an kickin at a stone,
no one to play with, nothin to do,
    same as yesterday an forty year on.

Peel the bark off a white pine branch,
    the color's pretty an smooth to the feel,
whittle a propeller to turn on a nail
    in the whistling wind, when the wind will.

Mom is off with one of her beaus,
    Sis is gone to work all day,
if the neighbors knew the thoughts I have
    they'd beat me up an put me away.

※

A terrible disaster befell me
long ago, no newsy story,
I was in love, my love was not requited,
I missed the easy boat of happiness,

since when many a thing possible
to those who have been fortunate in love
has been impossible for me who lack
conviction the world is ordered for the best.

A disastrous and terrible simple fate
I share in common with many other folk
and maybe we had all been better off
if we had died then when our hearts were broken.

※

SIRENS

Piercing sweet the trio thrilling
woo the sailors more than willing
    and on they come with rowing pressed
    while Vesper blazes in the west.

Half on a rock half in the brine
    a body lies: the fishes are
eating its ankle at the water-line,
    shaking the reflex of the Evening Star.

※

Where is she now and whose is she
my 'Ginny the 'Ginny
who was a world to me
and all the world to me?
but mistakes and trifling
that turned from sweet to bitter
were suddenly all greater
than our little love dying.
Our little home has monstrously
into two places grown,

and our little daughter doesn't know
into which doorway to go.

✵

A SPHINX

Here sullen lies their marriage bed,
they lie apart, in pain and hatred.

Never in foreign lands where none
spoke English was he so alone

nor she so pale with guilt and fear
in schools where they mistreated her.

The sheets are rumpled not from kissing
or making love but sleepless tossing

after they have lain an hour
immobile on the bed of fire.

Let us survey this Sphinx, this riddle:
there is like a chasm down the middle

in which have fallen into hell
years of their only youth—the yell

considerately muffled as they try
to sleep a little before day.

✵

ANIMAL SPIRITS

Sometimes since you don't love me any more
    I cannot find an animal spirit

to move my feet,
    or one quits and leaves me in the street
among the traffic's fearful roar

as if I were deep in thought, but I'm not
    —until the animal spirit that preserves
    me still alive
    takes care of where I am and slowly drives
my feet their way across the street.

※

What have I lost, having lost your love?
    Very little, very little.
    Busy with your private riddle
you did not have much love to give.
        Always you were impractical
        and came late or not at all.

I have lost caring for you hurt,
    long days of dread for you,
and guilty second thoughts that
    my influence was bad for you,
        but I was frank with you! to whom
        now I shall not show this poem.

If I begin tonight to cry
    I shall not soon stop crying.
Every day that passes by
    I am nearer dying.
        You cared for that, why I know not,
        but having lost your love I've lost it.

✻

SENTENCES FOR MY MOTHER, WIFE, AND WORLD

Cuckold by my mother
and cuckold by my wife
and cuckold by my world my only one,
most of what I do is deny it
while my soul is blindly wandering
where there are echoes of wailing.
Do I truly care for that
so much any more?

Forty years I spended
glaring at what I loved
until I stopped loving
my world my only one.
We have commenced to live
on civil speaking terms
since I do not care for that
so much any more.

✻

SENTENCES

I won't give thee my come
since thee does not regard it
the cream of my hot loins
some silly boy that I
picked up cares more for this
than my royal wife,
I have been spendthrifty
and thee has been ungrateful.

Let George do it let Jim do it
let Tom Dick and Harry do it.
As for me, I'll bawl my nothing
my ancient nothing where
there is no ear to hear.
Midnight is my mother.
I'll write her my complaint
on a yellow end of paper.

For some men fly the mail
between the clouds and the stars
and some are shrewd to garner
the things that money can buy,
I have among the Americans
the gift of honest speech
that says how a thing is
—if I do not, who will do it?

AT STANFORD

John said (he cared for me),
"Now get some sun, take it easy.
But no, you'll overwork as usual,
I'll get the sun before you will."
He was wrong, he fell in a rage
and they have put him in a cage,
while I lie here by the lagoon
with my shirt off in the sun
at Stanford College in the west.
My sexless spirit knows no rest
thinking of John who cared for me
and told me to take it easy.

A BAR IN NEW ORLEANS

In the amber light and black
    through the cigarette smoke
of the twelve potent faces
    softened to their vices
only Carl was one
    of the original sons
of Genesis, not to be sure
    Adam but the sore
runaways who yet had
    commerce with God
in the woods, and his crown
    of curly black hair shone.

COMMERCE *(MANNER OF WORDSWORTH)*

I wrote a book *The Dead of Spring* no publisher
would publish, so I published it myself
my generous friends subscribing and I have,
believe me, many copies to dispose of.
And yesterday I met in Tom C.'s bar
a gentleman from Georgia oh a rich one
descended from bankers of Napoleon
whom at the customary forty percent
gladly I sold a copy for two bucks,
the only money I made in New Orleans.
This money I have spent on Jack, a hustler:
he boasted he would eat two dozen doughnuts
but ate fourteen and a fat French bread
and drank a quart and a half of orange juice,
otherwise he had not a wide discourse.
I gave him six bits for the picture show

and cigarettes, of which he chose my brand.
Such was the commerce of *The Dead of Spring*
and the cotton-dealer that I met from Georgia
and Jack a brawny youth who shared my bed.

🌿

A HUSTLER

"No, Ronny, sit and talk.
Let's skip the sex. I'll buy your beer.
What good are your muscular arms
if you won't hold onto me?
I see your cock is hard
but you'll lie there like a lamp post."

Yet he was not ridiculous.
He kept his glum green eyes averted.
They looked at me dartingly.
His forehead was perplexed.
His solid frame was mute
but had a mute appeal that was alive.
He didn't want to go away. I said:
"Try to say it. What are you thinking of?
I'll find you words." I guessed that he would bawl
if father treated him gentle for a change.

He said, "I'm not thinkin about anythin.
Ast me a question so I have somethin to say.
Mostly when I sit like this I am
not thinkin about anythin at all.
Maybe I'm thinkin about so many things
I dunno what I'm thinkin about, it's sub
conscious, maybe."
                    "Don't you ever cry?"
His eyes were scalding hot; connecting sentences
opened the abyss of making sense

which he could ill afford. "Naw, I don't cry."
"What's bad about crying?" "Nothin's bad,
only you ast me, no, I never cry."
"Don't you feel like crying now, Ronny?"
"Naw, I don't feel it," Ronny said and wept
—one tear and panicked. "Why do you bother?
why is everybody innerested in *me*?
I'm just one o the fellers."
                              The conceit
shone brilliantly out of his sidelong leer,
he waited baited for a compliment,
his long hair was combed Puerto Rican style.

"Suppose you could, what would you like to do?"
"You'll laugh at me," he said. "No, I won't laugh."
"I'd like to be an actor." "Marlon Brando?"
"I don' need to imitate Marlon Brando,"
he said indignantly, "I'll act myself!"
"Why don't you?" "I am waitin to be discovered."

꙳

FOR G., AET. 16

"You're beautiful," I said, "I love you."
I met him half an hour ago
but he was and I did—
there were above a hundred thousand people
at the party and he was a bar-tender.
"Am I?" he said, "I don't know what to say—"
Since he didn't know me at all
he could hardly know that I was serious,
that I hoped he would be happy
as he no doubt deserved
because of his blue eyes and flowing hair;
and I wished that I could be one
who would make him happy.

I entertained even the wan idea
that I too in being one
to make him happy might be happy.
Instead I gave him my little lecture
on how to live cheaply in Hawaii
which isn't where I am going
and I kissed him despairingly
on the mouth and he said good-bye.
"Maybe," he said, "we'll see each other
another time." What did he mean by that?

꽃

Gene, John, Jojoy, Jerry,
Lor, and Hal were lovers I had
and all we were rarely merry,
sometimes we were sad.

Trusting, we were not betrayed,
shrewdly enough we sought our chances;
mathematically unmade
we were, by times and distances.

But now the circumstance and duty
that hurried us and harried us
are no more, but abide the beauty
and attentiveness that married us.

Oh the beauty and the madness and the strangeness
of my six lovers astonishes me
as I murmur their names I used to say
aloud on better mornings than today.

LONG LINES

It is not the same to eat candy and to sit down to a dish
    of candy and eat it.
It is not the same to get drunk and to buy a bottle
    in order to get drunk.
I tried to make love in the alley but they wanted
    to go to bed behind locked doors.
I have a bad reputation, they say I have no regard
    for persons
but I have paid fierce attention to each one of
    (hopefully) my simple friends.

ON THE BUS

Grinnin' an' singin'
    an' a hard-on in yo' pants
you gentle black boy
    what you been takin'?
where'd you get it
    'cause I'm hard up to be hard up.
I used to know a song
    but I swallowed in my throat.
Ladies, don't get scairt
    out o' your silly wits
he's high an' I am curlin'
    limp between my legs.
When I was ten and five
    I would've sprang alive!
an' *Stardust* was my song
    my inspiration.

MAKING LOVE, III

My world my only one, whom must I love
if I so hard persist and pursue
to become a happy man with you
just you, with only you, my obsession,
and I cannot imagine
another possibility than to make
such idle passes at my only world.
But you are coy, you make it hard
(as if we hardly knew each other)
even to declare my honorable intentions
and then you tell me, "Take it easy, guy!"
This I despise
and kick a rock along the road in rage.
I am beforehand disappointed
and late at night I end up sobbing
on the shoulder of my only one my world
for here you are—where else would you be?
"Whisper to me." What word must I whisper,
lovely, and what flower shall I bring?
where must I stand and wait to catch you in the mood?

LILACS

Young ass, is nothing like it! no,
neither April is as welcome
nor lilacs with their heart-shaped leaves
are not so fresh, nor is melody
so wholesome though men feed on music
and hum a tune while they make love.
But I can't tell you which is best!
music, lilacs, or young ass.

Lilacs with their heart-shaped leaves
are like young ass, soft and showy
in the back-yard where the laundry
blows in the breezes and the dog
can't stop barking, it is maddening
maddening! my reputation
never survived the April day
I sold my reputation for a song.

Long ago I sold my reputation
for a song, I never did regret it
for my song keeps singing on:
"If I can think it," I decided,
"I can write it down, and if I write it down
I'll publish it!" so I decided
one April day of bright young ass
and lilacs with their heart-shaped leaves,

and my song keeps singing on
though the rain is falling on my middle-age
and the dogs keep barking, it is maddening,
about my heels. I cannot shoo them,
nor no young ass ever in my back yard;
but the lilacs with their heart-shaped leaves
are glowing in the tender rain
in the slant shadows of the harrowing rain.

❧

I planned to have a border of lavender
but planted the bank too of lavender
and now the whole crazy garden
   is grown in lavender

that smells so sharp and heady
of lavender, and the hue of only
lavender is all my garden up
   into the gray rocks.

When forth I go from here the lust
I squander—and in vain for I am stupid
and miss the moment—it has blest me silly
   when forth I go

and when, sitting gray as these gray rocks
among the lavender, I breathe the lavender's
tireless squandering, I liken it
   to my silly lusting,

I liken my careless indefatigable
lusting to the lavender which has grown over
all my garden, banks and borders, up
   into the gray rocks.

❧

PRIMROSES

Some primroses I never picked
   (so they wouldn't wilt), the idea
of these pink flowers O permit me
   to give you, my not present dear.

The pink flush of these thoughtful primroses
   is the color of my grave surprise

when I do not laugh or weep at plays
    but watch how they are made, with enthralled eyes.

꙼

WHITE DOGWOOD

Pink dogwood is too beautiful
it makes me yearn for the reunion
of the separated and I hurt.
But dogwood white is my bland joy
I look at with an open face
of wonder in the sunlit woods
just on the border of the possible
and this doesn't make me unhappy.
A branch of dogwood blossoms
I sent to Davy Drood
to whom I gave my trust entire,
it was not he or I betrayed it.

꙼

ODE FOR AN ADULTEROUS COUPLE

For the illicit temporary joy
of this couple grinding against censure
that will prevail, for they themselves
approve what disapproves themselves;
nor will their hectic warmth knit or mature
anything enduring among our friends
but only incense discord and enmity—
and yet they must, just to live on a while—

shall not I, therefore, make it the occasion
to say in poetry the public word

that countenances and ennobles
because we say it on authority?
Weddings do not need epithalamia,
use and law gird them around, yet poets
contribute to the ceremonies;
but adultery is speechless and frail,

it hides in the corridor or timidly
brazens it out, the target of envy,
living on chance and so will languish
when three mischances happen in a row,
nipped in May by the Northeaster. So
be blest and happy, ————and————,
lovely (as lasting) as the darkly fiery rose
he gave to her, and she wore girlishly.

Look, sinking after the retreating sun
the lurid planet Venus shows her hour
over the rooftops reawakening
ideas of lust, if any let them lapse,
and night that mentions nothing offers now
opportunity to the conspirators
who have made an agreement where to meet
in the dark, on the abandoned dock.

A LITTLE EPITHALAMION
FOR A WEDDING AT OUR SCHOOL

Dragging its feet the spring
across the ragged grass
is April like a flash
and thick as thoughts the sparrows wing
into the sunrise of
Amy and Lew in love.

300

Now loosed the streams like incorrigible girls
meander where they must not go
and like bad boys the gales blow
across the world in swirls
this wayward morning of
Amy and Lew in love.

In the original colors lit
in Paradise to heat man's soul
the flowers of the field are slowl-
y burning to nothing bit by bit
through the long midday of
Amy and Lew in love.

With one paw raised and bared his teeth
my dog is arrested by the hush
of dusk, and in the whispering brush
the hare has vanished like a breath.
Sudden is the evening of
Amy and Lew in love.

Night speaks not. From pole to pole
the Milky Way flows motionless
and every star without distress
exists and all together roll,
the speechless midnight of
Amy and Lew in love.

꽃

A LITTLE ODE

What beasts and angels practice I ignore
but the best of human use is careless love,
    and surely bravery and cunning merit
    the prize, that are the method of success.

Congratulate us, friends, as home we speed
and play us music when the train arrives,
    for we outwitted obstacles
    and joy seduced and made us fearless.

"Happiness, not only the reward
of virtue," said Spinoza, "is itself
    a virtue." For we squander satisfaction
    whence there is much, disarming envy.

᭙

HURRAH!

Taylor, Don, Jim and John
hurrah! it is my lucky year!
for even in these dismal states
where Nixon and Kennedy are candidates
I found me something practical to cheer:
Jim! John! Taylor! Don!
Now let the envious and grim
who slander me, look at these
gifted and loyal beauties,
Don, Taylor, John and Jim!

I long between success and failure
hovered, but God with His large hands
and broad grin burdens me with garlands,
John and Jim, Don and Taylor,
hurrah! and if my busy pen
has well deserved of America,
to my amazement she has given
me of the best she has, hurrah!

For some can't and some stall
but we friends are practical,
and when I have been at a loss

my four friends have come across.
The effort people put into
deciding whether or what to do
is better used in showing how,
and fucking, and cooking chow.

But you young men, a storm of
gratitude and confusion
baffles me. I know you love
me just to sustain a while yet
your old artist and champion.
I stand before you with bowed head.
What now must I invent or fight
in order not to let you down?
teach me, for my classic wit
is out of touch with your new spirit.

※

I love you Donny
Peters your appearance
out of the night
in your wooly hat
and rough short coat
coming an errand
in my dark house
shone like a brief star.

When Urgent my prick
and Squirmy my
white body want you
and Heat the wild
pal of my youth
who badly scorched me
again like a ghost
dancing blazes,
my heart has stopped

you cannot share
my lust, yet you
abide my need
bitterly spent,
loyal friend.

So, very cheerfully
my fatherly
harness assume I
for this young fellow
whose eyes often
flash gratitude
he cannot speak,
whose pointed grin
makes me welcome.
Creator of the world,
make him again like Adam
and Holy Spirit
fill Donny Peters' sails.

Holy Spirit fill
Donny Peters' sails
and forward springtime
favor him to joy;
but me to glory favor
that suits unhappy years,
put on my brow a wreath
of Mayday mountain-laurel
and in my hand a branch
of dogwood from the grove.

✴

A CHESS GAME

The chessboard was reflected in her eyes.
Eager to win, first I looked in her eyes.

I made a Spanish move, an ancient one,
and broken was the red rank of pawns in her light eyes.
Then I lowered my eyes from that chessboard
and Love said, "Oh not her; conquer the king if you can."

My eyes I lowered to the checkerboard
planted with lords in particolored fiefs.
My red soul hated the black chesspieces
and first my knights flew forth, to dominate.
I hovered over the pattern like a hawk
and Art said, "Do not win. The pattern is enough."

Then the chess-game became luminous
and then I was not and then we were again,
and suddenly into the center came
of that luminous crisscross of mathematical
possibilities the Angel Fame
whose left wing was love and his right wing was death.

米

BUDDHA AND SHIVA

I. BUDDHA

This young man simply loves me, he
laughs because of me,
softening his angry mood.
I know myself, I'll do him good,
God grant it a long space.
Today when he lay in my embrace
there reappeared to my joy
his face of a mischievous boy,
and we each other's breath breathed in
till we fell back weak and drunken.
He is good to look at, touch, and taste
and placable and grateful and modest.

All this is so. Yet no hope
revives in me. I cannot cope
with a likelihood of happiness,
I have no future in success
but only dumbly to say "More!
more!" and not grow rich, being poor.
Except I hold it in my hands
I have nothing, and I make amends
for holding it by going away.
Yet when I come another day
my fears are groundless, my lover is glad;
in spite of me I cannot be sad.

Now being so has given me,
though not the reality, the idea
of the immense Buddha flustered
blushing, confused, sweetly pestered
by the great Universe he fostered.
And lo, for an instant I
am stoned by the humility
of not through thick and thin
controlling everything.
Both of us are at sea
and would to God we could be happy.

II. SHIVA

He scatters flurries of gentle rain
    and green leaves wears and yellow flowers,
he blows softly into the brain
    Desire, the devil that devours,
        he comes lightfooted at a march
        and sweetly blows the bugles of March.

Open the veil, and appears
    with diagonal eyes of meditation
the god that for a thousand years
    was not. Without a word or question

his level look accepts how we
look upon him hungrily.

Longing woke him up. His wrath
is sudden: blasted to the hell
of being is March. The heavens fell
and Longing has gasped out his breath.
The fist of Shiva's anger still
quivers where it fell to kill.

❧

A PRAGMATIC LOVE SONG

If I needed you I'd make the effort
not to lose you, John,
instead of being quick to quit
at every threat to my peace or pride.

I guess I never liked you
enough to risk missing you,
and yet I need you to need me
so I can come across and be in love.

The truth is it's God I need,
something to work in space and time,
a proof my only world is practical,
and you are real to me my proof

my difficult! my practical!
Proof? "Oh it's a mighty poor theory
that can't abide a couple of facts
to the contrary," said William James.

O practical, how skeptically
without illusory pangs of hope

we act in faith that we shall have
one future day an endless hour!

how generously, in the limits
of duty and honor, still I throw
myself away by the handfuls
on you who still repay me

with looks of love so burning
from your wintry pallor
I am confounded, but
speechless I am not

to whom is given to declare
among the Americans
just how a thing is,
and what I say I do.

※

Woman eternal my muse, lean toward me
again from heaven for these
comforters on the earth have died
or left me, and none others please.

You were Ariadne my leader
to where the monster lay,
I met him there, and you restored
me forth unscathed under the sky.

Three-person'd Fate, who draw my thread
and measure out and cut its length,
passing along from hand to hand
I rest assured in their strength.

I know you as Persephone
the queen of Hell and Flowers

who idly guide my course
to where is only guessed by me.

My limbs are shuddering
but I am not afraid
for it is I the requiem made
for those who died in the Dead of Spring.

MY FAMILY OF ARCHITECTS

※

The harmony of tones to me
   finally is lovelier
   than English does not compare
nor reasoning, even the speedy
middle term and definition pat
    as well I can; but chords of song
    content also the restless longing
of my bowels, when I am sitting at
our old piano adding one deep tone
    to the arpeggio or from a chord
    pruning an unnecessary third,
and look up noticing the day has flown.

※

A CLASSICAL QUATRAIN

For rage and dignity no words compare
with the Atlantic Ocean lashed by winds;
the love-gestures of juveniles are sweeter
than any words of mine. But for alcaic

speed and in the end a pat surprise
you must read Horace. John, the fertile fields

and the repetitive factories produce,
though many other things, no metaphors.

Sure, many a labor is heavier to do
and profit by than stanzas, but these are
my skill, shall I ungratefully
my gift of formal speech disdain?

By literature Scheherazade a thousand
midnights his prone violence appeased,
the homicidal hurry in his soul
embarrassed into an uncertain smile.

꽃

SENTENCE FOR DONNY BERRY AS THE DRIVER IN *STOP-LIGHT*

When Donny Berry fell to his knees
and crossed himself and saw the ghost,
Goodman was thunderstruck: the truth
he wrote was real in flesh before him.
His lips were dry, he could not swallow,
for grace had embodied terror.
Unhappy poets, beware to hear
your very speech real before you.

꽃

MY FAMILY OF ARCHITECTS

Sally found the leak
and I fixed the pump,
in a fit of distraction
Percy re-invented shoes.

We made a lovely wampum
border for the sweater
and tiled the fireplace
with a thunderhead and a moon.

Make do with what is,
not shy to invent it!
"the American Family
Goodman!" laughed Alice

(to my embarrassment
Mathew repeats it)
our family of architects
who think up something!

For the beautiful arts
are made of cheap stuff,
of mud and speech
and guts and gestures

of animal gaits
and humming and drumming
daylight and rock
available to anybody.

    🌿

FOR MY BROTHER
(MANNER OF PINDAR)

I.

By strings and pipes
speech used to be embellished
but I unmusically
my brother praise
though as of old he closes loose

space until it glows like silver.
Poems are pale in sound and use,
the spiritual art degenerates,
but crafts are usefully renewed.

With compasses and square
he has steep up a slope
designed these variations
of iron and glass
where when blood-red the days grow late
heavily breathe into the western
dining-rooms the used-up suns
falling, and the windows blink and flash
signals. What is the message?—

an artist is lucky who is busy
with what is necessary! He
invents what people do not know they want
but they see it come to be with surprise,

II.

pleased in the end.
So was the smithy Vulcan
lucky though lame.
Greeks understood that Beauty and Toil
need one another: by decisions
made in lust in the dead of night
a man lays out a boulevard direct
and dares a dome instead of sky.

No craft's without
the marriage of love and labor,
for, brother, as we are
embarrassed in the day
how shall we make the day alive?
But an irresistible unwonted
lust has created an offspring!

Naturally loud is praise! (why do I try
to aim beside a Theban archer?)

Scening the choreography
of society and solitude
with rectangles and yellow, red, and blue
and, whence things grow, the void, O go

III.

prudently, architect!
for as you draw we move.
Let no cross-eyed surveyor
injure these houses'
alignment, nor dishonest mason
skimp, nor carpenter improvise.
Be accurate to a good plan,
until it looms between the sand and stars
when quiet is the night.

We are a family
of architects, who marry
the crafts and an idea;
again my son and daughter
can see that what is built
was thought up by a man
for it was thought up by their kin,
they having seen a picture of the future
before it stands upon the earth.

But I, before the people come,
shall I discover how the people
may freely love and yet have peace? or must
our likelier children fight it out?

1934: A TRAIN WRECK AT SIXTY-SIXTH STREET

The iron El stood overhead.
Bronze Dante like a man of God
in the green triangle stood.
"Listen," thought I to the crowd
milling about,
"he wants to speak—" but the railroad
was growling and my thought
I could not yet speak out.

A pigeon on his copper head
sprang and sank therein his feet.
A living silence spread.
"Look," I whispered without breath
to the deaf,
"the metal man is quiet
in this clamor of death
like Ser Brunetto's shade
in the whirlwinds and the heat."

Snorting sparks, the train came forward.
Dante like a sword
raised his arm without a word
and the dragon cowered
and hid his light behind his shoulder;
he clambered down on haunches awkward
and crouched where Dante petted his deep-scarred
forehead gently. I stood proud,
I have had my reward.

GOLDBERG VARIATIONS

My memory of Harold Samuel
is fingering this packed counterpoint
unsmilingly with tact unusual
in the service of Sebastian Bach.

He's dead, Bach lives. Bach's dead, Music lives.
Music is dead unless the Spirit makes it live.
Inspire us, Holy Ghost, that all mankind may live.
My memory of Harold Samuel.

Listen. How closely are the following notes,
until we know not which is death or life
—what great chords! and forward—march!
My memory of Harold Samuel.

And tender song but oh surprisingly
different, and is it peace or tears,
peace or tears, which is it peace or tears?
My memory of Harold Samuel.

FOR JANET FAIRBANKS
(WITH NED ROREM)

Janet sang our songs because
(no other cause) she loved to sing
and loved our songs and loved for us
to make up songs for her to sing.

We loved to make up songs, we loved
Janet to sing the songs we made.
What shall we now make? death has made
her mute, has made us dumb. If we

make up a quiet song of death,
who now shall sing this song we made
for Janet Janet not, because
(no other cause) she loved to sing?

꙼

A SENTENCE FOR LAO-TZE

"Heaven cannot help being high
the earth cannot help being wide—"
I am awestruck by these words
of the yellow sage. I cannot—
I cannot help stammering
this speech of gratitude
with graying head bowed
like an old slave set free.

꙼

A CANDELABRUM
OF JACQUES LIPCHITZ

Our hands reach empty, hungrily
—there is no oil.
Thou givest in each hand a light.

More than justice, yet Thy mercy
is not gratuitous,
is wrested by our will to live.

Our arms are powerful, our lifted
hands are helpless.
Thou givest in each hand a light.

Ow! what shall *we* do with these curly fires?
   we did not think
to hold the miracle in hand.

FIGURES OF GIACOMETTI

There are figures of Giacometti
and a narrow head "I look."

Approaching and not noticing—going past
not noticing going past—approaching—missing.

I look along them and they are converging
nowhither neither whence they came.

Some seem aware they have gone past,
I look behind and they are looking back,

missing. The figures of Giacometti.
I look past them and they are looking past.

AN ANTIPHONY OF GABRIELI

He dared (what brass!) to bring the sea inside
St. Mark's was wide enough to harbor her.
The Duke dismissed his ring into the water
and took the Adriatic home his bride.

Northern furs and the stiff stuffs of glory
clothed their thews and did not weigh them down;

presumably their cocks were glad enough
for such a bridal and such a bridal song.

Were there such things? animals to assume
simply the magnificence that we wear well?
play it again! and I'll burst with pride
and my glad smile with a puff ignite.

Even so, without disparagement
of those admirals and merchant-sailors, we
we are the first and second generation
to fly the air and indicate the Moon.

❧

FOR L.v.B.

These, afterwards, monumental wrecks
horrible but not worse, nor otherwise,
than we predicted and consoled already
with such consolations as we wrested,
reject and rage, accept and bawl, and so forth
—when only the unloss would now have served,
that cannot be.

They cannot understand why thee is dear,
had never, no, not once! the loving-care
that we forbid, affright, or disallow
—but what kind of care is that, that we can nullify!
vulnerable to many things, not help!
It is as equal torture either
to notice it or not to notice it.

✺

The gaunt and fumbling style of acting out of
    desperation.
We do not have furs, lace, or cloth of gold
or anthems or address or gallant looks,
but we have the gaunt and fumbling style of
    acting out of desperation.

✺

MOZART'S CONCERTO IN D MINOR

What is the young man trying to tell me,
that he says clearly but I grasp poorly?
He's young and long ago—I have more world
but he lives nearer to my only world,
more intimate with the only world there is,
and what is the young man trying to tell me?
Is it always only death and shuddering?
but the coda is sardonical, what's that?
Maybe he is telling about hell
—that I cannot conceive—close to his eyes,
O my sweet angel, tell me, is it hell
close to your eyes? and singing to burst your heart
sweetly as, they say, the nightingale.
I do not grasp, have not experienced it.
People have told me that, though generous
and kind, I do not know it, do not fear it,
and so am callous to their real troubles.

ORPHEUS AND MOZART

The *Sinfonia Concertante in E-flat* exists
and by this token Fiddles, the happy brother and sister,
have entered in Creation like things of the Six Days.
Now Violin and Viola have a shadow in the stars
their strains and pizzicati beaming and falling bright
from Vega blue in Lyra heavy dews that drip
on the meadows on May-night.
                                                This all the gods approve;
but Orpheus that awful demiurge who stretched
animals lifeless on Cos except for their greedy ears
and people lay like dead until the spell was past,
speaks up in a stern mode unaccompanied
while the spheres hesitate to turn: "O Wolfgang Mozart
you have adventured on the sounds that always were
so they shall always like the first time sound,
and sounded who can quiet them or ever hear them not?
This piece in E-flat is miraculous
but, young man, are you wary for the broken human heart?
It is not with impunity we clang the spheres.
Consider it, young man: they who see too clear,
they who feel too much and speak too plain and well
ought to take care what they declare, for it is not
compassionate to mention what cannot be remedied.
But you, alas, have in you to revel in your wide-eyed
stupefaction speaking out of a white face
not stammering but shuddering with chattering teeth
a concerto in D-Minor and a quintet in G-Minor
and frightful Statue music more than needs—for what?
What advantage is it to say what no one ought to hear
nor is there a remedy between nothing and the sky?
Men will listen blank with horror and not applaud.
Music feeds on applause. Oh it is better far
to wreathe as you can spring garlands for Persephone
or dig in diamond-mines for the Plutonic fire;

best is to imagine wordless dances for Apollo.
Otherwise be still."
                    But Wolfgang Mozart says,
"Nor is it by choice that I rejoice in panic.
I cannot breathe. I know how I shall shortly die,
it has me by the throat, in the death-rattle
I am simply gasping out, croaking, these songs."

≱

The ending of *Tristan* will be interrupted
again by the discord
but the ending of *Otello* never never
never again will be interrupted.

≱

CLASSICS

Suppose *you* would invent a universe,
would you ever strew the Milky Way
or make the mammals fuck and generate
the way they do, so improbably?
On such a scale, in such detail,
it carries you away, how can it fail?
constantly daring. But if you figure
this is a galaxy, the sun a star,
fucking rearranges RNA,
et cetera, et cetera,
it turns out nearly as it is,
this extraordinary production
almost the only world conceivable.
Every classic, Jim, is odd,
stupendous, not altogether sane,
but through and through all of a piece.

※

THE PAST

Every gain has its loss, not every loss
     its gain but sinks into the waste
the primal pain unplastic the chaos
     without a future the astounding past

O monument of agony! if I could
     carve you a few hacking strokes
unfinished, you'd be worthy to be stood
     in Florence among the other rocks.

※

The Great Bear in the tingling sky
     I want to take and hoard for my own,
I am thwarted and I feel abused
     that I cannot. See, how every one

enjoys that beauty, only I
     am deprived in the darkness of the night,
I bitterly climb to my room
     and huddle in the sheets and write,

write my complaint till I forget
     the causes of my pain
in excellent sentences I make
     better than any other man.

※

We had a family vase
made in Bohemia, of glass

of ruby, of gold leaf, with blue
eyes as I look at you;
a vessel used to show off
the bouquets that the suitors brought
to mama, bloody roses, or
when we came back, we four
—this was before Arnold died—
the cornflowers of the countryside
so many hanging there like smoke.
Now this vase I was dared and broke.
And now my art is never enough
though I have wrote the Facts of Life
and made the ram of Isaac dance
and mourned for Arthur dead in France.

※

In fear and trembling and clarity of sight
among my enemies accusing me
whatever my tongue forms to defend me
is nailed inside my mouth.
What I most lately and most surely know
I do not have the ability to say,
so they keep darting arrant stares
and pointed words that I cannot ward off
and turn to each one after he has struck.

※

RED JACKET (LAKE SENECA)

I made a poem Monday
how the wake flows away in the water,
but Tuesday I spent making resolutions

how to survive the rest of the week.
The creator spirit breathes in me short breaths
only enough for some effort or other,
I am inadequate to be
a lover and a husband
a teacher and a friend
a man alive and a man of letters
not any of these and not them all
I cannot work it, I am beat.

So have I, as I crouch here in my boat
powerfully gasping my short breath,
summoned, as is my wont,
the local spirit to confer:
if maybe the influence of rocks
of lapping laughing waves
the far-off roaring of a falls
can quiet my revolving wits.

It is the Seneca Red Jacket
the orator (those dead were trapped
under the ledges in the depths
their bloated bodies never rose).
Smiling is he! pleased to be remembered
decked in sunny blue cornflowers
and hovering butterflies, otherwise naked,
in his scalplock one yellow quill.

"What must I do, Red Jacket?"
I ask without preamble
because I do not know
and we have no small talk.

Red Jacket answers, "Go away.
Quit cares for which you do not care
pleasures you don't yearn for
safety from empty fears.
Go find out where you are

who you are, what you are
You are not here, go go
away! away—away—"

his voice is drifting away
and I am drifting away
the water is eagerly gurgling
the lapping waves that laugh for joy.
"We men of gifted speech!" he murmurs
and his voice is like the present
the rainbow in the falls!
unchangeable and bright
while the future vanishes past:
"We men of gifted speech!" he cries,
"we aren't lonely when we are alone
we find out what is interesting
otherwise how are we orators?"
His smiling face is full of teeth
his pride is thrilling, why am I afraid?

"Devil! go back to hell!"
I shout across the roaring falls
"why do you tell me the advice
I give in my own heart
early in the morning
before I have sunk awake?
that Nature is against my way
which I will to make only to win
nor do I win."
                    But my
Red Jacket has advanced vast
like mist up in the falls
uprearing from the pool
he stands in the square rocks.
The thunder of his oratory
is louder than the falls
I cannot hear myself think
his premises are rainbows
and he demonstrates the pool

in a clap of silence
the eye rimmed with brown
with a terrible green center
like a bull's.

⚘

BREAD AND WINE

An empty container that cannot be filled is nothing at all.
    Smash you! *be* nothing.

My hope is no longer hollow
    ow! I am no longer disappointed.

The shards do not reproach me as violent,
    each broken piece has a bright outline.
I love you, immortal contents of the smashed
    empty container that could not be filled.

I am immortal drunken on the raw
    draught of my no longer disappointment.

Who is this tipsy fellow who is dancing,
    dancing for joy as though he were in love?

He has drunken the immortal contents
    of an empty container that could not be filled.

He smashed it on a rock. There on the ground
    the broken shards have each a bright outline.

He keeps repeating how he broke the jug.

I too feed daily on the non-being of Paradise
    of which a month ago I gave up hope.

So I have put on needed weight
    and people remark that I look younger.

I was distraught with longing for Paradise
    convinced that it was unattainable for me.

I came to my senses about Paradise
      at 142 West 23rd Street
      which building now is down
      and there is a parking lot.

Such is my bread and wine. Creator Spirit,
      let me make a song too, like Yuan Ming
      on his lute that had no strings, he was so poor.

※

    My way of composition is like a beast or fish over
which is cast a net. The animal with unexpected force
—not equal to *my* force, but I should never have hunted
him if I thought he had so much as this—he strains to
writhe away ever in a new direction. Before he was
quiescent, it is the tightening net that has infuriated him.
Writhe as he will, he nevertheless tightens the net: in a
paroxysm he rears up, into a posture unknown and also
against his nature. He tears a few meshes of the net. Next
moment he dies, with his limbs rigid in a fantastic
attitude and on his countenance a grimace. And it is this
grimacing dead body that I would offer to the reader as a
work of art—except that, in fact, it is only the net, with
its unequal strains and a few cords torn, that I have to
offer, for the live animal escaped and the corpse stank long
ago. Were there two?

✲

So far unspooling
a rosy cord
I lightly thread
the labyrinth inward
willingly admiring
the dead along,
walking straddling
like a four-legged bridge.
Wondrous so far, but warily!
for I must in the middle,
well I know it, confront
the Minotaur, myself
armed how? Who then
will give me heart, blind with blood
hoarse with hate,
to fight my way back?
In the crooked claws
of the monomaniac
my space is stiff
and does not stream about me.
Apollo who explain
and mother Aphrodite
forth, though I clench my fists,
woo my staggering steps
—you will, if ever I
made music out of hisses
and lost my will in longing
when my teeth were bared.

✲

TO A QUESTION
OF HELEN DUBERSTEIN

"Are artists schizophrenic?"
They do have a deep rift,
they satisfy themselves so strangely.

Though art-works aren't dreams,
yet this *is* like dreaming,
living in a world that they make up.

But the rift is earlier than schizophrenia,
Helen, cracked before they learned to speak,
their syntax is still leaky.

(Some are afraid that psychoanalysis
will castrate them, but it doesn't happen,
they carry on where they left off.)

With luck they get away with it,
dealing with people by their own rules,
and make a kind of psychopathic adjustment;

without luck they are liable to flip,
without the protection of family
loyal friends or steady jobs

to which, of course, they have never fully
committed themselves. (Don't marry
anything like that.)

Worst of all, if they run dry
—and they have no control of this—
they may jump out of a window.

Nevertheless, since reality
these days is way out crazy,
many artists seem exceptionally sane

trusting to their psychopathic cunning
—nobody's mere dreams
are as unreasonable as the New York Times.

MOUNTAIN MUSIC FESTIVAL

Thin-lipped, dead-pan
expert and energetic
are the melodious dulcimer
and the five-stringed banjo,
and quick and young heel and toe
the square dancing too
is not joyous nor joyless,
its calls are like talking
curtly to a well-trained dog,
"Stay Sophie, you stay here."
My heart is fit to break
for this objective music.
The fiddler with a foot
taps time without rubato
and otherwise stands there
stolid and square
with the mountain face
cruel to the niggers,
his baffled dignity
by-passed by history.
But once the measured music stops
that weaves man with humanity
the sullen mountains are strip-mined
to the same screaming vulgarity
as the audience and televiewers.

SENTENCES FOR
GROWING UP ABSURD

What I will I can't
and what I wish I mayn't,

what I ought I won't
and what I must I don't.
It's a non life I lead
past midway to the grave
in my city of New York
in nineteen fifty-nine.

Heavy silence has grown
around me like a wall
and I feel early
shut in my narrow room
where I lie waiting
from the rectangle of sky
the spades of stony earth
to hurtle rattling down.

In this unpleasing plight
I have composed a book
to show how youth is thwarted
by the world we made.
May they who read be stung
by wrath I never felt
for me but for these kids.
Creator spirit come.

STANZAS AFTER *SPEAKING AND LANGUAGE*

I will stand firm and say my say.
I cannot be stupider than I am.
If men do not make better sense
God and I must go it alone.

Yet tears well up, my voice is hoarse
for my citizenly army

in our shining helmets
—vanishing in the mists of waking.

What a beautiful idea
the Reformation was!
Mendelssohn's symphony—we Jews
naturally overestimated it.

From phrase to phrase will I make do
and choose the lovelier lilt of English
ever over the truth.

SENTENCES AFTER
DEFENCE OF POETRY

A man who fixed his eyes
with longing on the sun
might see the sun stand still
while he himself was carried
east on the turning earth
swept blinded into night:
so did I love some one
once, like Copernicus.

Stars are sweeping past me
—I can fix my attention
only on my sick body
and that is not still either,
I am upside down.
They say that God is still
—where? I am too stupid
to understand it like Einstein.

I made a golden disk
like a Keltic relic

that I saw in Dublin.
I do not love it,
it doesn't keep me warm,
but I hide and stare
at it and into it
flat and impenetrable.

It says, "Your eyes are going blind,
you have three teeth and cannot chew,
often you are dizzy.
Yet it is quiet here
in our neolithic cave
and you do love me
although you glimpse I am
a flat evil fetish."

I love the English language.
She has loved me.
I used to stutter, fear stuck
my voice inside my mouth
—my rebel double
fought with me she should speak.
Now I say fearlessly
what I didn't know I knew.

❦

Say my song simply for its prosy sentence,
cutting at the commas, pausing at the period.

Any poetry in it will then be apparent,
motion of mind in English syntax.

I willingly work with true propositions
to hack like wood, I don't like clay.

A platitude is true when Goethe says it,
it lies like iron on the page.

I know that the honesty of how I come on
is the insolent sureness of my heavy strength

but I don't know, I don't, if this has brought me home
to be a simple spokesman of the nature of things.

But I know, I know the chilly passing by
and the crashing presences of death
have made even more circumspect
my speech that was already careful.

❦

FOR MY BIRTHDAY, 1971

It is like a dream that I had a son,
I see objectively how the physician
came up the mountain to the scene
of the accident and shook his head.

I wrote a poem to reclaim
for my own at least my dream
but it became a work of art
in a book for everybody.

It took four years to say good-bye
and see it all objectively,
maybe tomorrow I will be gay
when I fly away to Hawaii.

❦

A cliché was true only the first time it was said.
A platitude is true whenever everybody denies it.

335

When you see it too simply to explain
you must give up teaching the course.

The young complain that I am talking abstractly
and I am saying my intimate experience.

Oh, we call it the artist's Third Period:
some of the chords are already angelic.

But they did not even notice
the omission that made us bawl.

EXILE

✳

HORATIO'S MOURNING SONG

Stateless, yet we have a flag
of the raw stuff the neutral color,
a march without a rhythm or key
our drum and trumpet muted play.

Unarmed, yet we have the power
of when the bottom drops out.
Lonely, loyal, murky-minded,
doubt-free we go our way.

Chuangtze is dead as I shall die
unnoticed by the wayside,
his spirit does not haunt the world
and his death-grip is relaxed.

✳

LONG LINES

The quiet hour when we have put the good-looking dinner in the
    oven
after busy little preparations and pinching pinches of spices

and we step out under the open sky in the green yard, it is
    sundown
quiet but neither still nor silent for the birds are chirping loudly
and the air is softly moving in the leaves, it is cool
—O love, my only one my world, I'd feel so lonely I could die
here in exile now for forty years, nor do I see the end
except for your kindly gestures in the regularity of everyday.
But when, O world, will our arbitrary and inscrutable master
who watches over every one of those chirping sparrows in the
    trees,
when will He recall me to my native home where I have friends?
Come in. The food is baked that I eat salted with my tears.

LONG LINES

The heavy glacier and the terrifying Alps
that simply I cannot, nor do I know the pass,
block me from Italy. As winter closes in,
just to survive I hole up in this hovel
with food that has no taste, no one to make love to
but fantasies and masturbating, sometimes sobbing
South! South! where white the torrent splashes down
past Lugano.
        Yes, I know
I cannot move these mountains, but how did I stray
by cunningly bad choices up among these snows?
Are most of men as miserable but only some
enough communicative to declare how much?
Balked! balked! the dreary snowflakes do not cease
drifting past my window in the demi-dark.

AN APRIL WALK

The end of music is
stillness and the end
of love being alone.
Rest absent from me O
creator spirit awhile
so I may my long-held
illusions reconsider
as I, leaving the others,
follow this quiet path

where weedy it winds brown
among the dogwood pink
and dogwood white, evident
trodden in former times
but now not many come
into the sacred wood.
Here I shall not meet
Adam, and I can listen
to the loud prophet-birds:

"Naa! naa!" they caw, "do not
doubt your lust and art!
Caaw! caaw! you can't anyway!
they have made you not more
and not less than you are!
Aanh! aanh! go on! try
to fashion into facts
the useful thoughts you have
for the Americans."

You evil birds! you cynical
comedians! I shall
—I also know the obvious
future—by the wayside
die in a ditch, and you
peck on my weak eyes

worn out by attending.
"Caw! caw! caw! caw!" they clamor,
"caw! caw! caw! caw! caw! caw!"

※

A VISIT TO BLACK MOUNTAIN COLLEGE, JUNE 1952

They lay as if in ambush to embrace me,
the ones who sadly saw me go away
and those who knew me only as a name.
Alas! they lay in wait to tear and eat
their totem with the callous arrogance
of hungry youth and crowded me their questions
though I was tired to drop—it is my doom.
Insoluble puzzlers about the war
—for the draft was breathing hot on them again—
how to dodge with honor or be jailed with joy;
as usual they were too fastidious
and too imprudent. (I had rougher thoughts.)
Others—or the same another hour—
baffled by sex: one didn't have a hard-on,
another had at the wrong time and place,
as usual; and there were timid girls
who needed babies but they met no fathers.
Yet others—or the same again and again
and oh! by now I knew them pretty well—
brought out their paintings and their poetry
for me to auscultate and teach each one
by showing what he did not know he meant.
So war and love and art were still the themes
that my young ones laid bare before their friend,
till finally I got away to supper.

We equals talked about the community
and this was great and sad, as usual,

340

still promissory, never glorious,
smoking with love that did not burst in flame.
And *still* they had not made themselves the play
we planned to answer the ambiguous Sphinx
that was destroying our community
—although the lake, as usual, lay hushed
and the Smokies ominously stood around
not growing old, but we were growing old.
If I were there, we should have lived that play!
therefore I was not there. I came away—

I came away having seen no new thing,
in tears and pleased because I was much loved,
tired and proud because I was much used,
discouraged because I was not rightly used.

ༀ

MARCH 1954

I have been fighting a grim war with spring
   and I am winning
although this year he did surprise me
   in February
with a patient and electric sun that also
   whether I would or no
endured another day, and this pure raining
   is a sweet thing
as it melts into being and falls out of the air.
   Yet I in my lair
lurking have recovered my advantage
   of willing what I don't want.
By harsh language and well-chosen malice
   I have frozen ice
even where it was not all the black year,
   and we live in fear
because I improvise a threat of danger.

We yet shall see whose banner,
mine or the spring's, will stream in glory
    over April and May!

Nevertheless he clamors with his fife and drum
    freedom freedom
and hot feet itch to march, the slaves revolt,
    the nobles are in doubt,
my Irony Cross and Scar although lovely
    aren't worth the trouble
nor is spite sweet food. O my eventful
    spring! do not be fitful
but lord it on us with a steady care,
    evenly endure.
Do not false-promise like America
    who is my dismay.

✻

FOR MY BIRTHDAY, 1954

Small money and less honor
my native city so notorious and lavish
ever gave me her earnest boy.
A half dozen times I and my brother
proposing with affection and swift thought
what would adorn her, have been slapped in the face
by contentious ignoramuses in power.
Such thoughts are horrible for me,
the facts of my forty-third birthday,
for I am not a lonesome man, I need
a sociable occasion and applause;
otherwise I despond, my aim holds true
but I lose fire-power.
                    Oh, my God,
for the one life and city that I have!
I have fallen out of love with New York City,

her blocks are merely boring till it hurts,
big because at a loss for an idea
the overgrown moron, and she has no sky,
and she has locked Lordly my river out
and faces in across a narrow alley.
Violent men and women in her bars
have an affrighted lust or none
and the adolescents I was eager for
to venture what I couldn't or didn't dare,
just hang around, it breaks your heart
how they have neither wonder nor ambition.
I'll get no epic subject here nor friends
nor even pleasure, why do I persist?
New Yorker theaters want no plays of mine.
Go elsewhere!
                    But I have no other tongue,
not as a poet or a lover speaks
simple in detail, as he paid attention,
and this is what I paid attention to
that never loved me and I no longer love.
My hairs are graying. I have failed, I guess.

꽃

THE FORD
Analects, Bk. xviii, ch. 6

Of the boiling river ripped by fangs of rocks,
on the tranquil shore, in the pink sun, are plowing

bitter Chang, with pity swollen-hearted
and rational Chieh-ni, deep hermits.

And here comes in his dusty carriage
Confucius, humanely wandering

from prince to prince: "These are the rules of Order."
Soon departing! when will his heart break?

"Tze-lu, go ask them where to ford this flood."
The favorite bows low to the lonely sages.

Says Chang: "Is not yon noble with the reins
Confucius?" "Yes, Confucius my teacher."

"He knows the ford! he knows the ford!
he wanders with advice from state to state!"

Says Chieh: "You see the flood! you see the fangs!"
—alas, Chieh-ni! the very shore is rotting—

"disorder like a flood has won its way,
the Empire is raging. Who will change?

who will change? from state to state withdrawing
your teacher is traveling in disorder.

Once and for all withdraw. Is it not better?"
Without another word he falls to plowing.

"I asked them for the ford across the river;
they mention a philosophy of life."

The Master said: "It's impossible to live
with birds and beasts as if they were like us.

If I do not associate with people,
with whom shall I associate?"

LONG LINES

At 20,000 feet, the earth below was overcast
the flat top of the cloud was like a desert dusted with snow.

344

At my sunny porthole I agreed to be resigned
as in a bright hospital where they would feed me well
but like one peacefully dying rather than convalescent.
The sky was royal blue to the skim-milky horizon
and the sun was awash in its own golden light,
I stared at hungry with my weeping eyes.
Then were my cares for my sick country quieted
though not forgotten, and the loneliness
in which I ever live was quieted.
Briefly I dimly saw below the wide meandering,
among the Blue Ridge Mountains, Shenandoah River,
and one friendly sparkle from a wave
like a signal to me leaped across four miles of space
saying "God! God!" or "Man! Man!" or "Death!"
or whatever it was, very pleasantly.

꿏

OCEAN!—

I don't like how I hunger
just for something uncorrupted,
weeping six miles high
just to see idle sparkles
signaling from a river;
inside I must be dying
so frantically to lust for life
above clouds, above eagles.
Indeed, these days my contempt
for the misrulers of my country
is icy and my indignation raucous.
Once American faces
were beautiful to me,
I was their loyal lover,
but now they look cruel
and as if they had narrow thoughts.
Their photographs in *Life*

devastate my soul
as their gasoline denudes
the woods of Indochina.
Let me go into exile
—a poet needs to praise.
It is wicked to live
where I do not care for the people.
What is the use of flailing about
like a wounded animal?
Nothing can come of spite and disdain.
Pilot! please fly on,
do not descend upon my native city.
Ocean!—

WATERS AND SKIES

Waters and skies
hours and seas
are in number plural
before they are singular

and so are gods
joys and sorrows.
But you, my joy
and grief, are singular

like the water from the well
of Bethlehem that David
was thirsty for and other
water was nothing to him,

nor though mankind is my race
can I stay my indignation
at my country's course
as if I had other countries.

Oh I think of leaving here
to go to Crete or Ireland
and what it would be like
to live in a simpler way

but I shall die of my depression
here where I have grown gray,
probably in prison
limited to the last.

Tell me, beautiful,
do any people live
by choices that they make,
or do like me all leap

to the bugle call,
although I just awoke
from a dismaying dream
and the battlefield is a bad one?

But God He is my home
and smiles upon His son
as I write down this poem
in my English tongue.

COMMENCEMENT, 1962

The insulted poor will riot in my city
without community. The air is poisoned
by crazy sovereigns. America
shamelessly has counterfeited
this ring and book.
                    Thwarted as a man
I grow deluded about my importance
because teen-agers look to me for words.

I am in fact confused like the abandoned
hut in the deep woods with dusty windows
and the town far away, the path grown over with
     blackberry bushes.

Nevertheless! hear the tumultuous west wind
restless in the foliage turning white
that will destroy God knows how much of the world
before retreating he whispers Good-bye
my frightened darlings, thank you.
                              He is whining
and sobbing, he will whistle through his teeth
and howl, and the big branches crack and sag
and wither. I remember Shelley's words,
"Make me thy lyre even as the forest is!"
Something is breathing me despite myself,
my speech is frantic.
                    I was too near-sighted
to see the look on the county-leader's face
last night I shouted at him to resign,
and when I called on passers-by on Broadway
"Help! help!" they stood only staring at
each other with impersonal alarm.
Misthrown! I was not meant to be the agent
but the historian of the excellent.

※

1965

The curses that this peasant spat at us
will torment and destroy us
deadlier than the gasoline
we rained upon her family.

I am afraid to be an American.
Even if we were right, no reason is

so final as the shrieking our marines
have listened to and they will carry home.

We read of things like this in history books
and shudder and get sick. Merciful God,
stop us, our leaders have gone crazy,
listen to them talking like computers.

🐝

Where is the little old woman in tennis shoes
    who knew all the annoying facts and figures
and stirred up trouble at the planning-board?
    They humorlessly shot her dead in Georgia.

Up here we used to laugh at her a little
    though she was generally in the right,
she certainly had no head for politics
    being only a little old woman in tennis shoes.

Today we smile at the thought of her.
    Isn't it strange how we are almost pleased
as we affectionately bring these daisies
    to her daughter and her grandchildren?

It must be because she was so old
    and soldierly, and in her way quite perfect,
quite perfect, she was in her way quite perfect,
    and therefore she is in her way quite perfect.

🐝

WASHINGTON, D.C.

I am, like Jefferson,
on the axis but across the lagoon.

SURFERS AT SANTA CRUZ

They have come by carloads
with Styrofoam surfboards
in the black wetsuits
of the affluent sixties,
the young Americans

kneeling paddle with their palms
and stand through the breakers
One World Polynesians
lying offshore
as if they were fishing for the village.

They are waiting for the ninth wave
when each lone boy falling downhill
ahead of the cresting hundreds of yards
balancing communicates
with the ocean on the Way

how beautiful they are
their youth and human skill
and communion with the nature of things,
how ugly they are
already sleek with narrow eyes.

I grew calm
watching the campfire's
rioting flames

but I am frantic
at the golden prophecy
blinking in the coals:

"They who destroyed
the redwood forests
will die in Asia."

God save from them
my son Mathew
gentle with animals.

꽃

AT MICHIGAN STATE UNIVERSITY

I quoted from a knowledgeable scientist
how almost certainly the atom bombs
will blow in 7 years. (He said 15
8 years ago, and we have drifted on
and upped the budgets.)
                    The old chaplain said,
"You're strange. You talk so pessimistically
and yet your tone—the way you are, proposing
to change the schools and so—is optimistic."

I puffed my pipe and mulled it. It was true.
I talk out with a kind of energy.
Now I said hesitantly, "My pessimism
is only on account of evidence."
—We smiled wryly at the epigram—
"Obviously I must have animal faith
or I couldn't sit here!" I shouted.
"It follows I believe in the Messiah,
because the sociologists and statesmen
are not going to do it."
                    He said nothing.

"Who can afford," I ended wearily,
"to be either pessimistic *or* optimistic?

You have to do your duty anyway.
A lot of my energy is rage."

"No, it is indignation," he said kindly.

❀

MARCH 1967

The woods below are still white
    but the streams and peeping puddles
are shiny liquid the springtime
    is breathing and in the blinking

puddles and ponds down there
    torpid frogs are likely stirring,
and many of the April young
    will burn their draft cards up

twinkling across America!
    Oh from three miles high of hope
it is hateful to go down into
    my dirty city but here goes.

❀

MORNING

The sun in front of me
as I ride east is rising
early in the day, we call
it Morning. Here are swans
on the Housatonic. I am bound
for New Haven to lecture the young,

an ambiguous moralist
but my lust is authentic.

My lust is loyal leads me
toward beauty early out.
Oh many do more damage
than I! few want the future
to be so very simple,
this morning on my way to New Haven,
an ambiguous moralist
but my lust is authentic.

I imagine Paradise to be
the beauty that I haven't
yet met in New Haven,
I call it Morning, it is my best map
my city plan where I wander
confused but do not stray,
an ambiguous moralist
but my lust is authentic.

ᛉ

NEW BEGINNING

Loping waltzing marching
happy, quick and proud
and hopping with excitement
we converged on the capital

the bass-drummer beat
and big the brasses blared
our entry was a rout
as if fleeing in disorder

"Peace" was our password
that stung from lip to lip

people spoke in tongues
the future had no shape

we two met in that crowd
that carried us along
I shall not forget the light
of recognition in your eyes

your name is New Beginning
I love you, New Beginning.

APRIL 1966

I see by how the young behave with me
my tired face, my searching eyes
put them off or are grotesque to them.
Yet I persist because my need persists
wooing, sneakily touching
or angrily asking—it is pitiful,
for they seem to like my company
but they avoid being alone with me.
Frustrated I redouble my attempts,
there must be *somebody,* if there are twenty.
My fading mind cannot recall their names.

I am not well. I lie down in distress
to ease my tightening heart. The telephone
rings from Boston, Austin, and Vancouver
colleges inviting me to visit
and be unhappy also there and die.

There it is, and I am quick to say it!
to say again among the Americans
how it is. We poets are like stone.

Give, God, me courage to endure
anyhow, as I have often been
other times in despair and done my work.
Stone is my tried way of being human.

Oh long ago I hoped to be like water
that seeps into low places and lies flat;
blue heaven, a white cloud, and the flock flying north
is the fleeting picture in it
                              —it is springtime
out of my window in California;
happiness would make me healthy here
but the nature of things (and I was a large part)
has in fifty years contrived this trap
in which I lie gasping. Prudently
I wrote thirty books and reared three children
—now it is sprung in April among flowers.

※

1945–1970

Men are under a curse, it is cause and effect,
I am not speaking superstitiously,
since they exploded in the mushroom cloud
the bomb in Japan.
Having put so much mind in it,
they cannot now turn mind away from it,
and they have contaminated to the spell
the mind of the world. It is no longer willed.

Surely some of the scientists foresaw this future,
some of them were wise men as men go,
yet right on busy in the dark they worked.
In the myth, as we tell it to ourselves,
it was Hitler who rent the veil
and let insanity begin to leak

into history. But our sanity
has been precarious for centuries.

Those people never knew what hit them.
Simply, a hundred thousand were atomized
and later the survivors' hair fell out
and then their skin fell off and then they died.
But lo the big surprise
Jack-in-the-Box remains
to preside over the diplomacy
of a new heavens and a new earth.

When my life-time ago I swore
—I've kept the pledge and I am sixty—
that I would never stay in the same room
with persons who mention war as a reasonable policy,
I didn't think that I would one day walk
the alleys of a lunatic asylum
named Deterrence, and my little daughter
will probably be the last generation.

"Whom the gods would destroy, they first make mad"
—yes, but what am I to do
with this fatal proposition
that is not political?

Creator Spirit, of whom I say no ill
and no dismay and you are still my fact,
yet I do not believe that you will spring
wet like the fountain in the waste for Hagar
among these men, for they are mesmerized.
Oh maybe the Messiah will come somewhere
and sound his horn Sleepers Awake,
but I have never had *this* crazy hope.

I do my duty therefore for *no* reason,
as Kant said, just to make sense.
It is easier in great things than in small
that crave joy-food just to live on awhile.

HALLOWE'EN 1969

O goblin with your yellow fiery eyes
and jagged mouth that frightened me to carve,
glaring out of our window at the street,
protect us from the candidates for mayor.

A VOYAGE TO KALAMAZOO,
NOVEMBER 6, 1969

Just as I am, yawning with a sore face,
is how I am alive this day at 8 A.M.,
and my gratitude therefore to the nature of things
always to the point, I say with every gasp.

Our plane is passing over cloudy Pennsylvania
but beyond Erie, says the Captain on the speaker,
we should be able to see down on Ohio
and the polluted lake, crossing to Detroit.

There is the Cuyahoga! the one river
in all the world that is a fire hazard,
too thick to swim, too thin to walk on it,
and this too is necessary for the management
of this universal instant 8:47.

By noon I can look at it in perspective.
Our busy little species has fucked up but good
my available space, but sprawling on a grassy border
of the parking lot, perhaps out of reach of the cars,
if I close my eyes
—as is tip-top these days for seeing in perspective—
the radiant sun is beating down on me
from heaven cloudless across all the Middle West

in the fall of my life crowned with copper oak-leaves
even in Kalamazoo at the Holiday Inn.

So! up against me blotted on the ground
the ground's great palm pushes, and sustains
the heavy weight that I am always falling,
and equipoise this is the very peace
of momentarily the universe
including me communicating
by Isaac Newton's lovely second law
called Rest.
               For me it does not last.
Arise and shine, I say, for you must urge
the high school Superintendents of Michigan
—after a formal lunch—to quit their lousy jobs.

SENTENCES

By boat and train
and car and plane
I went a million miles,
and twenty thousand drivers
brought me home unhurt
—mankind is good at this,
at traveling and conveying
one another home safe.

So thank you one and all
taxi-driver of New York,
navigator, engineer,
pilot of the atmosphere,
even though every year
the food is lousier
and the congested ways
make one weep with rage.

What is to become of
my extraordinary species
in whom I have such pride
and that causes me dismay?
I have loved to cross the sea
to Mauna Loa and Mauna Kea,
yet because of me and mine
there is no room for the Hawaiian.

Brothers, I am sorry
as I get older and wiser
a deepening confusion
is my only proposition
—"No no," says the old man,
"since he undertakes to be
a horse, he must run"
—he beats the nag unmercifully.

Darius, says Herodotus, invaded Greece
because he had a sprained ankle;
these wars are anyway so senseless
it might as well be this,
or that he had ants in his pants.

Karl Marx explains it by business profits
—that hardly ever eventuate.
Maybe it's a lust for suicide
guiltless because they go en masse.
Tolstoy was frankly puzzled.

But that erudite historians
and common folk who should know better
seem to take war for granted,
this I will never understand,
I'm queer. Yes! it must be that.

※

When our demonstration was a dozen
in front of Danbury jail
we furtively collected
—and made a brave loud noise!
—and slipped away in different directions.

When our demonstration was five hundred
in front of the City Hall
we were a resolute band
as we took our stand.
We wouldn't go underground.

When our demonstration was twenty thousand
far up Fifth Avenue as we could see
oh! I was astonished
and had the heady feeling
of being the sovereign people.

Now this demonstration is half a million.
I listen to it on the radio.
The speeches are lousy, they are half-truths.
Somebody I'm afraid has political intentions.
I'd thank them not to plan my future for me.

I'll find out two or three
and picket on the other corner.
I hope, I hope
never to walk alone.
But I'm not getting any younger.

※

Schultz, the neighbor's big black dog,
used to shit on our scraggly lawn,
but we feed him chicken bones
and he treats our lawn like his own home.

The kids of Fulton Houses in New York
smashed windows on our pretty block for spite;
we gave them hockey sticks to play with
and they smashed more windows.

The dog is an anarchist like me,
he has a careless dignity
—that is, we never think about it,
which comes to the same thing.

The kids are political like you,
they want to win their dignity. They won't,
but maybe their children will be friendly dogs
and wag their tails with my grandchildren.

TO MY ONLY WORLD

❧

TO MY ONLY WORLD

My one my world you are no kindlier
but you are fair today; you wear your sun,
in T-shirts your hockey-players run
with sparking shoes; the icicles you wear
are bright, the shadows are as blue as fur,
your girls are speedy as their roadsters turn
into a private road. My weak eyes burn,
I hear the echo of a ringing cheer.

You do not promise anything today
my world my only one, I am content
just to watch wistfully. And my dismay
is very like glory as I slowly walk
away into my solitude intent
and musical and we two frankly talk.

❧

Small in the blue
our yellow kite
whom we dispatched
a spinning letter

and frenzied swung
in seven coils
her knotted tail
is gone, our string
snapt:
        a thousand
meters over
the rough Atlantic
we offer her
to you strong Wind
blow us no ill,
to you rough Sea
where she is drowning.

ᵉ

I thought I woke: the Midnight Sun
    flooded the street among the trees,
    the people floated at their ease
to right and left, I moved alone.

A savage drone, the thrilling air
    of bagpipes poured around the bend,
    the valley echoed end to end,
I hurried after him to stare.

The meaning of dreams in this magic day
    was clear as they befell, without
    the need or use to think it out,
and where the shadows fell they lay:

shapes of gold-leaf that dully burn,
    such shapes the travelers display
as souvenirs when they return—
    "These are the shadows as they lay,

"we gathered them, this jumping mishap
    and this grotesque profile,

this crooked hand is a common shape
   stretching a startling mile."

※

The flashing pigeons as they wheel
   now bright now nothing in the light,
met by the from the other roof
   —long aimless hours of play or fright

—silently loud—Sally! must lead
   elsewhither than they seem to me
—around they wheel now bright now nothing—
   men do not try so restlessly

just to die—and from the other roof
   hundreds silently crying, suddenly
you cannot count the numberless
   glory sprang alive of our city!

stormier than white-faced leaves
   —and quiet like sand dunes in starlight
—wheeling in the sunlight into nothing
   on the left, and on the right—

※

GREAT

"Its true name we do not know. Were
I forced to say to what class of things it
belongs, I should call it Great."
—*Tao Te Ching,* 25

Bright was June but suddenly
our agile shadows vanished
hid or were kidnaped away,
we were confronted by no shadows.

Immediately fell the thunderbolt
I had a leaping shadow,
it rained. In what peculiar conditions
we men and women soberly live on!

The day is periodic with a night
willy-nilly dragged across the sky.
They say I used to live as a larva
in a salt sea in the belly of a beast.

When first the rocky crust of this hot globe
hardened, rain fell down from a dark cloud
hundreds of years in lightning-lurid sheets
and filled up the Atlantic Ocean—Son!

surely this was great! We call a man
great when he is like the olden times,
the fifty-mile-long stormcloud and its rain
great, peculiar, whether we will or no.

THE LORDLY HUDSON

"Driver, what stream is it?" I asked, well knowing
it was our lordly Hudson hardly flowing,
"It is our lordly Hudson hardly flowing,"
he said, "under the green-grown cliffs."

Be still, man! no one needs your passionate
suffrage to select this glory,
this is our lordly Hudson hardly flowing
under the green-grown cliffs.

"Driver! has this a peer in Europe or the East?"
"No no!" he said. Home! home!
be quiet, heart! this is our lordly Hudson
and has no peer in Europe or the East,

this is our lordly Hudson hardly flowing
under the green-grown cliffs
and has no peer in Europe or the East.
Be patient, Paul! home! home!

WELLFLEET HARBOR (*MANNER OF WORDSWORTH*)

I unbelieving saw a white spire far
   on the blue bay and thought I heard its bell,
   but veering in the wind it was a bright sail
instantaneously triangular.
      Again the bell jangled far and clear
      across the water to my astonished ear.

That white sail like a comma in the long
   proposition of the blue bay sped
   toward the bold headland that was blanketed
with furze and dune. I followed where she swung
      around the cape and like a period
      ended, and it was silent where I stood.

DYER'S POND, WELLFLEET

You're a sweet limpid pond
to trudge a mile around
   or swim across you idly
   a mile divided by π.

The hatchets of the boyscouts
ring like rifle shots

through the scrubby pines
where the yellow sun shines,

and through the water where we stand
we see white pebbles in the sand
  and green pickerel about our feet
  nosing if this be likely meat.

༄

A CYCLIST

The young Master of the Wheel at Danbury
absently, both hands, fondling his prick
through traffic thoughtfully—up on the walk
(the curb was broke an inch) before me *was,*
and alighted even as the wheels ceased.
I who ride like a ferocious fireman
thank heaven for this breath of breeze of art,
the hottest noon that ever made Route 6
mirror the forest upside down. But he
arrived with the swoop of a swallow.
I'd speak with him, except his only lust
is in his speedy ease. Now everywhere
by moments and through rips, through the brilliant
curtain of July I spy the Way
whereon we deviate but do not err.

༄

ROWING AND SEEING

The system of the wake
as on and away:
hard astern

is rough in the midst
of the undulating V
widening from the prow,
and parallel on either side
ellipses opening recede
of which one focus is the vortex
where the oar first bit
the other is the vortex swirling
after the stroke two feet deep,
the ellipses following at a man's height apart
are joined by strings of circlets dripping from the oars.

I lay back in my drifting boat
and looked straight up at heaven:
seeing was oval seeing oval shapes,
within the broad-spread oval of eyesight
the sides of the boat sketched out parentheses
across the long open oval of high shores
of Seneca vanishing northward; but
the dark vast oval of closed heaven
vertically overbrimmed my oval of vision
and was one branch of an hyperbola
wide wide away.

FROM A HIGH DUNE

Still—I light my pipe unshielded
quiet—I can hear the Boston mail
immense immense—the bathers bob
in the fringes of the globe-encircling sea.

The cannon of the range at Nauset
are thundering at the blue blinding day.
The rollers are rolling evenly in
from a hurricane four hundred miles away.

AT THE RIM OF THE CANYON

Because its colors and the shadow
kept varying and the toplofty crowns
flamed and faded as if those gigantic
rocks were living and breathing, their foundations
sunken out of sight—although the turbulent
torrent must be down there in his black gorge
like a yellow trout in hiding:

                         wonderstruck
by so much God the folk, as they came south
out of Alaska into Yucatan,
carried with them the supernatural
Grand Canyon that they met upon the way:
they built their pyramids at Chichen Itza
from after-images indelible,
small folk afraid to fall.

CHAMELEONS

Curled in from behind her
lightly her nape in his jaws
the swollen sac in his crotch
from under in her glued
the lizards are immobile.
His crest is flushing bloody brown
his throat is apple-green
otherwise they are pale
pale immobile silent.
Their beady eyes are somnolent
now their eyes are closed.
Slowly his left thigh and the sac
is pulsing half a dozen times
and a gleaming drop exudes where they are fast.

They are asleep, they break apart,
quick lizards, all pale.

꽃

THE DAISY

The daisy standing on her stalk as plain
   as a gawky girl getting up from a chair,
   now lies cut in the grass, her milk-white hair
drooping round her yellow brain,

her milk-white lashes closing round
   her golden eye the daisy is asleep
   where the slow snail and the caterpillar creep
along the grassy ground.

꽃

It froze and the ice in his engine
swelled and cracked the block,
calamity! a hundred bucks
for negligence, nothing but.
"Damn! I meant to drain her!"
Naturally we were sympathetic.
Yet think of it! it was the gentle water
the innumerable drops that have no shape
and so they penetrate the crevices
and now have leaked away in the sun
—in one pulse of power, in one night,
less than three gallons broke that massy iron!
Brothers, do not be desperate
although we live in an age of steel,
see how the gentle water cracked the block!
"Very nice. *Your* car wasn't hurt."

No, I couldn't afford to pay the damage.
"Yeah, *your* jalopy you could put away
in the junkyard!" he explained triumphantly.

No no! my car's a fine a splendid car!
she rolls along on every one of her wheels
fast as you'd care to drive in such a car
and breaks down just as you'd expect a car like that
—what can you expect from a car like that?
I have learned to take the world as it is
and everything is just what it is.
A stupid old age is pressing on me too,
what good are the appearances to me,
what good is speed?

POEMS OF MY LAMBRETTA

I.

This pennant new
   my motorbike will fly:
a sea of icy blue
   and a pale blue sky
      and in the sky the wan
      yellow midnight sun,

Sally stitched for me
   of sturdy cloth
and silk embroidery
   to flaunt when forth
      I roar, so me all men
      may know by my emblem.

II.

My new license plate
is thirty zip six
orange and black
and cost me two bucks.

Castor and Pollux,
from cops preserve me
and all encounters
involving insurance.

Through lovely landscape
guide my wheels
and may my buddy-seat
carry friendly freight.

III.

Dirty and faded
    is the banner of my bike
and tattered in the winds
    of journey like

my self-esteem my soiled
    repute my faded hope.
The little motor but
    briskly roars me up

the hills and not half-way
    like some on Helicon.
Yet I recall a day
    she balked and stood there dumb.

It was no use to kick
    and swear at her. At her
own moment lightly she
    coughs, and off we roar!

on glad our windy way
    nowhere, going forty!
Flapping is my flag,
    faded torn and dirty,

and on the buddy seat
    there rides Catullus dead
and speaks to me in gusts of shouts,
    I dare not turn my head.

IV.

Oh we had the April evenings!
I had to tear myself away
a hasty kiss and on my way
past past the Cadillacs
that passed the Fords that passed the trucks,
I never had to jam the brakes
for I am a New Yorker bred,
the light is green all my road.
High in the forehead of the South
before me blazed in the lilac dusk
the Evening Star and I was drunk
on speed and the memory of your musk.
That was before I had the flat
and now the goddamn clutch sticks
and you have gone to Bloomington.

彁

His eye is a burning-glass
that in the heart of tinder places
a real image of the sun
trembling, bright, alone
speaking to the power of fire
that is entombed there.

A curl of smoke means little but
when smoke begins to pour and vomit
look! with a puff as if
blowing itself alive
flames are crazy with freedom
which is the prize of wisdom.

HOW LIKE A GOD HE KNOWS

How like a god he knows
when to withhold his hand!
obviously he has
more than strength enough
but the thought he judges by
takes more into account than ours.

If he should lift his hand,
if he should flash his eye!
who turns his head away
and thinks no more of it.
And is our hero tired?
he is tired to the death.

WILD GLAD HOUR

Driven back on the walk by the riptide of cars
but soon I'll pick an opening and risk it
—bent under the burden of a bag of dirty clothes
gasping in this dirty January

:   the wild moment of the limit of power and patience
which we long for in life when we're wasting away

is easy to reach when strength and endurance
are sapped by despair and no prospect and pain

—O wild glad hour that I forecasted under
better better better auspices!
the blind I am with brimming of self-pity
do not contemn, for it is for a man.

"Lead me across! lead me across, you likely
lad, I dimly see the luminous emblem
of a breathing Dragon on your gray silken back
and in your voice I hear the memory of songs."

—I think it is the Messenger of Death
and hopefully hold out my breathless arm
while the fast wheels spit ice in our faces
and steam is pouring from the underground.

❧

4 PEDESTRIAN POEMS

I. THE OLD DOG

Nagging at my life
grieving for my lost youth
it was hard for that which was
to satisfy, nor did
nor do I make it easy.
Yet three months till the spring
opens up the world
by then my hair will be gray.
I met a grizzled dog
a big an old campaigner
boyishly wagged his tail,
tears started into both our eyes.
Great spirits of Style and Song!
O spirits! circumvented

in toils of circumstance
and never did we construct
Paradise! O paradise—
nagging at my life
grieving for my lost youth,
today has missed its glory
this is too bad (not fatal)
and so another day has missed its glory
too bad! too bad! (not fatal)
and when all days have missed their glory
it's very bad, and fatal.

II. THE DANCER OF THE ISLAND

Passing along the wharves
purposive and sure-footed
silent on soft shoes
and staying out of sight
a seeking or avenging
ghost, like a restless
unfinished one of Noh
maniacally still seeking
on faces alive in this world
ideal shapes of heaven,
vengefully to wrest
a stolen inheritance back:
to in that instant shed
these rags of nakedness!
tags of pedestrian speech!
and put the great robe on
put the silver robe on!
Dancer of the Island
and the rivers bordering
—question me, I am he;
please to undo the spell.

III. MARCH EQUINOX

The springtime that I breathed
hesitant, a horrible

snowstorm has choked her—
I hate the shut-in winter!
I am a man of streets
where I follow what is lively
stammering my wishes
my tongue is nailed with strangeness
"What is it you wish?"
My city is my home!
shelter does not comfort me
(nothing comforts me).
Shivering the northeast
has come around the corner
"Take it easy, buddy!"
Hungry for a young cock
thwarted I write about it
everything else is a lie
and I will leave whatever
and follow after chance,
any likely stranger.
So have I twenty years
monomaniac
withered, my face is lined
today before the equinox
no different tomorrow.
Austere is the praise
that I am able to sing
in verses out of my life
as burgeons the spring.

IV.

Not a song in my heart
but some in my suit-case
I am riding to Washington
to read for the record,
another useless
official function
while nobody regards
the use I really am.

But my cock though quiet
is reassuringly
fat in my fly
and my soul is deep
in thoughts of Monet blind.

༝

"IF ONLY I KNEW THE TRUTH,
I SWEAR I WOULD ACT ON IT—"

On the tedious ferry crossing through the obscure night
toward the darkly lurid dock at Barclay Street
on the dark Hudson River pelted by the rain
the orange lightnings thick silently flickered and flashed
there was no thunderclap
I was sick with ignorance and fear
not knowing if my wife had left me, not knowing if I wanted that
was I making a waste for spite, and wise too late, if at all?
"If only I knew the truth, I swear I would act on it!"
I was in confusion and fright
the rain was pounding the water
the lightning was obscure
there came no thunderclap
the boat did not seem to advance.

༝

"So be it, Spiteful! triumph in your spite.
God is love and can afford to lose.
You are finite and can have your way:
neither need you yield in the final point
nor, you victorious, will everybody else
be annihilated."

Blest art Thou, O Lord,
who allowest me to triumph in my spite,
guiltless. Rosy is my glow of gratitude
as upon sweet snow the sunset flush
—not warm, nor do the flowers of the field
flourish in that arctic, where one lonely
animal is erratic, with thick fur.
Him shall I hunt.

᪷

A ROUGH WALL

The rough wall with a stripe of sun
    opposite my open window
is like a rectangle of the rough
    rocky cliff in the country

and I'm convinced I'm in the country
    although I know it's a rough wall
with a stripe of sun, I am obsessed
    that I am in the beautiful country.

And today will be a calm
    and joyous day out of touch
with everything! not *I* will be
    doing whatever I am doing!

as now this rough and dirty wall
    with a stripe of sun I am serene
has moss on it and blades of grass
    although I *see* it's a rough and dirty wall.

So have a few weeks of the lovely
    city of Paris brought me to escape
into the country of wishes, and a few
    bad years into days that are calm.

379

🌿

I LIVED IN FEAR—

I lived in fear of a youth who was coming
to make me trouble in the moment of my pride
I lived in fear of his immense
father'd kill me I heard footsteps
mounting the stairs and my heart stopped
driven nearly mad by dogs
that barked when folk approached my house
I could not reason to protect me
my wits were smashed when those dogs barked
I did not know a way to fight
the enemy with my own hands
there was no friend to call upon
defenselessly I waited wishing
he would not come today either.
So passed a hundred coward days
of my existence that winter.

🌿

This abandoned road is dead,
I do not like its influence, I am afraid.
Go here. Must I go here? will I find
what I am hunting where it can't be found?
No answer. All is still among the trees.

Something is angry at my scuffing shoes.
I pluck a daisy by the road and eat,
her stem is bleeding, she is crying out.
Who lives there under that black fallen roof?
Go look. I won't! and must I go and look?
Nothing but broken windows and my heart
violently jumping in my throat.
Enter in at that abandoned door
whose roof has fallen down; it is yours.
Here I am home! the broken mirror of
the dresser without drawers doesn't bother
even to greet me, and the dusty bottle
has broken on the floor next to the table
without a sound. Oh, they will soon forget me
in the other world where I used to placate them,
as now I lie down in this bed I choose
upon these sagging springs.
                              How many hours
have dropped out of the time? for the stars
are peeping through the holes in the tar-roof.

꽃

I walked in tears down Dyckman Street
    my present and past were at my side
the future ahead by a couple of feet
    and we advanced with equal stride.

The past in his track-suit was attired
    dirty and sweating in the race
that he was losing and he was tired.
    Nevertheless, nevertheless

the present in unresigned unrest
    kept darting quick looks at the passers-by
and he was dressed as I was dressed.
    And to the future I thought to cry

"Wait up and let's talk!" but fear
   stuck fast my voice inside my mouth.
And so we were as we drew near
   the Hudson River that flows north and south.

BIRTHDAY CAKE

Now isn't it time
when the candles on the icing
are one two too many
too many to blow out
too many to count too many
isn't it time to give up this ritual?

although the fiery crown
fluttering on the chocolate
and through the darkened room advancing
is still the most loveliest sight
among our savage folk
that have few festivals.

But the thicket is too hot and thick
and isn't it time, isn't it time
when the fires are too many
to eat the fire and not the cake
and drip the fires from my teeth
as once I had my hot hot youth.

DANTË *(AFTER TITIAN)*

Defiance is fagged out, and oh
my stubborn integrity could now

willingly be bought and sold
for a tiny shower of gold

as Jove came down on Danaë
and wondering but not shyly
    she opened to his pleasure. With a clatter
    her slave caught the money in a platter.

꙳

A MEAL

Liver of Prometheus
fried in the sweat of Sisyphus

is the supper we have sat
down to table to eat.

The chairs are trembling with
our unexpressed wrath

and the innocent water
has turned sour.

꙳

AT THE SAN REMO BAR

Blue and slow through the gathering violence
the juke-box is turning disks of silence.
That smash hit *You Can Hear a Pin Drop*
and *Hush-a-Bye Baby on the Treetop*.
A man with neither will nor whim
has bought a nickel of *Interim*
and the sweat is standing on Richard's neck
at the quiet *Moment After the Wreck*.

The eyes I seek with gaze intent
are listening to *Embarrassment*.
On the house the patrons hear
Time's Winged Chariot Hurrying Near
but few *The Silence of the Seas*
Beyond the Farthest Hebrides.
The needle grinding in a groove
is spinning out *Don't Make a Move*
and every one's humming at the San Remote
the popular *It Has You By the Throat*.

The great black hound upstairs
barks and roars, our little dog
yaps and stands there trembling
something is at the door
I open and the epidemic
comes in my house and lays us low
my wife, my children, and me
swift, like a murderous ambush,
delirium and pain
dizziness lassitude and fever
and only slowly we are fighting
back our way to stand upright
assisting one another as we can.
Alas, I see one night
how Death shall enter my defenseless home
and one of us no longer have
a ruddy face and breath that comes
nor the ability to fight
back the way to stand upright,
while the others watch in horror
assisting one another as who can,
while the great black hound upstairs
is barking and our little dog
stands yapping there and trembling.

MY DAUGHTER VERY ILL

My little darling looked so pale today
   fading away
pining and thin like the transparent moon
   in the afternoon,
I cannot sleep, obsessed by Susie's colorless
   cheerless face
and bony body in my arms too light,
   she who was bright
comparable to the meadowflowers
   alas! that the mowers
passed and did not spare, their petals droop
   my shoulders stoop
for fear and neither can I breathe for fear.

   No, hear my prayer,
Nature! who alone healest and not wishes
   nor art nor pity,
and do thou Creator Spirit visit her
   with the quick future
that alone stirs to courage and to walk
   and to work.

FOR MY BIRTHDAY, 1956

Mars is near this month, whatever that means.
To me he looks not baleful but inquiring
peach-colored in the west. When we go soaring
yonder weightless, as I fly in dreams,
the tired earth will fall away betimes
and new and promising to our admiring
another shore will open for exploring,
that planet that in my reflector shines.

385

This project makes me proud and picks me up
and buoys me up with a patient hope.

But friends, who ask me what I want or need
on my birthday, teach me fortitude
to face the illness that has struck my daughter
who was like me full of knowing laughter.

❦

ABSALOM

In the roomy oak among the translucent leaves
    fluttering and the coins of light in motion
    where nesting sparrows chirrup in commotion
and hop about in fright and a voice grieves
—what is this golden moss that interweaves

the branches like an unaccustomed snare
    dismaying birds and gleaming brilliantly?
    Is it not human hair in the oak tree?
Absalom hanging tangled by the hair
immobile even to his frightened stare!

whom Joab like a fowler in the sun
    looming destroyed, spotting the green with blood,
    and David when at last he understood
the message mourned, "O my son Absalom!"
he wept, "O Absalom my son my son!"

OUR LUCY (1956–1960)

I.

Small as a fox and like
a little fox but black,
    our Lucy's white teeth grin
    among the rushes green.

The feathers of her plume
flutter in the warm
    winds that fitfully blow
    from the Gulf of Mexico.

And like a machine-gun
her barking through the pine
    echoes where people have
    set foot on our grove.

"Quiet, Lucy. They
may bring us news today,
    or if thieves they may
    drop something on their way."

II.

She was a happy little dog
because she loved three things only,
us and food and to go barking
forth in the world, feathers high:
of these she had a plenty till
the car hit her at Eagle's Bridge;
died without pain in Sally's arms
blood slowly dripping from her jaws,
we buried with a borrowed shovel
a cairn of stones on the river bank

—she who leaped with joy to greet us
and enlivened us with her lovely spirit,
how suddenly! there she was
and now is not in our empty house.

※

PHILOCTETES

"My past is a wound I will not close
but I keep it open and I clean it out.

"It will not infect me if I nurse it like a stranger,
yet I can't help sometimes shrieking in pain.

"I have come to this island to enjoy in solitude
the foreign body imbedded in my quick,

but now you—ai ai ai ai ai ai ai aiiii
auuuuu opopopopopopopoiiii."

※

GOLDENS BRIDGE

If I'd lie like the dog with my nose on the ground
then I think the tiredness'd slip from my shoulders
like the overflowing of the broad dam
easily at Goldens Bridge like thunder,
like the thundering along the humped hills
in the storm of spring.
                          Who is this friendly pack?
waders in the torrent, what wet hounds
awaken me and lick my salt? (the last
of April is still raining all around.)

"Good Furies! *I*'ll befriend you, I the man,
we'll dance the dances of the hounds and man
: they mean that the past with its curse is still blest
—when I lie like the dog with my nose on the ground—
and has brought me at last to not less than I am
—when the tiredness slips from my shoulders like thunder."

%

ALCESTIS'S SPEECH

I saw Ixion turning on the wheel
and Sisyphus pushing up the heavy stone
and thirsty Tantalus. These sights are telling.
All of the huddled dead are brought by here
to learn not to regret what they just lost.
And there was a warrior under a cherry-tree
wearing a sprig of blossoms in his hat,
swinging a heavy sword he fought and fought
and because it was in hell this continued.
But nothing follows from what I saw
because we are alive.

%

SENTENCES OF NIETZSCHE

The deeper sinks the sun, the longer grow the shadows:
when now in flashing mines, under the horizon,
into tortuous caves the day is nosing,
overhead is darkness. The first
stars are peeping: small are men
while *the labyrinthine man seeks his Ariadne.*
Sunlight that falls upon the dungeon floor
twinkles like living light: if I
interpose my hand, the fingers drip the fire.

The deeper sinks the sun, the longer grow the shadows
—now shines in the Minotaur's unblinking face,
and the labyrinthine man seeks not the truth but his Ariadne.

᠉

A COLLAGE

On a curtain of black gauze I made
a Milky Way of feathers of sea-gulls
and eleven scallop-shells for the great stars
Procyon Pollux Vega Regulus
Capella and Arcturus to the north,
and southward Sirius and Betelgeuse
Altair Aldebaran and Fomelhaut,
and all between I stuck red bearberries
on their green sprigs to be celestial meadows
and around I pinned a border of tiny starfish:
these jetsam corpses of the sea and shore
standing for, by their non-being, heaven.

᠉

Patience! gentle firmness! uncompelled
Duty! strengths—not by restraint
but flames of the establishment
and oily time, first natures. If I do

that which is ordained before dreams
men are astounded that my strength fails not,
the fools, it is resting in the rooted
rock that whirls forward with the world.

Winged beyond any seeming lightness
is rock, upborne more surely than a baby.

Fiercer than desire of the eyes
is the rage of punctuality of flowers

that when May breathes, blooming crease by crease
tremble open to the most space
delicately, as they have been trained
almost since when the air was on fire.

ꙮ

FEVER AND HEALTH

Fever is beautiful the twinkling
campfires of the resistance
the scorched earth and the strait pass,
though it is terrible to watch
the history of the disease
and the wrong banner flying.

But the loveliest thing the violent stars
roll as they rush is animal health!
the three gaits of locomotion
and the fourfold gamut of song
and practical syllogism
and hammering and careless love.

ꙮ

Driving north ninety miles
my daughter to college, a young lady
bright and competent, independent!
We stopped beside a reedy pond
and poured our coffee from a thermos
and ate the bread and butter we had brought.
I lit my pipe. "Well done! well done! well done!

foreseeing, moderate, and reasonable!"
in my loosed limbs I felt the approving praise.
The sparkles on the water surface
were mad with excitement, they exclaimed,
they leaped into existence out of nothing,
everywhere continually they danced, they shone.

꿏

"CATCH UP WITH THE PATROL—"

I caught me at it: fuming, frowning,
and tightening my tough bullneck.
"Relax!" I railed, "where's the fight?
look around, take it easy."
I looked and this is what I saw:
that I was struggling for my only life
as hard as any but not shrewdly,
losing the battle-line, distracted
by the domestic troubles of unreliable allies.
"Guard!" I cried, "who catch me at it,
may I pass?" "You know the password, pass.
Catch up with the patrol
that vanished in the fog in the ravine.
And—man," he said; I turned; he said, "Good luck."

꿏

MAY 9TH

When slowly stepped we down
from the Palisades, often pausing,
   and broad the flood beneath
   spread glittering north and south,

then clear we saw how we,
each creature in his kind,
   are noble of the world.
   If I compare these cliffs

to artificial palace-steps
I do not belittle them,
   for kingdom and domain
   are natural to us

when in such joy and size
we move that the daylight
   is the provided lamp
   for Entry and Pavane.

A CHRISTMAS TREE

I bought a tree a lovely
I went far for and carried home heavy
   and as up Twenty-Third we trudged
   the branches tickling my cheeks were

whispering, "Be cheerful! this
incoming year will be prosperous
   as you deserve, most excellent
   poet!" Crazy was the scent

of the fir-forest, and that tree
shook in my arms as when she
   still wrestled with the gusts of rain
   and tempest on the side of the mountain.

OUT OF THE TULIP TREE

Out of the tulip tree Haskell his green eyes
   tossed yellow blossoms to the girls below
   standing with upturned faces in a row.
It clouded over, wind began to rise,

it grew obscure, the leaves turned white,
   the air was quiet, full of tiny noises,
   the girls vanished with their screaming voices.
"Come down," I shouted, "Haskell, before light-

ning strikes the tree and you are shaken out
   by swaying boughs this way and that!"
   "Catch!" he commanded, "catch! catch!"
and he tossed down a rubber ball, I caught,

and he aloft and I on the ground under
   threw the white sphere back and forth, amid
   the gusts of wind and strings of rain, silently
amid the bursts of lightning and the claps of thunder.

FOR DAN, THE FURRIER

Dan, who adorn richly like duchesses
ladies with sleek furs in our northern snows
—the seal sadly that lay blotted on the floes,
the mink that darted in the leafless trees:
yet are not strong and murdered coats like these
fitter for males, that have been the clothes
of shepherds and woodsmen and made grandiose
the stature of kings during solemnities?

Then as I see on our not unvivid street
spare men among the falling flakes flit by,
I think, Let Dan resume to glorify
our knights with furs and make my city proud
like seaports whither came the Hansa fleet,
Hamburg, Luebeck, and Nijni-Novgorod.

꽃

Splendidly generous
these days, O Town and Chance,
on your pedestrian
you squander fun and money

fun and fuck and money
like water through my fingers
and teach me, "Don't cling!
something will turn up."

But Muse, do you also
whisper in my ear
a new song, otherwise
than my gloomy sermon.

Tell me a popular song
a gay one the Americans
will sing as by they pass
the while I blush for pride.

꽃

LONG-FACE AND BRIGHT-EYES

Long-face, why d'ye plod
like yo' feet was made o' lead?

Oh I got plenty o' reasons
dependin' on the seasons.

Bright-eyes, why d'ye stalk
like yo' shoes was made o' cork?
    Never give it a thought, not I!
    find out maybe by and by.

⚘

There is spring in my new shoes
and my speech is gurgling in the gutters
but when will my soul, when will my icy balls
warm and thaw out in the great winds of March?

When the interior sun of reason
arises and approves of me,
then will I breathe as of old attention
and red my penis spring alive.

Unknown teacher! teach me a prayer
and rite to help that mild sun rise
for she is caught under the horizon,
though glimmering, in the jaws of hell.

Hell cannot swallow her, she has
saving humor, and the truth
is still too tough for death to chew.
But O bright eyes, return! return!

⚘

No image or idea! if I
could fully fill the boat of space
in which I row, then would I touch
the adjacencies of the illimitable

sea where teem profusely
monsters my dog and wife
and children and the Americans
and such and such lobsters and crocodilia
as the Oriental Brahma
spattered jerking off
with for his bride
the Void.

THE DEAD CICHLID

Beautiful you are
livid! motionless and dead
although I shudder.

Trifling were the book
that left out the solemn song
of you livid dead.

THE OLD CAR BARN
UNDER COOGAN'S BLUFF

I saw through lacelike leaves
in the lemony yellow morning,
corroding the abandoned engines
slowly sinking to the ground.

There was a heap of rusty chains
and iron sheets returning to the ore
and overalls in the shadowy
car barn with a yellow lamp

was pounding on a spike
clink clink clink
the noises in small bubbles forth
floating burst in the silent sunshine.

Startlingly a rusty door
fell down an inch on its rusty hinge
an acetylene flash in the barn's black heart
revealed a crouching welder with a hood.

⚡

AN ODE TO LUCK

O Luck, oh when? you twinkling fuse
of here and now, sometimes called Grace
a world *for* them, and wistfully I watch.
I am not much in pain, not much afraid,
I am not guilty and I am not damned,
nor even bored, but I am simply bawling
for want of you, wing'd Opportunity.
Nor am I envious: I do have virtues

of which I reap or shall the slow-come prizes
(though I complain), even the cider breeze
of Fame by which I tingle may yet blow
my patient way. My character endures,
my destiny will not be accidental,
and common reason must prevail at last
—but when? when? when shall I awake
to a morning quick and can what I want.

Long I labored to make me Goodman,
did it in despite of pleasure and prudence,
to my surprise that face fits me,
force flows from me with effortless ease,
my hunch hits home, my whimsy works,

my rebel bluff says a relevant speech,
what I meant in malice my neighbor needs,
and grateful foreigners offer me gifts,

only a luck of my own I lack,
only a task to wake up toward.
O Opportunity! do come my way
in such a guise, glancing one, that I
may know you, for long study has estranged
me from the common uses, but appear
in a likely shape, sexy, operable,
and whether I will or no imperious.

For lately wary of my self I lay
within the world like the long trill on B
in the Sonata in the key of E,
and Day crowded my room! the furniture
that yesterday had climbed upstairs climbed out,
the house itself fell down, and common day
was my raw banner flying—but O Luck,
when? when? for I am simply baffled

by want of you, wing'd Opportunity,
O winged Opportunity to squander
myself and live again among the months
my kinsmen, we were born in the same womb
I knew them well, how we grew strong together
and broke at last into the common light,
yes rough March is my brother and sweet May
and June and hot July and all of them.

꽃

WAITING AT A PLACE

The hours I've spent waiting at a place
where somebody isn't coming there today

until too late. The more more hours waiting
where somebody is loitering or busy elsewhere
or wending ever toward the far horizon
from me further away. "Is he unmindful
of where I am waiting, or is he wending
to just a place where I am *not* there waiting?"
—so have I speculated many hours.

Rarely have I been in a sweet place
waiting that somebody came that way
where I was waiting. I have known few such hours.
The world is wide and there are many places
to be not where I am. But this strait place
where I am waiting, it is all my world.

This room is familiar yet peculiar,
not empty yet not peopled. Nothing ever
will happen in this room, except to me
age, rage, and disappointment. If I could
step out of here, where I have lived fifty years!
what would it be like, the exotic landscape?
I would not know the name of the country.
I might be fighting for my life and money!

Yes, for tonight waiting I fell asleep
and restlessly I dreamed a wild wish
of fist-fights tooth and nail fights with knives
in Uruguay, gouging out the eyes
of heavy Spaniards who clung to me
to rob my twenty-dollar bill. I broke
loose and got to where our sailors were,—
rapturously freed of the nightmare
to our barbed-wire enclosure! We weighed anchor.

※

I LOVE YOU, NECESSARY—

Waiting in pain on a subway platform
my train doesn't come wrong trains roar by
fracturing space what are the facts?
I have given up what I wanted to love me.
It's raw two men are talking loud
it isn't interesting what they say
the lights are lurid the facts are harsh
but I am quiet with my mortal facts.
People have said I am disoriented
but I am on this bench where I am
with not much left to the middle of my life.
Who are you come and stand beside me?
you keep me silent company
what kind of thing do you want? I look
without fear in your neutral face.
It isn't true the truth's too hard
too hard for what? what's my alternative?
The middle, in a play, is the passage
between the probable and the necessary
and the existing is the necessary
I love you, Necessary, you are strong
and big so I am not afraid of you
I do not feel like I am under arrest
and shrewd you are to give away your love
on the likes of me for I pay back threefold
yes! ask any of them how it was
loving me, the while they dared.

※

TOO MANY LIGHTS

He frightened me awaking with a scream.
I held his hand, he slept, I could not sleep,

I came outside the tent and was astounded:
for in great heaven opposite the full moon
downwheeling in the west into the sea
—and all the western sea was ablaze—
the Morning Star *was*, unexpectedly,
baleful, I knew not what, and Saturn over him.
There were too many lights in the night
already too clear, and I was afraid.

But I have made a fire and hot coffee
and there is a rosy flush in the east.

So always, Lord of Hosts, allay my horror
if I do for myself, as I grow old
and too wise, for it is unbearable
but a man cannot be stupider than he is,
he cannot not see that which he notices.
Marked was I from a child who learned his lessons
better than the other boys in grammar school,
but I did not hope the lesson I would learn
would be that men are screaming and it is hard to be happy.

·

WITH ARGUS

I go with Argus to survey my navy.
"Here's *Going Nowhere*, I've used her a lot
in coastal waters ten ay twenty years,
she's good and roomy."

                        "I'm afraid," he said,
"*Nowhither* is a ship with no next cruise."

"Look at *Truthworthy*, small, but all my life
I've sailed where people never dared to go,
Truthworthy does not founder on facts!" I boasted.

"*Truthworthy* is too small," he agreed.

"Then what about this *Nameless?*" I implored,
"although I know she's manned by maniacs
don't I fit with that crew? don't I? don't I?"

The shipwright looked at me with mild eyes.
"What's the matter, friend? You need a *New Ship*
from the ground up, with art, a lot of work,
and using the experience you have—"

"I'm tired!" I told him in exasperation,
"I can't afford it!"
              "No one asks you, either,"
he patiently replied, "to venture forth.
Whither? why? maybe just forget it."
And he turned on his heel and left me—here.

MY CAR WRECKED BETWEEN
BENNINGTON AND BRATTLEBORO

While they filled the tank with gas and checked the oil
I murmured my secret prayer to Castor and Pollux:
    "Not called on to do aught,
    only to have survived!"

Against my better reason I drove forth
hundreds of miles into the marble hills.
I had no heart to go where I was bound,
I did not trust my car to get me there,
and being careless of myself I went.

A bad road, a bad car, and a bad driver:
no accident! it was by accident
that hardly hurt I crawled out of that wreck.

I was not frightened as I slowly watched
my car roll down the gorge and I inside,
surely I was not unwilling to be dead
and for a moment shut my eyes and waited.

There was a peaceful moment it was still
and I looked at everything with mild inquiry.
My limbs were pinned, I calmly worked them free
and crept out of a window into the world.

Savior Twins! teach me still not to care
as sparkling bright in the blue-black ye shine.

2. HALLOWE'EN, 1953

Hallowe'en, and thank the Lord
my ancient my pathetic Ford
    sits passive in no city-street
    to hoodlum goblins' trick-or-treat,

where men at dawn will sadly stare at
the windows smashed the tires flat
    and on the windshield writ in soap
    unflattering, "Fuck you, you dope!"

Ay! but in fact my gray my serviceable
car that flew as fast as she was able
    is rusting in a deep gorge in Vermont
    where I wrecked her in a careless moment.

That forest is unhaunted by
tonight the wicked and the spry;
    the first early northern snow
    is on my dark wreck settling slow.

THE *WEEPERS TOWER* IN AMSTERDAM

I see I've come a pilgrimage. I didn't
deliberately wander up this street
but here is Weepers Tower. It was hence
his *Half Moon* sailed away in Sixteen-Nine
and waxed into the full moon of New York,

my Captain Henry Hudson looking for
a shorter Passage—but there is no passage—
sailed to the maw of hope and the dead end
of the river broad whose other name is Lordly
and has no peer in Europe or the East.

Still here sits the squat bricken cylinder
oddly sheared off one side by the street
with a stubby steeple and a gilt *Half Moon*
weathervane. But why the "Tower of Tears"?
Upon this edge did women wave farewell

and wait and watch?—but *nothing* comes from watching,
not even tears. The number of whose hope
appears is null on the horizon. (Neither
are we who hustle happier by and large,
as I assay the fortunes of mankind!)

So. I remember how a lonely boy
I used to clamber up the Palisades
and, looking down across the lordly river,
to daydream the eroding centuries:
Offshore the *Half Moon* lies, and there my Captain

questions the Indians at Spuyten Duyvil
yonder under the monarch Tulip Tree,
now also dead and gone (like my desires
rotted away, as I squat here writing
at Schreiers-Tooren in a foreign port).

He is sailing northward into Tappan Zee!
gloriously broad as the Pacific
Ocean not. The water has begun
to freshen, the saliva in his mouth
is saltier and bitter. This is not

either the Northwest Passage to the East.
Try elsewhere. Rapidly he is retreating
on the ebb-tide—but hanging from the cliff
in a slow agony the small boy watches
the lovely ship diminish.
                              He will rave
in the muffling ice, lost beyond Labrador,
the crosses of his spars stuck in the ice,
he will be lost, my Captain Henry Hudson
crazy my fearless navigator where
there is no passage, for there is no Passage.

He will have gone forth from this Weepers Tower
a one too many voyage to where crosses
of two masts and their spars are in the icebergs
stuck forever in the future perfect
that most bleak tense where winter comes on dark.

What do you want, my Captain? what you want
is impossible, therefore you must want nothing.
"I am looking for the Northwest Passage to
India; *if I had made the world
that would exist.*"

Oh many are the lovely northern rivers!
the Housatonic and Connecticut
and Charles and James and Thames and Roanoke
and the St. Lawrence and the Kennebec
and the Potomac and the sweet Delaware,

and not of them the least the lordly Hudson;
and all of them have made the fortunes

of famous towns as arteries of trade,
but all of them flow down into the sea,
all of them flow down into the sea.

FROM *A WAR DIARY*, 1939–41

I.

The background of the European peace
the foreground of my own enraged home
and in-between I as I am: I could
here and now almost at last lust
to wreck all at one swipe and separate
and buy the *Times* to read about the war.
—But I'll begin with me. I'll slowly bend
my bent on the pattern of the best
because I can; and with Virginia
tonight determine to confront the future
much as we can; and private good our strength,
a little help preserve the Western world.
But as I came to this assurety,
here was Virginia home and crazy drunk,
and when I tried to kiss her, she cried out,
"Let me go! let me go! let me go!"

II.

"Grim evils—" so I reckoned—"will not fail
to animate me, even to grim joy
when finally the bottom drops out.
These trivial risks I take, my timid lies,
render me powerless; the envious
biting of fools takes me by surprise
for a moment till I brush them off;
but let the Evil lift his honorable
brow and won't I match it?" So I boasted.

Now here's this general war we prepared.
—Why am I at a loss? and my anger
undermined by confusion? But I counted
upon an intimate calamity!
my way of life prepared
me adequate for that.

III.

Of us who heed the whispers of the soul
—none too faint in which to overhear
misery or justification—now!
how many hearing of the shrieking butchery
in Bucharest last night and the tomorrow
we cannot hinder—even the far future
bleeding of it being hard to staunch
by the most energetic therapy—
how many of us feel a wanton duty
to be ourselves plunged into foolish death
and we are only looking for a way,
lest there be so much rage and we quiet,
and the pogrom, we safe.
As yet, however, meditation turns
to rational self-sacrifices or
the honorable suicide of despair
in decent circumstances with a clean
weapon and no damage to property.

IV.

Relying on disasters of the war
to minimize my misery, and counting
these public penalties that none can doubt
as the proof and price of private wickedness
I otherwise don't much believe in—No,
we have to say it is our public crimes
that cause public calamity. And yet
my lust is moderated into impotence
by the embarrassing imagination of
the agony of Europe. How is this?

MASSACHUSETTS

Oh for a favorable wind to chase
these biting flies these spiteful Massachusetts
morals, so a man that has worked hard
and merits it can bask on this white beach
and soak in the strong sun of pleasure
that proves itself, and is a grounds to act on
though not the only one. But Lord! these flies
annoy and buzz and they are present
even when they are absent. I don't hope
for hot joy or much luck along the shore,
being not young and never was a beauty
though amorous and forward, but to have
my rights to animal idle like a man
without this hullaballoo and hateful laws,
suspicious looks and make me feel a foreigner
on my own bright American sea-coast.
Hate for hate, why don't they drown themselves?
Swatted it!—it's only a horsefly
with twitching legs dying in the sand.
Irritation creates metaphors.
Poor stinging bugs. I understand they must,
naturally they come at us insanely
for we are their life-blood, they live on us.
The prissy acid speech and the scared arts
of Massachusetts can't enjoy them much.
Ours is the future, be compassionate!
(I wish I had been happy in my time.)
Great sun of power, you do not strike me blind,
I calmly look past you and reel like drunk!
and let me touch you, pine woods of the dune,
for you are fragrant though your bark is rough.

WELLFLEET HARBOR

Visibly here the tide
creeps onto shore, almost
which particular lapping
wavelet is the utmost
and then the sea recedes.
The sun in my burning-glass
has moved a millimeter
off-center. Mars is rising
a little further west.
On on the summer
is hurrying away.
Next Thursday is my birthday.
I have already reached
a still point where I stand
hearing my heart pumping
my interior river round,
my friends drifting away,
the shoreline drifting away,
like a ship standing (as we say)
out to sea to sea.
Venus is not so high
when first at dusk she shines
descending with the sun
into the jaws of night.
All days are different days
monotonously flickering
past and faster by,
but there is one single night
and she is called the Night
starlit or dark the Night
my black brain, I have wrapped
myself around me like a coat
yet I am shivering in the night
though flaming like a werewolf in the night.

THE HURRICANE OF '54

The hurricane of '54
that knocked the spire off Old North Church
no damage did to me and mine
for the house that Williams built
and many friends drove nails
houselikely sheltered us
as at the streaming windows
we saw bay flood the meadow
dunes fly up in clouds
the fishing-fleet destroyed
but the elastic pines
wrestle the winds and win.
The storm was circular,
first from the east the blow
sought us out, it blasted
our south as laughing sun
leaked through the wild spray,
for hours west wall bore it,
as evening fell departed
the gentle gale from the north.
The barometer rose, the vortex
has left the kitchen, sea-gulls
are soaring from Blackfish Creek,
cars are roaring to Wellfleet,
the woods are pruned, the world
is washed, and the townspeople
will talk of nothing else forever,
a bore for years to come.
For young folk talk about animals
but old folk like to dwell
minutely on disasters.

ON THE LAKE

The boat rounded a bend and Urirotstock
towered in its snows. "Canton Uri!
da ist Canton Uri!" thrillingly
sang out the farmer native of Altdorf

and thrillingly today his memory
has pierced my torpor: please it God
that I will once cry for my towering city
such a cry I heard at Urirotstock.

Freedom of course was in it, and quixotic
labor endured as a thing of course
to live among those snows, and fatherly
anxious affection for his pretty daughter.

There is the Tell Marker on the right!
The Alps stand up around us and behind,
and worst in front, whose name is Obstacle.
Everything says, This world is not for cowards.

Everything is quiet on the lake
that is shining awestruck in my mind's eye,
and everything says, This world is not for thieves—
as softly we steam into Flüellen.

RED ROCKS, DENVER MOUNTAIN PARK

Into the foothills in their giant unrest
we went the dozen miles among ponderosa
and blue spruce to, in the deep snow,
the amphitheater hewn in the Red Rocks

where the fellow plucked a fiddle and his friend
high in the crevice heard it. In 1910.

"They built it in the Thirties," I explained
to the Australian, "W P A
project to make useful work."
                          The rocks
were gorgeous brothers and as red as blood,
one is called Creation, one the Ship,
and all around about us rocky mountains,
the rocky mountains were the Rocky Mountains.

"Since then this country," I said angrily,
"is dragging its behind. What *you*'ll observe
is lousy television." I was furious
because he just came from Los Angeles.
I was ashamed.
                 So I began to bellow
like a spokesman from the middle of the stage,
"Hello! Hello! hi! hi! can you hear me?"
A hail of echoes rattled on the floor.
"Certainly we can hear you," they called down
in ordinary conversational
voices like a Stradivarius.

My eyes grew misty—I had been surprised
by my own vehemence. My glorious
various country! where I go about
checking up like a proprietor
and write her jealous notes like to my wife.

※

SUMMER OF 1958

The astonishing races
the Australians ran

at Santry, and everywhere
this summer their swimmers
swamped ours
in wakes of water;
their batters beat us.
How glad and proud
must Melbourne be!

We loudly wonder
as if they wended
from another world
where gravity is less
and very slowly tick
four minutes to the mile,
those mighty kangaroos
and jolly wallabies.

When I was young we couldn't run
so fast, nor did we whip
moons like tops around.
We hardly could fly.
Aren't these new men lovely!
God grant them prudence
to their prowess equal!
My part it is
to decorate their glory.

※

EVENING (GAVOTTE
AND VARIATIONS OF RAMEAU)

The air is blue, that sun is gone
and the inverted sky is white in the pool
where the dirty shepherds and the tired women
are bathing solemnly. The water is cool.

A single happy cry—but from a fool
or sage I do not know—rings in the air alone.

The husband, whose intenser body-heat
has dried his body, says, "I am a man,
nothing frightful," frightening her again.
He finds their clean clothes in the dirty light
and as its outline fades sits on a stone.
But she is far and thoughtful. The animals bleat.

There are loud bells like holes
in the gray air, and there are calls
of corbies whence they are not to be seen.
The bathers' clothing on the hardly green
are hardly blots; and all this is the fact
that has you by the throat the moment you would act.

Sally is weeping in a young girl's voice
after the delicate happiness appears
and eludes, and laughing in a throaty voice
at the troublesome desires of the satyrs,
and far astray is grieving without tears
in a small daughter's white and homeless voice.

Now the bonfires are lighted and are jumping
among the treetrunks. The provincial wine
is blinking. "Shepherd, do you feel that something
was drowned?" "But I see no one missing." (Nine
long months are the long months of becoming
into this pang of life and the next day divine.)

Jolly hunters with their careless arrows
aim at the geese and bring down nought, or sparrows,
they are a menace in the rushes, oh
they are carefree as they come and go.
Around the fires the shepherds have murderous eyes.
No one is safe because no one is wise.

"Let us go home, my life, let us go home
where a small seed has taken root, to bloom
and be the golden square rose of the world.
Close things are mysterious. O Lord,
prosper us! for I have built a cot
of poor materials, hope, love, and art."

FROM *A GOAT FOR AZAZEL*

As forth he boldly dances
led by my silken cord,
particolored streamers
ravel our favorite.

His eyes benignly peering
shed radiance around
and his horns lie on his shoulders
as he lifts his triumphant nostrils.

Now have we come into a natural world
where there are no things that do not exist
and not by miracle the tree and beast
invent in the unfinishing creation
their beauty. And because they do not think
that the impossible is possible,
men do not find with fright how all their possible
has suddenly become impossible;
but happy wit and serviceable power
spring not by chance but from what a man is.

And here we see—how goodly and how gracious!—
the unsuspicious brothers sit together
(is this impossible?) each man exerting
without remorse his strength (is this so hard?)
and sometimes frankly frowning brow to brow.

If then some brother moved by simple thoughts
gives aid and judges by the facts of life,
and another notices the time is flying by
and comes across because our death is soon
(what amazes you? is this so difficult?)
they are not made the scapegoats of the tribe.

So. Into this natural wildwood heart
I led the happy kid and let him free.

THE EMBLEM

If a life must be lost, let it be the rescuer's
for that has a meaning, it is our Emblem.
Therefore since all must be lost, be a rescuer.

You may print a meaning on the underlying fact
or make an emblem *of* the underlying fact.

Martyrs who sign their deaths as witnesses
and the Faithful who died in battle for their faith,
these print a meaning on the underlying fact.

The Northerners chose just to die in a battle
and this was glorying in the underlying fact,
but we cannot say that it was meaningful.

The underlying fact is that they all are dying.
The meaning is Buddha the compassionate.

Warriors merge and drown in the sickening maws of the sea.
Seers and physicians are alert lifeguards
on the shore that itself is being eaten away.

Warriors as they drown in death shout "Victory!"
but a lifeguard when he rescues some one, curses.

A MAN FROM GEORGIA

As to this dirty broken man from Georgia
weeping and with a bandaged head, I gave
my pipe to smoke and thirty cents for breakfast,
neighborly words without disdain, but not
a bath nor clothing nor a ticket home
nor useful information—so myself
in need I get thirty cents of affection,
thus much I have in me to give and get.

I saw him later, washed and not too bad
but drunk on apple-wine. "Hey, I know you,
you're the good guy," he said, "the one New Yorker
ever give me a nickel. Thanks a lot, suh.
Have a drink." I drank it without grace
to be polite. I am the more confused
about the nature of things and my own role.
I could not shake him off all afternoon.

Bitterly he told me how three niggers
had knocked him down and took ten dollars off him.
No doubt they did, no doubt he provoked them.
"I thought," he said, "when I come to New York
I'll be a big shot. Lying there like that
like a shitty tramp. They left me in the gutter
to die," he whined, "bleedin.'" I remained
impassive, cheerful, optimistic.

I know that life is simple. It is hard
but simple. Living is not complicated,
but it is very hard and very simple.
I don't think anyone would say that living
is easy, though to some (I can imagine)
living which is to me horribly hard
is just that easy, but they wouldn't say so,
people like that wouldn't say anything.

EPODE. THE NEW BUS TERMINAL

I thought, "Why, I'll go in and see this new
this marvel where the buses overhead
roar to the provinces. It's not all finished
but through the rags I'll see the flesh the better
like this lad with a rip in his pants—"
A mason's boy was polishing the cornerstone
and I admired the progress of his work,
but he was busy.
            So I came inside
out of the lousy season dignified
on calendars as our first month. And why
am *I* freezing in this Hanseatic town
fit for fur hats, and I am no merchant,
when that bus is bounding over the viaduct
southward to Key West?
            To my surprise
I was enchanted. Gleaming escalators
were elevating travelers through the ceiling.
Everything was shining and in motion.
The chromium handrailing took a thumbprint.
Then I was standing on the mezzanine
lordly overlooking the Grand Concourse
where I could window shop the passersby
—with one eye on the prowling cop—and smoke
my pensive pipe in peace.
            Glory to God!
rough-scored with plaster like the Milky Way
came by that mason's boy; he looked at me,
our glances met, he smirked—as thirds at last
in the A-Minor Adagio of Haydn
fill out the wide skip in the melody
and this arpeggio is the climax,
he frowned self-consciously. I followed hard.

God damn the labyrinth that we have built!
laid for us—by us—we become confused—

I lost him in an unknown corridor,
inside my soul and on Fortieth Street.
There is no reason to an American plan,
we are leased out to shops, we dig in subways,
the ancient simplicity is gone!
Gone is the interesting from this house!
That chromium was tarnished long ago.
Those buses leap to no good south and west,
black care drives with the driver as he drives.
How did I give this stupid Terminal
even my provisional assent?
Yet let me praise the star-eyed mason's boy
who meant as much as I did to make sense.

※

MAY

My darling Sally is
        and what for me in April
        she did was amiable,
maybe May will more than this

open to me her heart
        to my delight to my
        wandering wonder my
lost onward steps and newfound art.

Then Persephone
        the queen of hell and flowers
        will idly guide my course
to where is guessed, not known, by me.

My hands are shuddering
        but I am not afraid
        for it is I who made
Alcestis and *The Dead of Spring*.

※

DREAMS ARE THE ROYAL ROAD
TO THE UNCONSCIOUS
Freud

The King's Highway to the Dare Not Know,
but I beg my rides and well I know
that boring road where droning hundreds
of cars fade by in hundred-hundreds
of mirror windows all too bright
to see my face, and when the bright
morning breaks I lie like dead.
An old-time surrey, an ancient dead
horse and his farmer stop by the way,
they'll take me one mile on my way
—out of my way—is this the Way?
I used to think I could be happy
but is it possible to be happy?
what is it like? like Plato oh
I'll copy it at large and oh
plan a city where all the distances
—where? whither? —are walking distances.

※

The wheel Charles left me, that I christened
"Johnny Wells," and Charles would know why,
I do not keep so scrupulous as he
used to keep everything except his life;
and yet our Johnny still outstrips
lesser wheels on the dusty road,
though I do not ride so tirelessly far
as Charlie used to do before the accident.

※

In the fussy details
of my overworked existence
I am looking for the ticket
I put in the wrong pocket
and for your kind letter
under the heap of trash
the Board of Education
sends me every morning.
I lose my temper quickly
since John went crazy
and you went to Cambridge.
Sometimes I just sit
defeated while a tear
rolls slowly down my cheek.

※

How like a wildflower untended
among garden flowers no fairer
is Susan and these kempt
children, beauties all.

Surely a wild strain
of blood and wit—well we know—
is in her, fitful fearful
gay willful and tearful.

In our unhappy home
still sometimes the sun
and wind and fresh rain blow,
and these nourish our darling.

※

A raw day in a foreign land
   when the baby was sick
I quarreled with my wife, she stamped
   her heel with a click.

I zigzag from overworking
   to days that have no use at all
but joy and peace of mind elude me
   because I am a fool.

※

SABBATH

The end of Your six days' improvisation
was rest and the Sabbath became Your purpose.
You didn't need to finish up, and didn't,
but unlike us You were free to leave it off.

I write these conversations with You
without awareness of Your presence, Lord,
much as I wake early with a hard on and fuck
although I am not with it. But there it is.

Last night young Burton Weiss who was my son's good friend
made a big deal of the Princess Sabbath
with a white cloth and lights and bread and wine
working himself into a kind of joy
as he went off to make peace between the Jews
and Arabs. Grant that he comes back alive.

423

꙰

A PLANE TO PITTSBURGH

The ills of this world are mathematical, as Kafka said. I notice
3 fellows boarding the plane that I'd like to sit next to me, but
the 96 seats are assigned at random, and even discounting the
pairs who sit together, the odds against my happiness are over-
whelming. So it proves.

Oh, I keep at it. Disturbing my obnoxious seat-mate, I get up and
walk the aisle and ask for a match. I beat my brain for a pretext
to exchange seats, but nothing is plausible. Anyway the weather
is rough and the pilot keeps flashing "Fasten seat belts."

So I give up and write these sentences to pass the time, to make
do. The evils of this world are mathematical, they are mathe-
matical. The goods, I have found, don't fall into my lap. Some
people have a lot of luck. Others, worse off than I, don't have
a chance even to make an effort.

The blond with the squinty eyes was best, though not the best-
looking. Blue collar class. There's quicker savvy in a boy
like that. For a short flight. And there's Pittsburgh. Yes, and
another thing: the lower class boy would have had less prejudice
against how old I am. He would have fewer notions.

Kafka himself was in the actuarial business. He *would* know.

꙰

The sky was hazy blue, the planes like fish
were pointing up and down the air chalk-white
red and green, it was as gay and bright
a carnival as any child could wish.

I was a rider on the aeroplane
to Cleveland bound on business that I do,

and in that city would I visit too
people I love so much it gives me pain.

We flew so high! three miles above the earth,
the tiny lakes were shining and the streams
meandering reflected the sunbeams.
All added to my wonder and my mirth.

❈

KANT

Immanuel Kant that beautiful old man
that character, the most manly and modest
intellect we ever had in the West,
I'd like to taken him to where the Alps
descend in the dark lake in Canton Uri
and watch the terror and the tears of joy
awaken in his knowing eyes. And where
the blue bay of Vesuvius would made
them sparkle and his wrinkles flush with pleasure.
And where, if I could without alarming him,
a teasing pack of pretty Arab hoodlums
hospitably refuse to let him quit
Tunis without a fuck, immensely flustered.
All this I wish I could because I love
that little man who never left Koenigsberg
and well he merited a sabbatical.

❈

DON LARSEN'S PERFECT GAME

Everybody went to bat three times
except their pitcher (twice) and his pinch hitter,

but nobody got anything at all.
Don Larsen in the eighth and ninth looked pale
and afterwards he did not want to talk.
This is a fellow who will have bad dreams.
His catcher Berra jumped for joy and hugged him
like a bear, legs and arms, and all the Yankees
crowded around him thick to make him be
not lonely, and in fact in fact in fact
nothing went wrong. But that was yesterday.

꽃

AJAX

Ajax is dead our pet white rat
he died during the night
and Minos his identical twin
in the cage never before alone
will not live very long.

I have brought the body in a box
to throw it in the river
a dirty end for rat or man
but it is still my lordly Hudson
and solemnly I bring the body here.

꽃

TWO POEMS

He slowly beat his feet
until the rhythm locked
the rafters, and the house
rocked from side to side.

Go! go! "Who? me?
what a I done now?"
"You ain't done nuthin,
like you is on fire."

"Call out the fire engingines!"
he pled with knockin knees
and he pissed in his drawers,
was a puddle round his shoes.

2. STRIDING BLUES

Like a pair o empty shoes
    paddin across the floor
I got the stridin blues
    don' know what for.

Across the hardwood floor
    back an fore, afore an back
all the house is shakin
    like the 1906 earthquake.

Wings sproutin on their heels
    they're crawlin up the wall,
the plaster ceiling has a crack,
    a shoelace is danglin down.

❦

LINES

"Sun-bathing?" No, I lay down in the shade,
now it's too much trouble to move over.
"Oh, you were trying to keep out of the heat,"
he strenuously offered. I said nothing.

"Well, thanks for a good talk," he said briskly
and strolled down to the river where McCoy
was holding his patient line and thoughtfully
playing with himself in the sunshine.
"Catch anything?" our eager friend exclaimed.
The Irishman obligingly spread wide
his legs and fell asleep.
                              Some citizens
are busy producing goods and services,
others of us are not even consumers.

FALLING UP

The bubbles of gas
speed up in the glass
   just as the sparks
   leap up in the dark.

Nothing is so fair
as this law of t square
   embodied here
   in my glass of beer.

Even more beautiful
is the invisible
   inertia that sinks under
   with inaudible thunder.

NEW YORK

Always something new, and now these signs
peremptory green and threatening red

"Walk" "Don't Walk" "Walk" "Don't Walk"
jump up and down like soldiers on the street
City Hall thought it up.
But people circumspectly watch the traffic,
drop a modest eye around the corner,
and flit through a disappearing crevice.

"Circumspect" like crossing Ninth Avenue
"Modest" like asking for a raise
"Nimble" like disregarding bad advice
we walk, if merry were, our merry way.

However, we have unhappy faces
(though human compared with the Americans),
for my native city has become worn and dirty
like an old shoe that doesn't even fit.

꽃

A REVIEW AT WATKINS GLEN

Trim squadrons oiled and lit by beer
the Central New York Volunteer
        Firemen come marching by
        from Seneca to the Fairgrounds.

Here is something rarely seen,
Tioga has an engine green!
        hurrah for that bold emerald
        aglow, four hats on either rack,

my vote goes to Tioga. And
Horseheads has the loudest band.
        And Hector and Ovid and Virgil
        do not discredit their namesakes.

They climb up ladders into space
and haul the hose with speed and grace
    astounding, drunken as they are
    beside the sparkling water.

☙

THE SIEGE
Aristotle, Politics, *II, 7*

To ferret Eubulus out of his nest
for honor, justice, and the rest,
Autophradatus came in panoply
horse and ship, land and sea.
Atarne-town prepared for death,
armed in turn and held its breath.

At twilight came a messenger
to the besieger to confer.
"How much will this siege cost,
the armor and the engines lost,
the rations and the daily pay?
Make up an itemized account
and for sixty percent of the amount
Eubulus will go away."

Autophradatus with a frown
—bad at figures —marked it down,
whistled, had the bugles blown,
and left at the crack of dawn.

☙

"*Now* what can you say?"
cackled the septuagenarian,

"I've proved it can be done!
Not in jail, nor in disgrace,
I did not die by violence
nor ruin myself as you predicted.
Victory! victory!"
—So cried the king of beasts
in his social cage
and the angelic choir
covered their heads with their wings.

FLIES

I flicked these flies impatiently away
and suddenly I knew
how I could lie there like a cow
indifferent to flies: "They don't sting.
The whispering tickling is a sensation
like any other—like the soft trade wind.
I need not choose to be annoyed
by tiny toes—"
                    At least this happened.
But I continued into a mere fancy,
"—which if indeed, beauty, they were your
wandering fingertips along my shoulders
and on my forehead, etcetera,"
I went from the mistaken to the stupid.
Couldn't really stand the flies and I went in.

THE BONE

With narrow eyes, sucking on my long pipe,
I see the time is over-ripe

to change the animal I am
from dog, who's friend to man, to be a man.
My tail will no longer thump the floor
and I will not wait hungry at the door.
I used to like to sniff at Lassie and Lad
and try to mount them, but a dog is sad.

Our zoo is rich with the wild and tame
totems that we devoured and became.
Perry's a moose: moose are misunderstood,
they stand the spread-horned monarchs of the wood
until the hunter fires and they fall dead
and their horns above the mantel spread.
My Gene's a monkey who flies up a tree
and pisses on the passers by with glee,
but George is a brown bear rough and surly
who oughtn't to get out of bed so early.
Glenn, a stallion whose nostrils flare
shies away skittish as a yearling mare.
Sally's a kangaroo, her one word *Ouch*!
she vehemently jumps, but in her pouch
she guards a secret that she will release
one day in the land-cut-off Antipodes.
Fritz, who's an elephant, says every hussy
would be a panther or other glorified pussy,
and that pussy of his pounces on the harp
and like her claws the melody is sharp.
My little boy, I guess, is a wild-jackass
who hee-haws as he kicks me in the face
—all amiable animals!
                This middle-size
spotted mongrel, jaunty with enterprise,
has barked his bark. But now the man
must choose what beast to be, for he can.
Look in the glass: I do not like him much,
the man, I am not used to being such.
What would it be like to be like that?
He doesn't show the horror in my heart
but maybe the impatience—his lips are taut—

he seems to say, "Dog, finish! there's no use
to worry the bone once you have the juice."

※

He got arrested because he was lonely
and they have put him into solitary.

He went mad to be like everybody
and they have made him mayor.

※

Can one straight forward march and bawl and bawl?
See, can one not!

※

MOSES
Pensées, viii, 458

On the yeasty water the wild torrent
of vice, of need, despair, disgrace,
to death, to death, the jaws of death

little Moses in a bowl
sits dry of flesh and sure of soul
through it all

—to whom the Princess from behind
her stylish linen hood will smile
and he shall stand within the Porch
of Heavenly Jerusalem.

※

WELLFLEET HARBOR WIND SUN SPACE

North Wind across the dunes and bays,
sweep away hatred, be praise.
    Hatred has been half of me
    but it's boring, praise is free.

Hot Sun, who makes earth green and tan,
give heat and color to this man.
    The blank morose where I have been
    is dull, I long for tan and green.

Great Spaces of the bays and islands
and ocean crashing down from the horizon,
    without effort here you are,
    make me be here who have been far.

I am a native, on my home
rocks of the world I play like foam,
    my quick spirit gives delight
    and little children send me soaring like a kite.

※

The day was clear as day
March like the start of spring
everywhere the sky
spread wider than the earth

the clouds were shapes of vapor
in the high atmosphere
the light came from the sun
the heat of it was warm

the clouds rested secure
at the height they were,

just this density
choosing just this pressure.

that past day was
it is written down in words
how my only world
went with me as I walked.

※

The noise of my neighbor's buzz-saw lopping branches
is driving me mad and drives me out of my house.
The noise of the busy sea does not destroy me
so I sit on the beach deafened by the surf
by the square of its nearness. But there is a point
midway at which my neighbor's buzz-saw
has become the pleasant sound of the woodman in the woods
in the North Country, among country sounds,
loud crows, the low of Henry's cows.

At the right distance, at the right nearness,
your voice is lovely, O my only world,
let me sit by you. I am sick today.
And hold my hand a moment.

※

AN AMATE TREE

Tree . . . the others went to Xochicalco
to see the ruins and the ball court, what a strange
species we are . . . but underneath the tree . . .
I meant to buy some silver and turquoise
downtown, for it's absurd to come so far
and not mix with the people in the square . . .

but that canopy of foliage
is *like* a city, the quick yellow finches
traffic mainly in the upper planes,
the ravens have perched in the denser zone
of six and seven stories, the melodious
racket incomprehensible as Spanish,
no, Nahuatl. There are a million exits
to the blue fields where the swallows wheel . . .
I never *will* get up to meet the bishop . . .
but it *is* odd that we voyaged to the Moon
before exploring this amate world
where very little that is going on
makes any sense. Is it accessible?

LINES, HOKKU, AND LITTLE PRAYER

The icy Missouri slowly wending toward the east
through the quarter sections of snow-covered prairie
I saw from seven miles up, a veil of cloud
whiter than the snow cut off the view
endless to the horizon and I was alone
then there after my many friends I well
deserve watched over me hospitably
including one who was very sweet to live with.
I hope when next I fly these windy ways
that I will see the blazing Mississippi
south,

       the meanderer
    to hunger at from on high
       his leisurely course

      through the continent,
    be easy my spiralling
      spirit my long lust.

No, neither with my eyes closed and You
a presence warm that near I know
        nor in the busy world and wide
        where I am Your friend open-eyed,

but vaguely peering out to see
a small room and I am drowsy
        and You seem to be everywhere
        in the room, if You are.

※

MY FAMILY 1969

I.

There came of joy a gleam of tears
when Daisy struck the A major
in *Entre le Boeuf et l'Ane Gris*
in D minor, and she ran
from the piano and swung on her swing.
        She swung on her swing
    weightless oh but not fleeing
        into outer space.
And I am so glad for her the sunflowers
tower three times as tall as she in August
and the Connecticut is still sweet, where we live.

II.

Studying astronomy
noon and night
her forehead is furrowed
by puzzling problems

the effect of the impact
of meteors on the Moon

the hydrogen exploding
and the Doppler shift

the signals vanish in a hole:
surely Sally
is possessed by the ghost
of her star-drunk son.

III.

Mowing down many hundreds
of dandelions on the meadow
I have plucked one to bring to the grave
of Matty after his winter sleep.
He was my golden weed: we deemed ourselves
among the common of this world,
and we were splendid. So I say
to whom? in the speechless language of flowers.

IV.

Through flat and uneventful days
scratchy with chronic ills
I straggle pleased: rich and ripe
berries though small I find to hand
a preface for Alexander Berkman
and praising Speech at the M.L.A.;
the Governor invites us to St. Thomas
which is better far than February
and I shall go to Mexico in March.
The animated talking of Sally and Daisy
in the next room is lovable
and I will go and tell them
—unlike me! it is an event!

✳

Awful is the grief
welling up when the only
    world is relenting.

✳

Like a soldier again dragged
out of sleep before dawn
hurrying east in the cold rain
—I often think of those who have worse duty
although I never did much please myself—
to salute her my sweet my dear one
who was the soldierly of all my tribe
and—You knew, God—one of the kindest women
who lived her life in noisy New York City
these seventy years of an ungentle century.
Alice was old-fashioned.

✳

THE CORONA

Sun! — the thing with its engulfing jaws
was eating up my sun, we beat the gongs
and shot our arrows that went up halfway
in vain, the wan light of our darling faded
small and blew the chilling gale of death.

There was a sudden flash of diamonds
like those in Pluto's mines and it was dark.

I do not know what countenance we looked
at one another, for we could not see.

439

Was all this only upward of an hour
since first I noticed how it is with me?

Then shone the petals lovely in the sky
and I was amazed.
                    Do I now therefore wish
the blinding sun had not been resurrected
although we could not live by the pale vision?

※

The Columbia, daughter,
is such a river!
The Hudson is majestic at Storm King
but this is like the salmon to the shad
—both are delicious—they fish them with nets.
The once hot head of Mount Hood
is snowy in the cloud
and the slender column
of Multnemah falls
by Galileo's law,
you could time it down with Matty's stopwatch
(if it weren't broken in the drawer)
—the water seems to jump in pulses
—it crashes evenly into the pool
without let from melting April
and the ground is carpeted with cherry blossoms.
Each place in the world, girl,
is lovelier than the others,
death is therefore poignant
to me as I grow old,
but still I saw this scene
with all my loyal wits
about me, although dizzy.

꽃

My poor one! Ocean.
Poisoned by mercury.
You who were so vast
you were our boundary.
The big fishes are sick
with mercury and lead
where the waves pound down
and leap in spray off Makapuu.

Before I die
I shall go to Scotland
and hear like Felix Mendelssohn
the horns of Fingal's Cave
where the waves pound down
where they leap in spray
where the waves pound down
and where they leap in spray.

꽃

Out of every wave lapping over the ledge
of lava flames a streak of emerald.
The flat sea is turquoise
—a streak of emerald—
transparent to the coral floor
—a streak of emerald—
a man o'war like a drop of blue ink floats
—a streak of emerald.

INDEX OF TITLES AND
FIRST LINES

If I undertake to say, 85
If I'd lie like the dog with my nose on the ground, 388
"IF ONLY I KNEW THE TRUTH, I SWEAR I WOULD ACT ON IT—" 378
If the raccoon gnaws ten percent of the corn, 46
If they were to say, 56
I'm ever ready, 59
I'm not in pain, I owe no debts, 92
Immanuel Kant that beautiful old man, 425
Implacable! there is no uglier, 108
In a panic and compelled, 88
In anguish I started from sleep, 89
In Copenhagen one in three, 281
In crashing waters, 53
In error, incompetent, 121
In fear and trembling and clarity of sight, 324
In how few hours I, 73
In July the tawny hawkweed, 42
IN LYDIA, 210
In such a stink of filth, 107
In that company I was malcontent, 9
In the amber light and black, 291
In the bright twilight, 57
In the fussy details, 422
IN THE JURY ROOM, IN PAIN, 18
In the little mirror, 63
In the roomy oak among the translucent leaves, 386
In the Universe of Correspondences, 197
In the variations of the Arietta, 146
In this black cloud it is confused, 121
IN TRAFFIC, 263
In twenty poems, 233
Into the foothills in their giant unrest, 412
INTRODUCTION AND BALLADE OF MUSICIANS, 253
Irises in hand, 53
Isn't somebody calling "Paul Goodman"? 130
"It could have been worse," 62
It froze and the ice in his engine, 370
It is like a dream that I had a son, 335
It is not the same to eat candy and to sit down to a dish of candy and
    eat it, 295
It is nothing new, no, nothing new, 130
It is peaceful coming home across the meadow, 42
It is smoke and dust, 61
It isn't Delphi, though it has, 45
It was because of need, Lord, 225
It was good when you were here, 43
It's one thing to cope with a problem, 220

It's poignant and gloomy to me who am grounded, 218

With drooping groping toes, 125
With narrow eyes, sucking on my long pipe, 431
With unerring finger he put, 158
With unremitting energy, 240
Without horns or style, 380
Woeful was the winter, 122
Woman eternal my muse, lean toward me, 308
WORLD, ELEPHANT, AND TORTOISE, 202

Yes, weariness and grief, 87
Yes, when I was twenty, 16
You are lithe like the doe I do not see, 229
You ask what is the bay with the statue, 120
You ask, What is the use of the chiefs? 245
You notice, Lord, I am half pleased, 95
You said my lust was like the insistent, 126
You see how these young fellows, 109
You teach quick and very hard, 95
Young ass, is nothing like it! no, 297
Your face, your profile while we fuck, 268
Your fists are ablaze, 55
Your kingdom is within me sure, 75
"Your ordinary mind, that is the Way," 44
You're a sweet limpid pond, 366
"You're beautiful," I said, "I love you," 293

※

About the Author

PAUL GOODMAN was born in New York City in 1911, and
died in 1972. After graduating from City College in
New York, he received his Ph.D. in humanities from the
University of Chicago. He taught at the University of
Chicago, New York University, Black Mountain College,
Sarah Lawrence, the University of Wisconsin, San
Francisco State, and the University of Hawaii, and
lectured at various universities throughout the country.

Many of his articles appeared in *Commentary, Kenyon
Review, Resistance, Liberation,* and *The New York
Review of Books.* Vintage Books has reprinted a number
of his well-known works of social criticism, among them,
*Growing Up Absurd, Utopian Essays and Practical
Proposals, Compulsory Mis-Education & The Community
of Scholars, New Reformation: Notes of a Neolithic
Conservative,* and a book on linguistics, *Speaking and
Language: Defence of Poetry.*